Unseen
Flesh

Unseen Flesh

GYNECOLOGY AND BLACK QUEER

WORTH-MAKING IN BRAZIL

———

NESSETTE FALU

Duke University Press *Durham and London* 2023

Project Editor: Bird Williams
Designed by Courtney Leigh Richardson
Typeset in Garamond Premier Pro by Westchester Publishing Services

Library of Congress Cataloging-in-Publication Data
Names: Falu, Nessette, [date] author.
Title: Unseen flesh : gynecology and black queer worth-making
in Brazil / Nessette Falu.
Other titles: Gynecology and black queer worth-making in Brazil
Description: Durham : Duke University Press, 2023. | Includes
bibliographical references and index.
Identifiers: LCCN 2022055563 (print)
LCCN 2022055564 (ebook)
ISBN 9781478025184 (paperback)
ISBN 9781478020240 (hardcover)
ISBN 9781478027157 (ebook)
Subjects: LCSH: Lesbians, Black—Medical care—Brazil. | Gynecology—
Brazil. | Gynecology—Psychological aspects. | Sexual minorities,
Black—Brazil—Social conditions. | Gender identity—Brazil. | BISAC:
SOCIAL SCIENCE / Anthropology / Cultural & Social | SOCIAL
SCIENCE / LGBTQ Studies / Lesbian Studies
Classification: LCC HQ75.6.B6 F358 2023 (print)
LCC HQ 75.6.B6 (ebook)
DDC 306.76/6308996081—dc23/eng/20230417
LC record available at https://lccn.loc.gov/2022055563
LC ebook record available at https://lccn.loc.gov/2022055564

Cover art: Untitled, watercolor on paper. Courtesy Ani Ganzala.

For mi abuela, Luz,
For my Sands, Val,
For my Brazilian sistah, Júlia,
For all your courage through breast cancer.

Contents

Acknowledgments
ix

INTRODUCTION
Bearing Witness to Unseen Flesh
1

ONE
The Virgin Who Lives within Her Erotic Worth
21

TWO
Unseen Flesh:
Gynecological Trauma, Emotional Power, and
Intimate Sociomedical Violence
51

INTERLUDE ONE
Angela
77

THREE

The Social Clinic:

Mapping the Social and Colonial World of Gynecology

79

INTERLUDE TWO

It Doesn't Matter

111

FOUR

Are *We* Ethical Subjects? Seeing Ourselves in Shapeshifting Ethics

113

FIVE

Bem-Estar Negra:

Lésbicas Negras' Beautiful Experiments of Worth

141

Notes

169

References

179

Index

195

Acknowledgments

My journey is full of twists and turns. Many beloved people have laid hands on it. Truth be told, I never dreamed of being an anthropologist. A dancer, yes. A fashion designer, yes. Not an anthropologist. But then, neither did I foresee going to the New York Theological Seminary for a Master's degree. Yet, it was the seminary that would sponsor in 2007 my first one-month immersive visit to Salvador-Bahia, where I stayed with Marlene Moreira da Silva who introduced me to the Brazilian Black feminist movement, to Candomblé (an Afro-Brazilian religion), and to the important Brazilian Black lesbians in my life, first and foremost Erica Rocha. I am grateful to the twists and turns and all the people in it.

First, I want to thank all the Brazilian Black lesbians and *sapatonas* who contributed to this book and to my journey. This book would not have been possible without their sensitive and intimate sharing and the ways they guided me during fieldwork. I honor you. You are all fierce, beautiful, and full of life. I pray to the orishas that your stories touch others and that the book brings justice where it is most needed. May this world be a better place if someone listens. Also, I thank deeply the scholars and community organizers in Porto Alegre for their hospitality, insights, and sharing of abundant materials.

Graduate school at Rice University sprung the biggest twists and turns. I started in a religious studies doctoral program and ended in cultural anthropology. I thank Anthony B. Pinn, my first advisor, and Elias Bongmba for nurturing my transition into anthropology. I thank the Department of Anthropology faculty for welcoming me into a world I wouldn't have imagined. Cymene, we loved our platform shoes. Nia, it's never too late. I now cite and write about reproductive justice. My advisor, teacher, and friend, Jim Faubion: There are no words to describe the impact you've had on my transformation. Remember when I told you in your home that I must have always been a closeted anthropologist. We laughed queerly.

The Center for the Study of Women, Gender, and Sexuality at Rice University gave birth to me. Though I began my commitments to Black feminisms in seminary, the Center became a home where those and new commitments deepened. Thank you Rosemary Hennessy and Brian Riedel for being you during difficult and fun times.

This research was generously funded by the Ruth Landes Memorial Research Fund. Also by the Social Science Research Institute and the Center for the Study of Women, Gender, and Sexuality at Rice University.

I thank the people and academic spaces that supported my research and intellectual transformation. MUSA-Instituto de Saúde Coletiva—Universidade Federal da Bahia feminist scholars—Marinho Lili, Cecilia McCallum, and Estela Aquino who supported my visa, opened space for presentations then and over the years, and gave feedback and mentoring. The Sarah Pettit Dissertation Fellowship in the LGBT studies program at Yale University and the faculty, including Inderpal Grewal, were also immensely supportive and provided space to write and grow. I thank my dear friend Monica R. Miller for her support, especially during my Visiting Scholar positions at Lehigh University. The postdoctoral fellowship at the Institute for Research on the African Diaspora in the Americas and the Caribbean (IRADAC) at The Graduate Center, CUNY, is where the transformative critical work in this book began with Herman Bennett, Juan Battle, and Ruthie Wilson Gilmore.

Over the years, the countless iterations of this book were guided by many people. I must first thank Dána-Ain Davis. You have been a golden blessing, friend, mentor, and Black lesbian to think and grow with. There is too much to say, but I will say our Mother Oxúm loves us fiercely. I have only deep gratitude for my community who have read versions of this book and given feedback: Christa C. Craven, Rosemary Hennesy, Traci C. West, Beatriz Reyes-Foster, Rachel Vlachos, and my transformative, raw, honest, guiding book conference at the Easton's Nook with Christen A. Smith, Dána-Ain Davis, and Bianca C. Williams. Many other scholarly conversations and support shaped the book: Jafari Sinclair Allen, Erica C. Williams, Kia C. Caldwell, Emanuelle Goes, Juli Grisgby, Chelsi West, Ugo Edu, Sarah Franklin, Dorothy Roberts, Deborah Thomas, John L. Jackson, Janis Hutchison, and special gratitude to my dear friend Ezekiel Dixon-Roman. The early Reproduction and Race Working Group: Daisy Deomampo, Natali Valdez, Risa Cromer, Christa, and Dána, with whom I conferenced substantively on different parts of the book; the University of Central Florida students and faculty: Alexis Chamarro, Trinity and Suzanne,

Joanna Mishtal, Reshawna Chapple, and Richelle Joe; and the people of the Department of Anthropology, who supported this book journey during my faculty time there; and immense gratitude to Ann Gleig and Jeanine Viau, who helped me to more than survive but live. If anyone is missing, you know my heart.

My developmental editor, Laura Helper, is a beam of light. Laura worked with me for seven years. You are a special human being and super talented. I thank Martin Manalansan for introducing me to Ken Wissoker, my editor. Ken, you have watched me grow through many twists and turns since 2015. I thank you for your patience, encouragement, and unyielding support. I am extremely thankful to you and to Duke University Press for granting me ownership to the Portuguese rights for the book. I look forward to transnational conversations and the reproductive justice work to be done.

Life is not possible in this academic world without your people. My Alpha Kappa Alpha Sorority, Fall 1989 line sisters are a true string of pearls in my life. I am especially thankful to Julie Johnson and Stephanie Gayle for tolerating my texts and tears, cheerleading every win, and giving comfort when they lacked capacity. Writing during the pandemic was no joke. My line sisters saved me, and so did Easton's Nook's virtual Saturday writing mornings during the pandemic. Thanks Jacquie and Nadine for your generosity.

I deeply love my friends and family who made space and cheered me on this journey. Three people fed my soul when it was depleted: Merle Anslem (bestie), Eleanor Moody-Sheppard (Big Momma), and Destyn Martin (my nephew). Your excitement, proudness, and centering words filled my cup full every time for a long time.

To my mom, Ivonne Castro: it is finally here. I wish buela and buelo could hold it in their hands too.

This book is dedicated to my everlasting loves for whom I honorably cared during their breast cancer journeys until their last breaths: my line sister Valerie Holden and my buela, Luz Santana Castro. I also lift a beautiful soul, a Brazilian Black woman from Salvador whom I also had the honor to support during their breast cancer journey, Júlia Couto. May the orishas keep us close while you rest in peace.

INTRODUCTION

Bearing Witness to Unseen Flesh

One typical hot March day, I jumped out of my taxi in front of Estação Calçada in Salvador-Bahia, Brazil. Estação Calçada is the central station of the only train line transporting people to and from the *subúrbios* (middle- or working-class neighborhoods) and *periferias* (outskirts of the inner-city or working-class and poor neighborhoods) in the lower city *(cidade baixa)*. It is close to Feria de São Joaquim, where locals buy a range of things from meat and produce to essential Afro-religious provisions. Salvador is understood by its inhabitants to be an urban, densely populated Black city. The train station is in Largo da Calçada—the first *barrio* to connect the lower city to the *subúrbios* that accentuate Salvador's deep racial and class divides. Amid the buzzing commercial district in the lower city, you can see the stark contrast of white Brazilians dressed in business suits rushing to work while Brazilian Black vendors hustle in the streets in the summer heat. Many Black and working-class Brazilians moved through this train station while Juliana waited for me at the station's entrance.

Juliana was well known in the community for her deep commitment to Black women and LGBTT (lesbian, gay, bisexual, transgender, *travesti*) social movements. I was eager to connect with her to talk about Black lesbians' experiences with gynecology and well-being. After a warm embrace and double cheek kisses, the Brazilian way, she took me to her small office inside the train station.[1] I had met Juliana during a *roda* (circle of discussion) planning resistance work to combat gender and racial violence in July 2007, during my first monthlong stay in Salvador. I was an exchange seminary student interested in African diasporic religious life. That summer, Black women took to the streets and marched into the Assembléia Legislativa (state legislative building) to advocate for the new Lei Maria da Penha, a 2006 federal law against domestic violence. Subsequently, I saw Juliana at *vigílias* (public gatherings to denounce Black genocide and femicide), marches, and other protests led by Black women, including many by Black lesbians. We stayed connected through my subsequent visits to Salvador. When during my fieldwork in 2012 I ran into Juliana in my neighborhood, Bairro Dois de Julho, in downtown Salvador, she had a huge reaction to the focus of my research: the negative impact of gynecological practices on the well-being of Brazilian Black lesbians. "There is a lot to think about regarding that medical experience that we don't talk about," she said with an intense facial expression.

Unseen Flesh is a story of Brazilian Black lesbian *worth-making*. Worth-making is the human energy expended or consumed to create pathways that sustain and claim agential living. Therefore, this ethnographic account seeks to intimately describe my Black lesbian respondents' everyday lives amid structural violence in gynecology. This Black lesbian worth-making is anchored by love, erotic power, religiosity, and family care as much as it is marked by trauma and struggles for survival. My storytelling constitutes what Brazilian Black feminist literary scholar Conceição Evaristo (2017) refers to as *escrevivências*, or the ways that crafted narratives reflect real life, even when their futures are conjured by imaginings of a freer world. These are stories of Black lesbians conjuring selfhood and well-being against a social and cultural backdrop and official historical record that would find them *unseen*. My participants' lives are windows into the unseen experiences within medical spaces and radical transformations of reproductive well-being. *Escrevivências*—literally, *written lived experience*—honor subjective and interpretive lived realities, validating memory work and imagination. Evaristo's stories center Black women's ways of navigating their intimate worlds and narrate their range of corporeal sensations and sensory knowledge-making. She unapologetically does not prevent herself from reimagining the realities and dreams of Black women, who care for and love themselves and others (women and men). Her *escrevivências* have long been employed as a method for the study of Brazilian Black experience and are exemplary of worth-making storytelling that seeks to rupture racism, poverty, and violence at the seams (McKittrick 2020, 44). Juliana and other Black lesbians I followed closely saw their social traumas within institutional spaces as both individual *and* collective struggles. Here, likewise, their stories, in and out of medical spaces, are taken as evidence of Black lesbian living. Juliana's retelling of the story about another Black lesbian highlights how Black women care for and respond to other Black women's social traumas and how they carry the responsibility to each other. In this book, Juliana's intervention to navigate a healthcare system that devalues them is a critical, intersubjective mediation.

At Estação Calçada, Juliana shared her deep concerns about the lack of attention to Black women's and lesbians' reproductive issues, such as menopause, and the prejudice against trans men. However, when we shifted our conversation to the subject of the gynecology exam itself, Juliana's demeanor became agitated. I sensed that she had a traumatic story to tell. Having experienced a number of these difficult conversations, I noticed an emotional burden weighing on her. But the story she told was not directly about herself. She shared the experience of a "very young" Black lesbian in her early twenties (whom I will call Gabriela) who recently telephoned Juliana, enraged and crying after a visit with a white female gynecologist.

By this time, my own gynecological issues pervaded my fieldwork experience.[2] I appreciated sitting under an air conditioner with cool air to ease my hot flash from an abrupt postsurgical menopause. Six months earlier, I had returned to the United States to undergo a hysterectomy with ovary removal. I was diagnosed with widespread endometriosis that had been kicking my ass with fatigue, pain, and heavy bleeding. This unexpected major personal event only drew me closer to my participants. Our interconnections (Juliana, Gabriela, and me) are interwoven life stories—*escrevivências*. Juliana told me the story that Gabriela told her, thus constituting a transnational Black feminist praxis of shared storytelling and affirmation across age, nationality, and other borders. I invite you to witness these stories as one way to fight against invisibility and unseen worth.

I tell these stories now not just as an ethnographer and a Black lesbian, but as a person who has administered the speculum exams in the United States. My own clinical experiences reimagine their interpretations within those closed spaces and how power is fraught in those relations. My clinical lens played a part in conceiving the framework of *Unseen Flesh*. My experience as a physician assistant informed how I navigated the field, analyzed the data, and wrote the book. I practiced medicine for seventeen years in the United States across specialties of neurosurgery, internal medicine, HIV, and oncology, and after immersing myself in Brazil's health care, I can bear witness in my analysis to the unseen-ness in medicine and society of the profound emotional and social trauma occurring within gynecological spaces.

Gabriela had sought medical care for vaginal bleeding that had persisted continuously for nearly a month. The gynecologist's first question, in a curt tone, was, "You are aborting. Are you aborting?" The young Black lesbian, shaken by the doctor's cold demeanor, emphatically replied, "I am not aborting. It is impossible to be aborting. I am a lesbian." Then, according to Juliana, the doctor leaned toward Gabriela and presumptuously asked with a smirk, "Tell me something, did you cheat on your girlfriend?" Gabriela swallowed her tears until she left the clinic and called Juliana. By the time I talked to her, Juliana was still furious and emotionally raveled by Gabriela's preventable trauma. She called the doctor's arrogant questioning "injustice in the delivery of care." I do not disregard the responsibility of Brazilian physicians to rule out complications of abortions (spontaneous or procedural) if suspected after a proper history-taking examination. Unfortunately, abortions are illegal in Brazil and are too often electively conducted under unsafe conditions; many Black women subsequently suffer medical complications such as infection and even death. However, Juliana told Gabriela's story to expose a different pervasive injustice: the abuse of power in gynecology that silently torments many Black lesbians. The gynecologist's presumption and insistence that Gabriela needed an abortion because she had cheated on her girlfriend with a man, which led to an unwanted pregnancy, was a mistreatment of a patient and, therefore, an abuse of power. This inappropriate behavior misdiagnosed the prolonged bleeding. It was dismissive of Gabriela's lesbian identity and sexual subjectivity; worse, the gynecologist's cruelty was rooted in the unchecked anti-Blackness, anti-queer, un/gendering, and classist power imbalance that pervades these medical spaces. Juliana interpreted the gynecologist's behavior not just as uncompassionate and inappropriate but *grosseira* (brute) and violent. She said that Gabriela cried for two days, traumatized by the experience. Then, still concerned about the bleeding, Juliana took Gabriela to her own gynecologist for evaluation. Juliana's white, LGBTQ+-affirming gynecologist found a sizeable uterine fibroid causing the prolonged bleeding.

Unseen Flesh bears witness to the emotional weight of gynecological experiences. This ethnography shows how Brazilian Black queer women are subject to iterative mental, emotional, and physical traumas within gynecological spaces. It understands that emotional weight as evidence. In this book I think with Dána-Ain Davis, who theorizes emotional weight as evidence of medical racism that leads to harms such as prematurity and infant mortality, to interpret how Black lesbians are forced to build and constantly recenter self-worth in their everyday lives toward survival and well-being. I argue that they consequently transform how they exist and are seen in medical spaces and in the world.

Unseen Flesh visualizes Black lesbians' existence behind the veil of gynecologists' assumptions and *preconcietos* (prejudices), however well-meaning their intentions to deliver public *and* private health care. Juliana described a Black lesbian body as "um corpo invisibilizado" (body rendered invisible). The term *unseen* indexes my participants' perceived invisibility and the invisibilizing forces within those spaces. Where they sat on the examination table, Black lesbians repeatedly felt invisible, erased, and unheard by their gynecologists. Juliana understands this unseeing, for example, as the indignity and disrespect experienced by older Black women in menopause. But the experience of Black lesbians is specific and particular due to their racial, gendered, and queer sexual positionalities. Gynecologists' hidden logics of unworthiness of respect, professional conduct, and, as in Gabriela's story, appropriate care is triggered by first seeing them as Black bodies, then as women (or in their nonnormative gender expression), and then as lesbian (or homosexual).[3] These multiple social positionalities matter because they inform how Black lesbians experience becoming unseen by gynecologists who devalue their full humanity. As Juliana said, the erasure of older Black lesbians' existence within medical spaces further triggers invisibility. This ethnography demonstrates how people's experiences and scenes are a lot messier than we imagine. This messiness evidences how their coming out to gynecologists is not the safest thing to do; but for some Brazilian Black lesbians, it is the right thing to do.

In this book, I trace an unspoken racial calculus operative within gynecology and within standard (heteronormative) reproductive discourses that is as homophobic as it is anti-Black and classist. Like Dána-Ain Davis (2018), who coined *obstetric racism* to explain how racism exists in obstetric care in the United States, I understand my respondents' narratives also to interrogate how *gynecologic racism* reflects pervasive anti-Blackness, sexism, homophobia, and classism in Brazil. Gynecologic racism manifests in how Black women are treated—or not—during exams, for example, by "not being touched" or by "not being given eye contact" and by receiving far less time during office visits than white women. These issues have been documented by Brazilian Black feminist epidemiologist Emanuelle Freitas Goes and coauthor Enilda R. Nascimento (2012). The routine pelvic exam ought to facilitate a feeling of safety with eye contact and by gently and respectfully explaining, before touching any body part, what is to be done. It is crucial to disentangle forms of power and potential gynecological violence. Obstetric violence names many reproductive injustices experienced by women across ethnicities, classes, and geographic regions.[4] Like obstetric violence, discourses of gynecological violence maintain racism that is rigidly unseen.

The unseen abuse of social power in Brazilian medicine is rooted in post-slavery plantation logics (McKittrick 2013). Lamonte Aidoo (2018) uses the notion of "slavery unseen" to expose the challenges of "understanding the real conditions under which Brazilian slaves lived due to willful concealment by whites" (5). Aidoo explores how slave owners enacted violence against Black male and female homosexuality using different forms of societal power. These societal powers ranged from medical discourses and the eugenics movement to the same-sex rape by white men and women of Black enslaved people. Aidoo's understanding of the long sociohistorical trajectory of unseen social conditions and abuse of power helps me bring into visibility unseen bodies today. Unseeing is a matter of influential people adversely seeing and treating Black lesbian bodies within medical spaces.

The vast sociohistorical ties of contradictions and anxieties in gynecology about race and homosexuality and the ongoing bleeding of colonial power into society and gynecological spaces call attention to Black lesbians' flesh. I use the concept of *flesh* to underscore the wounding and scarring of Black queer existence by the manipulation of medico-social power. As argued by C. Riley Snorton (2017), "flesh is, above all else, a thing that produces relations-real and imagined, metaphysical and material" (40). I appreciate Riley's analysis of the history of racial slavery and gynecology in the United States and the gynecological experimentation by James Marion Sims on many enslaved Black women, including Anarcha, Betsey, and Lucy, to understand how sex and gender produces racial arrangements (32). Flesh as object or subject is then manipulated and expressed through power relations. Riley helps me think about what actually remains after flesh is instrumentalized within economies and systems of medicine such as injury and pain.

Flesh designates Black lesbians' embodiment of injury at various scales. The physical pain that aggressive gynecological examinations causes is a critical corporeal dimension of power. But following Hortense J. Spillers (1987), I distinguish between *body* and *flesh* to shift our attention to the subjective and social aspects of Black queer existence within subject positions in medical spaces. Spillers's ideas of Black "flesh and body" points to that which lies between "captive and liberated subject-positions" (67). The notion of the flesh is the blood, fluid, narrative, language, soul, and much more concentrated cultural and symbolic significances that mark the captive body (Shange 2019; Spillers 1987; Snorton 2017). Then, flesh is the concentration of meaning about skin color, race, sex, sexuality, gender expression—understood as excess and turned into the otherness of Black queer bodies. Gabriela's captive subject-position under the grip of power, can also, in contestation of that power, shift into a liberated subject-position—which I explore in this book. Black lesbians' flesh, despite all crimes committed against it by society, is not a site of powerlessness. Their flesh is escaped and regenerated energy, spirit, soul, and body with capacity to revolt with knowledge production and action. Gabriela's sense of self in the moment and after the release from that captivity raises questions about whether her captive subject-position in that medical space is fully released after she leaves it. Gabriela cried for two days (maybe longer), indicating ongoing trauma even after the respite with Juliana. Her tormented memory is unseen flesh. It is a primary narrative tugged by hidden traumas, old and new, that turns emotional existence within these spaces upside down. Black feminists have long insisted on centering the embodied experiences of Black lesbians (B. Jones 2021). I follow this long tradition to rethink radical forms of evidence (Falu 2021) that situate our nonnormative narratives.

I establish unseen flesh as the excess and otherness produced by physicians resulting in body and flesh trauma and examine how the weight of that excess is carried by my participants. I redefine the medical term *gynecological trauma*, which usually refers to genital trauma experienced during medical procedures or sexual assault. My broadening of gynecological trauma, or what I refer to as *gyno-trauma*, expands that definition to encompass the adverse subjective, social, and corporeal effects produced by gynecology at the social intersections of intimate violence. The concept of gyno-trauma further shows that the biological and social in medicine are always intertwined. Gyno-trauma is unseen flesh; it is Black/queer/woman/female/masculinity/age/classed excess. The emotional work, quests for freedom, and resistance practices in self-care and self-worth are also unseen flesh narrated in this book. I explore the ways Black lesbian unseen flesh illuminates how notions of unworthiness are woven into the fabric of society and medicine.

Bearing Witness to Worth and Worth-Making

Unseen Flesh is an anthropology of Black lesbian worth that brings to light the uneven intimacy of power relations. It tracks Black lesbians' journeys to make and remake the embodied substance of well-being, where Black flesh and body conjoin, to define worth and worthiness despite devaluation by the world. What are the ways we gather, produce, and theorize Black lesbians' worth in its quotidian sense? This anthropology of worth acknowledges that the human labor of knowledge production and reactions within medical spaces are intricately tied to Black lesbians' work of making self-worth. This book argues that Black lesbians incrementally enforce their worth within the intimate violence in gynecology, steering how they evaluate, protect, and chart their well-being within medical spaces. Such anthropology cannot apprehend worth and worth-making solely within the vacuum of institutional spaces. Black queer women retool themselves in worth every day, wherever they resist Black death and push for "Black aliveness" (Quashie 2021).

We understand unworthiness: Black women's reproductive lives are a commodity and monstrosity to society. But clear distinctions must be made with how Black lesbians experience Blackness as un/gendering and queerness through devaluation within medical systems. Cathy Cohen's (1997, 1999) earlier essays on transforming a radical queer politics is instrumental for rethinking how Blackness is nonnormative, deviant, and in this sense, "queer." We also understand the idea of a female flesh "ungendered" by Spillers's interrogation of gender and race differences in the Middle Passage and slavery. Black female flesh is un/gendered as ugly, unattractive, undesirable, monstrous (Spillers 1987). Christen A. Smith reminds us about Brazil's police terror and notes that "un/gendering is not the removal or cancellation of gender but rather its disavowal" (2021, 27). In Brazilian gynecology, gender is dismissed as "immaterial and unimportant," rendering Black women continually *out of place* in these spaces.[5] This is a transnational experience tied to carceral and punitive tactics within medical spaces and health care. Health care's complicity in carceral and punitive tactics is embedded in the lack of accountability for the anti-Blackness and anti-queer violence within medical spaces. Gynecology is also the "arrivant state" (Lara 2020) in its colonial power, managing the intimate levels of being: queerness, Blackness, the femme, as well as the spirit, soul, and body.[6]

In this book, Brazilian Black lesbian worth and worth-making troubles an un/gendering/queering of Blackness in the fullness of its queer desire. This is distinct from worth and worth-making for Black heterosexual women and white lesbians. I follow Ana-Maurine Lara (2020, 4) in saying that to desire Black queer decolonization is to desire queer freedom and Black sovereignty. For Lara, queer freedom is not possible without Black sovereignty. Black lesbian life in all its expressions of queer desire in unseen flesh—the Brazilian Black lesbian femme or masculine-expressed female body. I take up Black lesbian worth and worth-making to show entrenched, iterative prejudice against Black lesbians' nonnormative sexuality and gender expressions. These intersecting prejudices intensify anti-Blackness, necessitating a Black queer analysis of race, gender, class, and homosexuality (a widely used social category in Brazil) in medicine and society studies. Black/queer storytelling shows how making gender and queerness is a lived Blackness that chronically reverses the un/gendering and deviancy of queerness (Allen 2016). Their Black/queer existence must be defended when others unsee it, intentionally or not. I show the quotidian critical sources of worth in agency, contention, and erotic power (Alexander 2007; J. Allen 2012a; Lorde 1984). Scholars often view agency and resistance as dynamics that obscure the analysis of extreme subjection (Weheliye 2014). However, I urgently address the unseen agency rooted in Black lesbians' pursuit of well-being for better or worse. I understand their retooled self-worth and agential labor as spirit: mental, corporeal energy for making a Black queer life.

I do not take an ordinary path to understand the relationship between medical experiences and the social world. The book foregrounds Brazilian Black lesbians' theorizations of three key terms frequently used in their interpretations of the quotidian: *vivência* (lived experience), *bem-estar* (well-being), and *preconceito* (prejudice). These terms offer a viable analysis of worth and worth-making. Juliana's and others' insights highlight the negative impact of a rigidly heteronormative gynecological discussion on lived experiences within those spaces. The first routine question posed by a gynecologist is expected to be, "What contraceptives do you use?" followed by, "How are you today?" This beginning sits at the baseline of Black lesbians' critiques of their medical experiences. These heteronormative moments are significant turns that position Black lesbians (and, in varying degrees, also white lesbians and Black heterosexual women, who sit at their intersectional margins and violence) within a more profound intersectional experience of erasure and negation.

Bearing witness to worth and worth-making is Black/queer freedom work. In 2011, I began to recognize Brazilian Black lesbians' buried emotions about their experiences with gynecologists. I realized that Black lesbians and people with gender-nonconforming female bodies in the United States grappled with far more invisible power relations, to the extent that coming out was relatively neither urgent nor emotionally impactful. I focused on Brazil due to the ease and audacity with which physicians behaved unprofessionally. I suspected this was due to colonial specters and the sanctioning of broader violence creeping into those spaces unchecked. As an ethnographer, I was initially most interested in how Black women engaged within their ethical orientation to claim space and navigate their experiences as open lesbians and Black women during gynecology visits. However, I learned that the sense of "claiming" justice within interactions was more than identifying what unfolds medically and socially within an interaction, space, and time in gynecology. The multilayered fieldwork experience—followed by long, in-depth contemplation of all the information collected (from interviews, newspapers, public materials, events, discourses, policies, photographs, and more)—led me down a different path toward seeing how Black lesbians make and remake self-worth, individually and collectively, against violence in the quotidian, within interactions, and on larger scales. After all, when gynecology causes multifold trauma, the effects are immediately sewn into the everyday lives of Black women.

Bearing witness to how my participants grappled with and elevated their worth is an ethical relation that opens multiple parts of ourselves. I came to understand this relation by diving into the depths of Black women's negative emotions: anger, shame, disdain, and fear. Like Bianca Williams (2018), who grappled with her reaction the first time a participant cried, I wrestled with deep emotions. My participants often cried while sharing their interconnected experiences, and I often cried with them. I am an ethnographer with training from a social justice seminary in New York City to hold space for, listen, and connect to the energy and words of others. I keenly see others through their unseen parts. When I cried with participants or sank into my emotions without tears, I recognized that my emotions were pathways to my knowledge production and connection with what participants revealed.

Some Black women responded to the unwelcoming of their bodies and identities by not seeking care when medically necessary or by silently enduring an aggressive speculum exam from a glaringly *preconceituoso* (prejudiced) gynecologist. Many similar stories about disdainful, presumptuous, and abusive interactions with gynecologists drive this book. These stories are acutely traumatic at both the physical and subjective (emotional, cognitive, and spiritual) levels and are layered with post-traumatic stress. Black lesbians' varied responses of self-care and self-worth to gynecology should be read not as negligence but rather as responses to entrenched societal prejudice and toxic encounters.[7] This is bearing witness to unseen flesh.

Intimate Violence: Gynecology's Intersecting Logics of Preconceito
Because of skin color preconceito, thousands die of hunger, violence . . .
Hate sinks further in the world every second.
You think you're superior, you hurt the mother who is holy, you hit me in
    the face,
Man mistreats a child. The sin of the sinner is skin color prejudice . . .

Because of color prejudice, if you are poor, you are already a thief.
But the doctor who robbed never goes to prison; the killer cop has skin color
    prejudice.
Ignorance spreads through prejudice of our skin color . . .

It's because I am black that I will hide
It's because I am white that I detest you
It's because I am Indian that I will be extinguished . . .
Awake (Desperta).

These are selected translated verses from "Desperta (Preconceito de Cor)" by the famous Brazilian Black diva singer Margareth Menezes. She was among the first artists to forge ideals of Black power and antiracism into popular music. These lyrics remind us that racial prejudice is powerful enough to produce intimate *and* systemic violence. She vocalizes doctors' crimes, shielded by racial privilege, while Blacks are presumed criminals. For Menezes, racial prejudice goes beyond bias or preconceived ideas. It is an epistemological mechanism rooted in anti-Black violence on all scales. *Unseen Flesh* uses the term *preconceito* in part because during my fieldwork, it was a buzzword in public discourses that explicitly denounced racism, sexism, homophobia, and other forms of systemic oppression—in contrast to the United States at that time, when the word *prejudice* was largely absent from the public discourse.[8] I also pry open this term because, like Menezes, my participants discussed preconceito with profound, palpable disdain, and they positioned it as a significant culprit for their negative experiences with gynecologists. One participant, Luciana, said to me about the gynecologists, "Para com sua preconceito!" (Stop with your prejudice). This statement expresses more than resistance to prejudice; it is a call to abolish it and its entrenched effects, which lead to volatile interactions and institutions. For my participants, preconceito was a social tool to disintegrate Black life. As I took more significant notice of how pervasively the term also circulated within the social movement and government materials, I understood *preconceito* as a catchall term for structural violence and power relations.

In Brazil, the diffused, elusive singular term *preconceito* too easily erases or marginalizes the experiences of Black nonnormative sexualities and gender-nonconforming female bodies. Brazilian "afro-nationalism" (C. Smith 2016, 6) has disrupted racial democracy with greater Black visibility and interventions to racial injustice.[9] However, institutional spaces, such as medicine, maintain ideologies and practices inherited from Brazil's history during slavery, after slavery, and in the twentieth-century, hygienist and eugenics movements. Kia L. Caldwell (2007, 2017) has focused extensively on the impacts of racial discrimination and social exclusion on the health of Afro-Brazilian women. Caldwell traces the slow progression since the 1980s of an intersectional approach to advocating for reproductive justice for Black women, prioritizing issues such as fibroid tumors, sterilization, and maternal mortality (2017, 118). Caldwell also interrogates the normative futility of color-blindness within Brazilian health care. She advances my analysis of intersectional preconceito as a multifold ideological feature of the gynecological encounter that materializes broader injustice within society.

In Brazil, while a significant number of women consult gynecologists more than necessary, approximately thirty-three million women do not go to the gynecologist at all or delay their visits.[10] It is no secret to the public health sphere that gynecological spaces abuse power. In 2015, Sheu Nascimento, a Black lesbian community organizer in Bahia, published a piece in *Bloguerias Negras* that called out how Black lesbians' experiences of exploitation in gynecology are silenced within broader reform platforms that combat racism and *lesbofobia* (S. Nascimento 2015). An intersectional preconceito analysis exposes gynecology's intimate violence and toxic culture.[11] Intimate violence differs from intimate partner violence such as domestic violence and sexual assault. It produces gyno-trauma in gynecology rooted in abuse of power toward the Black lesbian body marked by "gender '*dominado*' (dominated), race '*inferiorizada*' (made inferior) and sexuality '*abnormal*'" (de Oliveira 2019, 117; see also Prado and Machado 2008). Intimate violence in gynecology is a sort of neocolonial "monstrous intimacy," which Christina Sharpe defines as "a set of known and unknown performances and inhabited horrors, desires, and positions produced, reproduced, circulated, and transmitted, that are breathed in like air and often unacknowledged to be monstrous" (2010, 3). Like Sharpe, who interrogates postslavery subjects, sexual trauma, desire, and how the Black body is read by gynecologists in subjugation, I read Black lesbians' trauma, the intimate violation of their bodies, in both the present and sociohistorical sense. I read their trauma in this way to *reject* gynecologists' and academics' separation of Black lesbians' sexual and reproductive body parts from their subjective selves.[12]

Still, intimate violence is not without hidden intersecting logics that manifest what Brazilian race scholar Adilson Moreira calls institutional *microagressões* (microaggressions) (2019, 52). Moreira's work focuses on the pervasive, entrenched "recreational racism" of jokes and insults within Brazilian workplaces, media, and institutions. He points to the ongoing need to dissect interlocking logics of oppression reproduced within institutional spaces with chronic social and corporeal trauma in marginalized patients such as Black lesbians. However, Denise Ferreira da Silva also cautions us about the mechanism of racial logics within societies that draw from libertarian ideas only to maintain "exclusion and obliteration" of Black bodies (2016, 185). Here, Sharpe, Moreira, and Ferreira da Silva are instrumental in illuminating the entanglement of intimate and systemic power through Black lesbians' lens of the unseen racial logics that differentiate exclusionary existence from the obliteration of worth. And so, Brazilian queer freedom and Black sovereignty may never be possible in gynecology. But a mapping of Brazilian Afro-diasporic queer desire, Black decolonization praxes crossing into and out of those spaces, is the much-needed evidence of survival in worth and worth-making.

Shadowboxing Fieldwork

I name my Black queer feminist methods *shadowboxing fieldwork* (Falu 2021). Shadowboxing the field does not ignore the shadows in which Black queer women live. It analyzes within those shadows Black queer women's challenges to "state power, conventional discourses and politics, and the stereotypes that obscure their political agency" (James 1999, 8). I retool Black feminist Joy James's notion of shadowboxing to legitimize my radical warrior decisions, experiences, and labor when applying my multiple identities to identify evidence that I deem relevant to this topic. Shadowboxing the field turns over rocks, regardless of size, on the fertile ground of insidious power, which includes discourses. In 2011, I became interested in how health care (both public and private) would ensure the rights of all LGBTQ+ citizens to be free of prejudice and discrimination.[13] The Ministry of Health finalized its political and reform agenda in 2013 with a policy titled *Política Nacional de Saúde Integral de Lésbicas, Gays, Bissexuais, Travestis e Transexuais*, which purported to be an intervention on the part of Brazil's public health care system (Sistema Único da Saúde, or SUS) to combat the inequities that impact LGBTT people and their health.[14] These documents asserted that prejudice and discrimination lie at the root of LGBTT health inequities. This national public policy reinforced a commitment to eliminate such inequity. The ambiguous implications for such social reform to effect change for the LGBTT population became more apparent after my 2013 visit to Porto Alegre in southern Brazil. Porto Alegre, a large urban city with a much smaller Black and Brown population than Salvador and a higher number of private health care users, had significant lesbian activism around health issues. In 2011, lesbian activists in Porto Alegre initiated a Municipal Reform Agenda for Lesbian Health to extend the national reform platform. White lesbians who mobilized these efforts told me that they attempted to hold gynecologists in Porto Alegre accountable for developing and implementing new policies and strategies to eradicate homophobia in health care. Those efforts had not succeeded by the time I arrived, and their municipal reform intervention was paralyzed. They reported that gynecologists did not believe in "lesbian health" issues and did not want to take seriously the impact of prejudice on lesbians' well-being and decisions to seek health care. Despite these defeats, these lesbian activists were far more advanced in promoting public discourses and dialogue with the medical community than activists in Salvador were. Such mobilization is intricately tied to how racial relations are forged sociopolitically: anti-Blackness would demobilize such efforts in places like Salvador if taken up by Black lesbian activists (see Carneiro 2020).[15] The Porto Alegre visit confirmed for me that being a Brazilian white lesbian is a racial privilege that opens doors to financial and political efforts to mobilize policy work.[16]

This invisibility within the white feminist movement and policy work provokes Brazilian Black feminists to use Sueli Carneiro's longstanding notion of "enegrecendo o feminismo" (Blackening feminism) to recognize how unseeing racism mobilizes whiteness in power relations (Carneiro 1995, 2005, 2020; Santos 2014, 163; Caldwell 2007, 151). For Carneiro, "enegrecer" feminism is to mobilize intentionality in addressing the oppressions of Black women through an anti-racist agenda (2020, 3). Racism is often tricky to explicitly isolate as a discriminatory practice in health care (Davis 2018; Hoberman 2012). Carneiro (2011) would agree that Brazil's public discourses are critical vehicles for "whitening" (*embranquecimento*) medical racism by not forcefully addressing—if addressing at all—a normative system within public health discourses steered by white lesbian feminists and activists. The feminist discourses about lesbian health have fallen short of taking up Carneiro's anti-racist agenda. The 2006 document *Saúde das Mulheres Lésbicas: Promoção da Equidade e da Integralidade*, given to me during my fieldwork, was a pioneering publication for its focus on the health of *mulheres lésbicas* (lesbian women), yet it focused mostly on white lesbians, or lesbians homogeneously.[17] The research and propositions in this publication are a significant point of reference within national policy agendas, facilitating awareness of the implications of health policy for this subpopulation. The report includes quantitative research on health and mulheres lésbicas—but for the most part, its structure situates *homosexualidade feminina* in public and local discourses to understand its history, vulnerabilities, and social formations.

The report focuses on preconceito as the basis of the social conditions that negatively impact lesbians' health and access to health services. It draws attention to "the invisibility of female homoeroticism; the invisibility of feminine sexuality in itself; and the degree of prejudice (*preconceito*) that we have, today, in relation to homosexuality" (Prefeitura Municipal 2011, 4). Yet it almost disclaims recognition of other disadvantaged populations identifying as *homosexuali-*

dade feminina by its very minimal charge to recognize "racial/ethnic or class" as substantial categories of preconceito. It contains almost no data on Black lesbians—another sign of Black lesbians' (and Black women's) invisibility in health policy and health research. This type of national lesbian health policy points to the challenges facing local discourses to specifically explain what constitutes preconceito in relation to anti-Blackness within health care or institutional spaces.

Through my Black queer orientation to the field, I latched onto a lesser-known document within public discourses about Black LGBTT life. *Negros e Negras Lésbicas, Gays, Bissexuais, travestis e transexuais: construindo política para avançar na igualdade de direitos* was published by the Secretaria de Políticas de Promoção da Igualdade Racial (SEPPIR), a state-level constituency for racial equality established in 2003. The pamphlet envisions the intersection of racial and sexual identities and rights in a way that reinforces the relationships between citizenship, social well-being, and preconceito.[18] The document emphasizes that at the intersection of social identities, racism and homophobia impinge on the well-being of the Black LGBTT population. It poses the question, "What does it mean to be Black LGBTT in Brazil today?" The answer lies in an "attitude of life" and "a proposition of transformed (self and communal) politics." An attitude of life is central to worth-making when one is subject to multiple forms of systemic oppression. Nonetheless, such public documents and agendas that center discourses on race and racism illustrate that even a world free of homophobia applies unevenly to the fullness of Black LGBTQ+ well-being.

Brazilian Black lesbians see themselves as Black women first and as lesbians second. Another, more widely circulated 2012 document, *Saúde da Mulher Negra: Guia para a Defesa dos Direitos das Mulheres Negras*, delineates the structural conditions and inequities affecting health: biology (individual factors and reproductive capacity), social and economic relations (impacts of racism and patriarchy), environmental conditions, and the efficacy of the SUS.[19] The areas impacting the health and existence of Black women in Brazil were at the top of my participants' minds, particularly as all of them have kin affected by inequities in those domains. This report reminds the public that health, in general, is not about individual actions but about a "complete well-being that is physical, mental, and social." Its opening question is "how to define health (*saúde*)." Undoubtedly, an agenda for Black women's health starts with sensory and corporeal aspects such as "sensations, sentiments, visions, the comfort of the individual body and collective bodies" and, for Afro-Brazilian women in particular, an "embodiment of sacred body spiritually." It is critical to draw on such a report with a structural framework of intersectionality to explain Black women's health challenges with "patriarchal racism, institutional racism, and environmental racism" as the driving forces limiting and destroying Black women's lives.

Public discourse and the material mediums to communicate and translate social conditions are invaluable sources for Black queer ethnography. Among a plethora of examples of discourse production, I never found a booklet on Black lesbian health and well-being. These public materials, alongside the many spaces, events, and people I sought to learn from about Black lesbian life and Black life in general, are what I consider shadowboxing the field. "Shadowboxing the field" also refers to how I followed necessary, unconventional, "radical" Black feminist pathways—including tuning in to television and music, art and sports, social movements, and marches—that interconnect for Black queer analysis and all of which trace back to worth-making in gynecological spaces. As a physician assistant and an ethnographer, I understand that people do not leave parts of themselves at the clinic door. When we inquire into the stakes of life and living, methodologies that uproot power and make available the normative and nonnormative are most often seen by ethnographers who are also at the margins in the academy.

Unseen Flesh is undoubtedly a feminist ethnography forging radical and materialist feminist strategies to intercept forms of power (Davis and Craven 2016). I found that women wanted to talk for hours. They talked passionately, robustly, and ragefully. They shed tears or erupted in laughter. I did not take for granted the open sharing of their private lives in an incredible amount of detail. I interpreted their openness as a sign that the topic was highly significant to them. I conducted over sixty interviews on this journey from 2011–2013 with Black lesbians, physicians, and other informants (including medical staff, activists, and Candomblé religious leaders). The twelve Black lesbians I followed closely were out about their sexuality in all realms of their lives.[20] A Black/queer feminist ethnographic approach takes seriously the invisible intersections of identity, knowledge, praxis, and presence (as well as absence) transforming women and gender-nonconforming Black female bodies for liberation. I follow Jafari S. Allen (2016) in what it means to deterritorialize "Black/queer" narratives in anthropology. I agree with J. Allen that "queer may never do what some defenders claim it was meant to do—include a more capacious coarticulation of a number of embodied and embodying categories of normativity, like nationality, gender, region, class, and ability, as well as sexuality" (2016, 618). In Brazil, the term *queer* arrived in the academy from white LGBTQ+ scholars. My participants did not identify (at that time) with the term, nor is it necessary for them to adopt it. Nevertheless, a Black/queer analytic is crucial for honoring their erotic subjectivities and erotic autonomy (J. Allen 2011, 2012b; Gill 2018; Lorde 1984; Wekker 2006; Alexander 2005, 2007). Black queer ethnography draws on the agential sociopolitics claiming space to exist in the social world.

Freeing Ourselves: *Bem-estar* and *Vivência(s)*

The visual guide and handbook *Freeing Ourselves: A Guide to Health and Self-Love for Brown Bois* (Cole and Han, 2011), produced by the Brown Boi Project in Oakland, California, facilitated my conversations about the myriad ways Black and Brown nonnormative bodies are cultural producers of well-being rooted in resistance and ideas of freedom. The guide's vivid photography and images depict sexual health and well-being across topics such as sexual practices, mental health, and pregnancy. The photos (and the book) elicited from my interlocutors expressions of a deep sense of self that I interpret as an evaluative and transnationally self-reflective ethical condition of their lived experiences as Black lesbians of the African diaspora.[21] However, Black/queer freedom is not a given in representational politics. In this sense, this is a reproductive justice project centering and reimaging Black queer reproduction.

Ethnographers' Black/queer politics inform our presence and knowledge production in the field, coexisting with transnational African diasporic feminist strivings in solidarity. As cultural anthropologists invested in the study of diasporic Black life, we pay attention to how the quotidian moves us to imagine different futures. We thrive within narratives, images, ideas, and material culture that create speculation about what ought to be, or not be, for Afro-diasporic people. I agree with Jessica Marie Johnson, who, in telling a story about Black women's intimacy during slavery (and into the present), asserted there is much "more than confronting violence" (2020, 12). Like Johnson's story, my exploration of the erotic, desire, familial relations, and *luta* (struggle) responds to Sueli Carneiro's (1995, 17) claim that Brazilian Black women "have to do more than just hope for a better future. What we have to do is to organize, and never to stop questioning. What we have to do, as always, is plenty of work" (see also Carneiro 2003).[22] *Unseen Flesh* captures the "plenty of work" (Perry 2013). I propose a renewed *olhar* (gaze) that dismantles the myth of Black women as "towers of strength who neither feel nor need what other human beings need, either emotionally or materially" (Smith 1995, 256).[23]

Black lesbians know that they cannot use the "master's tools to dismantle the master's house" (Lorde 1984, 110).[24] Neither are they interested in forging new identity politics within spaces of power as liberatory strategies. Instead, they embody "lesbianism as an act of resistance" that rejects modes of servitude, and they engage in decolonizing, solidarity practices, and self-formation to define their quality of life as legitimate cultural critics (Clarke 1981, 12). This book joins the growing scholarship on Black queer studies that gives rigorous, loving, committed attention to varied theoretical frameworks for the study of Black queer life (A. Allen 2015; Avilez 2020; Johnson 2018; B. Jones 2021; Keeling 2019; Quashie 2021; Strongman 2019; Sullivan 2021; Tinsley 2018). This book brings to Black queer studies renewed social analysis and humanistic insights for Black queer existence. It is worth contemplating Black/queer futures with *bem-estar* (well-being) and how striving for it is a promise to ancestors and *orixás* (African deities) that they will not die a social death but only grow in beauty and joy (Falu 2020, 51). What word breathes life into our daily existence? That word is *us*.

The Book's Offerings

Unseen Flesh begins by digging into a world of vivências to explore sexual health as liberatory and foreground women's concept of *viver minha sexualidade* (to live my sexuality). I turn to Black lesbians' self-identification as virgins to interpret vivência as erotic power. Black lesbian virginity is a disruptive positionality for gynecology (and the sociohistoric making of sexual health in Brazil that constructs the healthy ideal family) since my participants are trying to live their best, healthy sexual lives. Chapter 1 introduces a lived bem-estar by centering the meaning of Black lesbian vivência(s) and turning to the notions of sexual health broadly and a body politic that exposes a social disequilibrium within a gynecological encounter. The chapter also establishes the language used by Black lesbians, interpreted in forms of erotic power to claim space and knowledge within the challenges of derailing speculum exams. Chapter 2 introduces my term, *gyno-trauma*, to rearticulate gynecological trauma and to emphasize the emotional and social pain and labor caused by gynecology. It charts Black lesbians' negative affective experiences with intersectional preconceito to rethink the intertwined facets of redefined gynecological trauma. This chapter considers various modes of "staying in your body" (Cox 2015) and resistance, such as body-scanning practices of "sousveillance" (Browne 2015), to convey Black lesbians' activated social gaze and orientation to their bodies within gynecological spaces and interactions.

The ethnographic interludes before and after chapter 3 cross the reader temporally and spatially. These interludes represent an entry and exit, passage points, of sorts, into and out of gynecology's "contact zone" (Pratt 1992) shaped by the sociohistorical legacy of slavery, eugenics, and a sanitary society and structural power. Here, I examine how gynecology, both sociohistorically and in the present, is an imperialistic, colonial, and modern contact zone. These splices of sociomedical history are the sociological and anthropological hauntings in what I name the *social clinic*. This chapter interrogates gynecology to look for sociohistorical ideologies entrenched in a contemporary colonial, racist, sexist, heteronormative, and homophobic space. Through these histories of gynecology and medicine, I interpret the intricacies of language, symbols, and power relations and the nuances of physicians' socialities, which are sometimes contested and sometimes unseen by Black lesbians. I open with Luciana's story of reading the intimate violence of anti-Blackness and heteronormative gynecological experiences. Gynecology is where gender is constructed, race is made, and sexuality is deployed. Through the dichotomy of private and public, gynecology reveals contradictions worth contemplating. The sociohistorical ideologies and institutional practices ingrained in gynecological spaces mirror broader hegemonic forces. The social clinic functions as a microcosm of the social world from which intimate violence emanates; there we can see gynecology as part of a larger social laboratory in Brazil.

Chapter 4 brings us into the world of worth-making in intersubjective relations and examines how Black lesbians respond to the social world, with its preconceito and violence beyond—and because of—the gynecological encounter. Ethical and political resistance spheres are the unseen social world where Black queer women want to be heard, seen, and be taken seriously as subjects who forge "shapeshifting" ethics (Cox 2015). I refer to how Black queer women shapeshift their value systems in protest, advocacy, and social movement work in response to institutional violence. In their activism and other resistance and abolitionist work, they are animated by a desire to effect change within public discourses and communities—specifically, to eradicate injustices. I describe their interventions—protests, social movements, and new directions in public discourses—to give a glimpse of Black queer women's empowerment and sustaining of themselves and others; again, these are their responses to preconceito and to living with structural violence. By looking at Black queer women's collective organizing work and how they occupy spaces, I understand them as ethical subjects, which allows me to track their shapeshifting efforts to eradicate injustice across all spaces. I offer a framework to understand the ethical relations that the Black queer women have to themselves and their intersubjective networks.

What is Brazilian Black lesbian living? Undefinably beautiful experiments (Hartman 2019). If Black lesbians, like Black women, are already from the future, chapter 5 centers on the ancestral inner energy reminding us that Black women's lives are radical. I conclude the book with "beautiful experiments" to frame my theorization of *bem-estar Negra* through the lens of the Black lesbian's most intimate ideas, places, relationships, struggles, and dreams. The notion of *bem-estar Negra* raises the analytical bar to ask, "How are we beholden to and beholders of each other in ways that change across time and place and space and yet remain?" (Sharpe 2016, 101). Through an anthropological lens of Black lesbian worth-making, Black lesbians' past, present, and future together become an African diasporic trajectory of possibilities, creativity, reimaginations, and erotic playfulness about what truly matters: their collective well-being.[25] All the chapters work together to analyze how Black queer bodies move about in the world, in and out of violent spaces, and zealously seek our attention to humanize, reimagine, and recreate a different world.

I am inspired by M. Jacqui Alexander's expression of her book map section, "If I Could Write with Fire: A Word on How to Read," for this section on the book's offerings (see Alexander 2005, 9, 18). I cannot tell you how to read this book, but I write with *fire*. I offer an opportunity to listen to the melodies and feel the sensations, full of turns and twists but all interconnected, to help understand Black lesbians' experiences making meaning of their worthy lives. Like Alexander, this is the Spirit in which I offer this book.

I

―――――

THE VIRGIN WHO LIVES WITHIN HER EROTIC WORTH

Vivência (Experience)
In a daily attempt
We try in crooked lines to find
The exact meter
Sustenance.
What is right, I believe
It is for us to succeed in our mistakes
Be fortified
Through our weaknesses.
With time
The armor
Acquired in battle
Is nothing but
Then a shield defense
Of ourselves
Of our actions
Hastily made
So . . .
Learning from experience,
We'll get struck
On wisdom.
—Cléa Barbosa

"I will need to get my house in order after my grandmother dies, get my *concurso* [training and exam for a government job] completed, and start to *viver minha sexualidade* [live my sexuality]."

These were Marcia's anguished words to me during her grandmother's deteriorating final days. As we sat at our usual bakery for coffee and cheese-and-turkey hot sandwiches, Brazilian style, she explained that by "viver minha sexualidade," she meant finding love or romance, doing her political work, and enjoying her friends. We routinely met for coffee after her long days of paid work and community/political organizing. She constantly returned to self-reflections, showing intensifying anguish about her life. Finally, I would break the tension by teasingly asking her, "And sex?" She would giggle fiercely and say, swaying her index finger, "Noooo, my love. Not me right now!" She was adamant about staying single for a while and just dating; that, too, meant living her sexuality. However, Marcia was an out lesbian and very active in LGBTQ+ politics and activism, which did not seem enough to live her sexuality. All the while, I grappled with *how we live our sexuality* and what that meant for Brazilian Black lesbians. I learned that "living your sexuality" is a much broader and more subjective practice than finding romance and love, a partner, or sex. It means, among other things, to struggle, defend, survive, and be creative; it means to expect and demand respect for our inner being as Black queer women and, in Marcia's case, as a Black lesbian virgin.

Lésbicas Negras (Black lesbians) develop and deploy quotidian living strategies to counter, or simply to recognize (there is power in silence), medical-social experiences that reproduce gendered, sexualized, racialized, and classed oppression. In analyzing these strategies, I ask, with Naisargi N. Dave (2012, 17), "How are cultural norms newly imagined, deployed, and inhabited in and through the politics of sexuality?" My interlocutors perceive their sexuality in the broader context of their daily routines. They use the expression "viver minha sexualidade" to describe their struggles with the social norms and violence that attempt to restrict their sexual freedom as Black queer women.

The politics of sexuality are always gendered and classed. Moreover, sexuality's coexistence with the raced inscriptions (Wekker 2006, 5) of Blackness makes it the most devalued locus of being and self-worth in Brazilian society. At times Marcia felt a void in her life, captured by how she described her erotic visions and worth-making. Only by finding a woman (or two) to love (*amar*), make love to (*namorrar*), and enjoy companionship with would she truly *vivendo a sexualidade dela*. Finding love and romance in a relationship is culturally tied to how some Black lesbians express their sexual freedom; I interpret these self-expressions through their social conditions and ability to enact freedom. As a result, their intimate relationship to their sexual subjectivities often spills into gynecological clinical spaces to forge their sense of self-worth, not just in being treated but also in staying grounded in their worthiness through erotic power.

The story I tell in this chapter begins to capture lésbicas Negras through their formulations and reformulations of the notion of *viver minha sexualidade*. I center how Black lesbians theorize what it means to live well and grapple with pushing the limitations of doing so. I rearticulate the Portuguese notion of *vivência* as more than experience in its literal definition. For Brazilian Black women and Black feminists, *vivências* are the lived realities that encompass how their Black bodies experience freedom, survival, or violence, with all three often intermingled. The notion of *vivência* raises existential questions about how Black bodies exist, thrive, endure, and celebrate life, and about the belief systems tied to that vision and outcome. To live well is to live within our worth and worth-making, or erotic power.

In this chapter, I argue that these Black lesbians readjust to particular terms of engagement by (re)making themselves, claiming renewed subject positions in erotic power, and reformulating racialized sexual subjectivity in and beyond the gynecological encounter. By *gynecological encounter* I refer to Black lesbians' orientations within their multiple positionalities and power relations during the gynecological clinic visit. In conceptualizing their lived sexuality within multiple positionalities as Black lesbians, or their *vivências Negras*, as I have argued elsewhere (Falu 2019), I rethink it as an embodiment of erotic subjectivity and autonomy (Alexander 2005, 2007; J. Allen 2011, 2012a, 2016; Lorde 1984). This framing situates how Black lesbians pursue embodied sexual health as liberatory and as a way to make self-worth for well-being. The forthcoming sections are concerned with Black lesbians' theorizations of viver minha sexualidade that evaluate, navigate, and demand ways to exist through their sexuality and Black bodies in gynecological spaces and their worlds.

Specifically, I center Marcia, the thirty-nine-year-old Black lesbian who identified as a sexually active lesbian virgin; her concerns were similar to those of other Black lesbian virgins I engaged with (Falu 2019). Virginity is a discursive identity and an embodied practice, critical to how such Black lesbians evaluate the problematic normative systems of gynecology. I ground the notions of *virgin* and *virginity* through linguistic and philosophical meanings within a gynecological encounter to grasp them as queering liberatory terms. These worth-making terms forge knowledge production for Black lesbians to protect their vivência and redefine normative ideas of sexual health. We rarely reflect on how gynecology can be and historically has been a violent, racist, and heteronormative system. Viver minha sexualidade is a critical concept for interpreting small acts of refusal that reject these kinds of violence to forge instead a corpo-reality grounded in human value. Black lesbians are more than patients. Their lives speak to how to decipher a gynecologist's manner of welcoming and un-welcoming and the necessary conditions for coexistence anchored by self-worth.

Unseen Vivências

When I first met Marcia, in 2011, I was captivated by her insight and depth of knowledge about LGBTQ+ movements, histories, politics, social realities, and cultural production. She talked for hours about everything from Brazilian LGBTQ+ history to the minute details of people's lives. Everywhere we went, even walking down the street, someone knew her! Her social and political re-lationships and networks opened the LGBTQ+ world to me in ways that others could not. I followed Marcia to theater shows, live music shows, *debates e mesas* (public debates and panels), and government and social events where LGBTQ+ folks gathered. She was flirty and charismatic. I only wished I had paid more attention to how she flirted with other women, but then again, she was that smooth in her affectively sensual interactions. Above all, she excelled in en-gaging her sociopolitical world and its people. Her praxis of community care and knowledge exchange touched many lives. People either loved or despised Marcia for her loud views and outspokenness. Still, she was utterly devoted, dedicating unpaid labor to mobilizing LGBTQ+ and Black social movements.

Her extraordinary presence within these social circles was an intricate path-way (one not always immediately apparent to me) to affirm her feminine sexual and racial politics. One evening in October 2012 she invited me to the Quinta Possiveis Sexualidades film festival at the cultural center. Marcia was most in-terested in the short film *Quem Tem Medo de Cris Negão?* (*Who Is Afraid of Cris Negão?*), about the life and death of a Black trans woman in São Paulo. Most attendees were white LGBTQ+, some were Black gay men, and a few were trans women. Marcia circulated around the room with her provocative charm, soaking in every aspect of the event: the people, film, and vibe. All the while, I asked myself, "Where are the Brazilian Black lesbians?"

After the screening, we got coffee at a restaurant in my neighborhood. I was eager to get Marcia's thoughts on the sparse attendance by Black lesbians. As usual, Marcia spiraled with reflections about her own lesbian life and in-volvement in social movements and politics. I quickly began to care less about not meeting more Black lesbians and, instead, gained perspective on what the evening at the film event meant for both of us. Marcia shared the news about a twenty-two-year-old Black lesbian, Daiane Almeida dos Santos, killed the day before by a heterosexual male neighbor in a suburban neighborhood in Salvador. The neighbor had a dispute with Daiane and her nineteen-year-old partner, Djeane Ferreira Lima. The next day, the neighbor and another man invaded the women's apartment and attacked them, fatally stabbing Daiane and severely injuring Djeane. We also talked about the murders of two other young Black lesbians in August 2012 in Camaçari, just outside of Salvador. Daiane's murder had not received much attention in the media. Then Marcia told me that when she was in her early twenties, her father was killed while working at the gas station he owned. Over twenty years later, she remembered how he accepted her homosexuality at age sixteen. Marcia said, "Every day we live to kill the lion (*matar um leão por dia*). I am not ready to be in a relationship." I understood Marcia's need to remain separate from the demands of a relationship while caring for her grandmother, sorting out her professional life, and knowing the risk of violence against lesbians. A relationship was a responsibility on different registers that she rejected. I experienced countless heavy conversations with participants contemplating sexual freedom amid entrenched intimate and structural violence. Black lesbians do not separate their sexual desires from the desire to escape or eradicate everyday violence.

To be Brazilian, Black, lesbian, female, woman, feminine, or/and masculine, and to hold all these positionalities—and more—at once is the focus of this chapter. I also include being a virgin. It is impossible here to give each of these subjective positions the attention it deserves. Nor should we disconnect them when we spotlight any one term; parsed embodiment work knows they are fused. I resist the tendency to relegate these concepts to identity politics. Doing so obscures the fuller life created and experienced by African diasporic people. There is deep color livening our intersecting identities as beautiful Black people, as captured by Alice Walker when she said, "Womanism is to feminism what purple is to lavender" (1983, xii). What would it mean for a Black queer feminist query to honor the purpleness of life itself separate from the social categories that bind us? The richness of Walker's analogy about Black women's lives offers permission to arrange, with care and justice, the lived experiences and reimagined possibilities of Black lesbians in Salvador. If Black lesbians are to white lesbians what purple is to lavender, I stand on solid ground when I say that purple accentuates the depth of our intersectional selves.

At this colorful junction about mattering Brazilian Black lesbian life, I pay close attention to the word *vivência* (experience) used by Brazilian poet Cléa Barbosa (2012).[1] Her poem "Vivência," which opens this chapter, invites us to interpret a deeper intersectional existence at the margins (and mercy) of power structures but not at the margins of life sustained. As expressed in the poem, *vivência* captures the "crooked lines" of lived experience and the pathway of "sustenance" into its embodiment. The uneasiness of *lived* experience, not simply experience, has a temporality that brings past and future into the present in "fortitude, armor, action, and wisdom," as noted in the poem. Audre Lorde (1984) warns that for Black women, "poetry is not a luxury" but rather a "revelatory distillation of experience" (37). She states, "It is a vital necessity of our existence. It forms the quality of light within which we predicate our hopes and dreams toward survival and change, first made into language, then into idea, then into more tangible action" (37). Lorde and Barbosa understand that wisdom is at the core of our inherited and forged legacies binding us transnationally across time and space. Poetry is never a luxury if fortified by our wisdom shaping our optics to navigate and resist structural worlds. I follow Lorde and Barbosa, among others, in embracing this notion of vivência.

Sexualidade and Sexual Health in the Erotic

Black/queer scholars and anthropologists have theorized the notion of the erotic to rethink how Black/queer subjects push against the constraints of heteropatriarchal systems (see Alexander 2007, 2005; J. Allen 2012b, 2011; Gill 2018; Lorde 1984; Wekker 2006). For example, anthropologist Jafari S. Allen reminds us that the "erotic can push us toward a more holistic understanding of subjective agency" (2011, 80). Like Marcia, my participants defined sexuality in a subjective agential holistic manner to encompass "living affectively," "caring for the body with awareness," and "moving freely with sexual desires in private and public." Marcia was my first interviewee, and she adamantly said, "Sexuality is not in the sexual act itself but must lie within the plentitude of body, mind, and spirit." Like others, she perceived sexuality as touch, embrace, and everything involved in loving a woman's body—including her own. These perceptions are critical subjective nuances forging corporeal space for joy and pain, pleasure and care, survival, and freedom.

The embodiment of the notion of sexual health disrupts normative societal perceptions and capitalist heteronormative systemic norms.[2] When I began to inquire about the idea of sexual health, I discovered that it was a relatively new concept to my participants and within Brazilian public health discourses. Public health issues related to sexually transmitted diseases (STDs) and sexual dysfunction, for example, were deployed under family health and sanitation discourses. Brazilian lesbians were curious about the risks of contracting STDs such as human papillomavirus (HPV) and herpes simplex virus (HSV) during oral sex or by sharing sex toys within their sexual relations. My research always sparked these discussions. Their gynecologists did not have answers for them, even if they dared to ask. Women picked my brain for hours, knowing that I am a physician assistant (or *médica*, as Brazilians called me) with a wealth of medical knowledge about physiology and the management of medical conditions. Brazilian gynecology is invested in these public health discourses to control women's bodies (J. Gregg 2003) and to pathologize self-care within Black cisgender and queer communities. When I interviewed Nanda in 2011, she said, "Nessette, to be honest, I never heard of this term 'sexual health' (*saúde sexual*) until you mentioned it." I was intrigued by the nonnormative perceptions of sexual health and the associated nonconforming epistemic practices of a lived experience beyond mere survival. Yet Brazilian Black lesbians have significant language for it, such as *cuidar minha sexualidade* (to take care of my sexuality), which disrupted even my own Westernized relation to the discourses of sexuality and sexual health. How does a Black lesbian take care of her sexuality? Does doing so disrupt normative views of sexual health? I address this question by interrogating the erotic as embodied power (Alexander 2007; Lorde 1984) that moves beyond sex into a more profound subjective value of the self rooted in resistance against domination and violence. Through these terms we understand the social forces of viver minha sexualidade.

Audre Lorde's conceptualization of the uses of the erotic helps us think about the rooted forms of these vivências within their sexual liberatory stances. For Lorde (1984), the erotic "is a resource within each of us that lies in a deeply female and spiritual plane, firmly rooted in the power of our expressed or unrecognized feeling . . . as various sources of power within the culture of the oppressed that can provide energy for change" (53). Lorde's notion of the erotic as power emphasizes the need for women to draw on their inner selves—"our internal knowledge and needs . . . those erotic guides from within ourselves"—as sources of empowerment and freedom (53). Lorde's interpretation of the erotic is a road map to situate Brazilian Black queer women's knowledge production in the deepest parts of the self and, in this case, in self-defining and existing as a Black lesbian virgin. Brazilian Black feminist Joice Berth similarly helps me think through erotic power in her argument that "processes of empowerment are not just stimulated by external triggers within the quotidian but also an internal movement of consciousness awakening our diverse potentials to define our strategies to confront the systemic practices of domination, machismo, and racism" (2019, 25). I understand Berth's concerns (also shared by Lorde) with triggered empowerment and awakening by how Black lesbians tap into this erotic power to lead their self-care, advocacy, and resistance after experiencing institutional violence. Black lesbians are driven by—and, more importantly, devote themselves to—their erotic power to awaken their intersectional positionalities as sources of freedom to define *vivência*.

One day Marcia insisted that I attend a public forum on violence against women. I was hesitant to take the long bus ride to the Universidade do Estado da Bahia (UNEB), anticipating another academic performance by white Brazilian scholars and feminists. Indeed, most speakers were white Brazilians. But I was unaware that UNEB (a state university known for its grassroots social resistance) was hosting twenty days of events at campuses across Bahia to raise awareness of the International Day to End Violence against Women on November 25. If I had declined her invitation, I would have missed a priceless moment to witness Marcia's impromptu participation on the panel to represent her group, Lesbibahia, and assert her value in addressing the audience.[3]

At the opening event, a Brazilian white trans woman diva sang fabulously. Marcia appeared confident, sitting on the stage with the panel of three women and three men, including lesbians and gay men. Marcia's short address was consistent with how I understood her social justice views. She said, "Our spaces of poverty, our areas in poor suburban life (*periferia*), for sure, these spaces are becoming more violent. So, from this view, I accept the invitation to dialogue with you all. What do we want to see ten, fifteen years from now if we accept that a person can be killed for [being a woman] loving a woman, or [a man] loving man, if you are a Black woman or poor with fewer resources than others. So, we must respect differences if we want change."

Marcia's public message illustrates how Audre Lorde's analytics of the subjective, such as the erotic as power, render visible how marginal women tap into their sources of empowerment. Marcia recognized that she inhabited the center of the Venn diagram comprising the three overlapping circles of other panelists' identities: white lesbian feminists, Black heterosexual women, and Black lesbians. In Salvador, many Black lesbians and Black heterosexual women are aligned in solidarity because race and racism are their ultimate shared struggles. Marcia was willing to be the Black lesbian face in spaces where race and racism were not at the forefront of the battle. This radical presence forged erotic power.

The stakes of erotic power when sharing spaces, even collaboratively, with non-Black lesbians were made evident by the two plenary lesbian speakers (one Black and one white). I grew accustomed to Black women in Salvador engaging the work of Audre Lorde and bell hooks to think through social life and justice. I also learned how Brazilian Black women influenced by Lélia Gonzalez, a Brazilian Black woman anthropologist, activist, scholar, and feminist, chart a Black feminist transnational tradition of critical thinking through non-Brazilian Black feminist epistemologies. This transnational knowledge production returned far more self- and communal value for transformation and empowerment to manage embodied distrust of society than most Brazilian white women's epistemologies. Critical thinking about intimate issues must also feel safe and nonviolent to women's subjectivities. At the panel event with Marcia, Professor Denise Botelho, a Black lesbian, for her plenary speech delivered a powerful presentation about love. She said that the fact that "many Black women do not have the opportunity to love is rooted in how colonial expansion stripped their ability to show and express love. Colonial expansion depended upon this intimate violence to create social conditions that did not fully emancipate us" (Botelho 2012).

Viver minha sexualidade, then, means that Black lesbians hold themselves accountable for the self-care of their sexuality as Black queer women, recognizing the sacrifices and risks in defending their existence and right to love, starting with themselves. The capacity to exercise sexual freedom pushes through the limits of anti-Blackness and racial conditions. This self-care is their erotic power shaping their inner selves, which then drives their social practices. This is worth-making. Professor Botelho (2012) introduced herself by saying, "I am a woman, Black, lesbian, and mother," whereas the white plenary speaker identified herself only as a lesbian. On our way home on the bus, I asked Marcia how she interpreted Professor Botelho's identity claims compared to the other woman. Marcia said, "She did not have to because she is white. White women do not need to identify their struggles. Black women do." These social practices express erotic subjectivity to conquer oppressive spaces with uneven racial and class relations and, as Marcia would say, to "matar um leão" everywhere. Gloria Wekker (2006, 5) reminds us that a Black diasporic understanding of sexual subjectivity also requires an understanding of sexuality as gendered, classed, and, more importantly, raced. As stated by Shaka McGlotten and Dána-Ain Davis (2012), Black sexuality belongs to racist and anti-racist discourses because "it is effectively everywhere permeating all aspects of cultural life, including the spheres of mainstream political and popular culture and transnational black diasporic spaces" (7). For McGlotten and Davis, Black sexuality is central to Black living as much as to the sociopolitical landscape of the African diaspora. For example, Marcia understood her Black sexuality to be affected by all aspects of mainstream life, and thus her earlier public message was a demand for respect for her being. Her source of empowerment charging the public to take the necessary risks to pursue physical safety against violence.

Erotic subjectivity is the optimal self-expression of corporeal safety. It is the material body and the inner self: feelings, thoughts, energies—holistic bodily security attained by defending life itself and the lives of those who breathe air into us. Viver minha sexualidade is a highly developed relationship of the self to itself; further, it generates awareness of responsibility to the self and others in the quest for modes of freedom. Marcia often reminded me that her grandmother was the first person to unwaveringly accept her homosexuality when she came out at sixteen years old. While a grandmother's unconditional love can ground any person with affirmation and legitimacy, Black women crucially embody for their grandchildren the norms and codes that shape self-love, struggle, survival, and endurance for navigating societal injustice. Marcia was always clear that she held firmly to her grandmother's affirmation in navigating how others addressed her sexuality. Families do not always welcome homosexuality, particularly Black families; Marcia was privileged to be anchored by that affirming legitimation. It taught her to live her sexuality at an early age and manage the risks and dangers of living life as freely as possible in a world entrenched in homophobia and racism. Marcia's erotic subjectivity is her embodied power drawn from all dimensions of living through her Black lesbian sexuality.

How do we reimagine sexual health that is intricately tied to the social world in terms of caring for one's sexuality? This vision requires a nonnormative view of sexual health beyond sexual practices and public health alarms. Luciana defined sexual health to me as "uma forma de liberdade" (freedom). If sexual health is a socially liberatory domain, and not centrally tied (if at all) to disease or medical health, then how Black lesbians demand recognition of their multiple identities and bodies formulates Black lesbian philosophies and practices to create or salvage their sense of human experience. Black lesbians define their combined sexual health and bem-estar as how to live their sexualities, tending to their various subject positions (raced, classed, gendered, sexual, ageist) within their world. It is anti-racist praxis to resist anti-Blackness, that is, not only confronting preconceito but freely expressing their empowered sexual subjectivities. They viewed sexual health as *cuidado de bem-estar* (care of well-being) or *uma forma de estar bem* (a form of being well). While there was often an explicit or implicit sense of sexual health tied to preventing STDs or caring for yourself by going to the doctor and treating STDs, our conversations consistently led to deeper, more robust, and broader forms of self-reflection.

At first, during fieldwork, I focused on how Brazilian Black lesbians interpreted sexual health as the idiom in our conversations and interactions through which they measured and analyzed their existence. Sexual health served as a framework for perceptual self-care or caring, a self-motivating way to forge justice, improve their lifestyles, and minimize the effects of life stressors such as disease, family issues, and poverty. For my participants, sexual health has much to do with sharing the pleasures of a healthier sexual life with same-sex lovers. It has even more to do with socially engaged acts of freedom, viewed from a racially and socially conscious understanding of well-being. Alexander's (2007, 2005) concept of erotic autonomy is critical for reflecting on sexual health as an empowering social category of making well-being for Black lesbians. Marcia did not have a live-in partner or any sexual partners. She did not want a relationship amid her family obligations, although lesbians in Salvador love to move in together quickly for financial reasons or to make a relationship official. I would tease Marcia with this idea of *casar* (living together even if not legally married) to elicit a response about her desires.

> ME: Marcia, are you secretly in a relationship? You are so popular.
> MARCIA: (laughing) No, my love! I do not want a relationship right now. Lots of women want to sleep with me, but I am waiting for the right time. I do not want anyone to pressure me to move in! I need to focus on myself and my grandmother. I need to get my life right first. My last relationship ended two years ago and lasted six years. No more!

Marcia's shimmering body language suggested that she yearned for a relationship despite her adamant rejection of it. These acts of refusal were ways to exert agency in her life. I also follow M. Jacqui Alexander in believing that the "erotic conjoins the spiritual and the sexual" (2007, 157). Marcia's 107-year-old grandmother had taken a sudden turn and was dying. Marcia was at a crossroads examining her past, present, and future existence without her grandmother. Yet the erotic self was not on hold or erased from her life. On the contrary, she expressed it through her erotic autonomy. Alexander's interpretation of erotic subjectivity as a dimension of the autonomous self—erotic autonomy—is critical for rethinking embodiment within a Black lesbian life "fully embodied with our many vulnerabilities" (156). For both Alexander and Marcia, sex is not just about how we use the body for pleasure. Instead, sex is about liberating our Black lesbian sexuality on our terms, including through our vulnerabilities. Therefore, sexual health is more than a set of practices to prevent STDs or tend to sexual medical dysfunctions. Sexual health becomes a dimension of our erotic autonomy and the ability to freely choose with whom, when, and how to live through our sexuality and bodies.

Marcia's and others' terms of engagement regarding bodily advocacy pivoted on claiming sexual health as liberatory existence amid often oppressive social conditions. I rethink sexual health as a means to self-express by any means necessary the devaluing forces that penetrate the body and the need to release them. In this sense, sexual health as liberatory is what Black feminist Lorraine O'Grady posed as "the reclamation of the body as a site of black female subjectivity" (2009, 321).[4] Black female subjectivity is always placed subordinate in otherness. It is also "self-expression" that stands as a "stage that cannot be bypassed. It is a discrete moment that must precede or occur simultaneously with the deconstructive act" of the subject (322), which, in Marcia's case, power and violence attempt to subordinate. Like O'Grady, I am concerned with how Black female subjectivity is not just shaped by systemic oppression, like racism, but alerts us of lurking, imminent danger to harm it or to close the opportunities to express and feel it in wellness. O'Grady gets us to think about how the deconstruction of the self also injures or obliterates parts of our being. This view of reclaiming subjectivity as situational and positional is critical to appreciating the ongoing healing and worth-making from self-breakdowns and self-questionings in institutional spaces and society. The idea of reclaiming subjectivity allows us to appreciate how Black lesbians in this study express their critiques and protect their lived experiences through demands, observations, and praxes beyond insisting on respect for their identities. Black lesbians recognize their objectification and the social relations that devalue their humanity and existence. In many self-expressions, Black lesbians revere their capacities and insist that society recognize and respond to their self-worth.

For Marcia and others, their pursuit of Black lesbian living within their *lesbianidade* (lesbian lived experience) is also understood through their notions of sexual health as vivência, *como você mente vive, ou como se relaciona sexual mente e cultural mente* (experience, how we live, or how we relate sexually and culturally). Marcia's joy when occupying cultural spaces of resistance can be read as enabling her sexual health as vivência and as a self-care practice of worth-making. Through our conversations and time spent at activist and sociopolitical events, I also understood that a chief facet of self-formation and embodied knowledge about sexual health is to be found in resisting preconceito. Sexual health disrupts our normative understanding of protecting our sexual bodies to allow us to rethink the embodiment of sexuality for more unrestrained sociopolitical expression. For my participants, sexual health is a lived experience with high stakes and the potential for much gratification. Given the extent to which the city of Salvador can be an oppressive environment for Black women, articulations of their sexualities are means of "self-governance and strategy of existence" (Biehl, Good, and Kleinman 2007, 5) in the pursuit of liberatory experiences.

Marcia's daily rituals included taking early morning walks along the beach. We often ate ice cream or dinner at that beach in Ribeira. She would tell me, "Preciso uma respira com orixá [deity] Yemanjá" (I need a breath release with Yemanjá). Marcia was not an initiated member of Candomblé, a major Afro-Brazilian religion derived from West African religion, but often visited a Candomblé priest or priestess or attended ceremonies open to the public for spiritual cleansing. The deity Yemanjá is associated with the ocean, and Marcia found relief and sustenance in the ocean's life force. When I asked how she cared for her sexual health, she referred to these activities first and foremost.

My intervention in sexual health to situate vivência as the erotic subjectivity of the Black lesbian body illustrates that the sexual self is made possible only by unloading the social burdens carried within and freeing the inner self from many social realities. As Keisha-Khan Y. Perry reminds us, "Black women who live the very real material nature of the intersections of gendered, racial, and class inequities hardly debate the need for radical social change in Brazil, nor are they passively waiting for that change to take place" (2013, xviii). Perry's work anchors Black women's vivências in their racialized and classed everyday lives in Salvador. I keep in mind that Black women, both heterosexual and lesbians (feminine and gender nonconforming), too often live their quotidian lives "picking up the pieces," as noted by Perry, managing everyday violence that includes police brutality, socioeconomic deprivation, and gender violence. The stakes are often life and death; their lives are weighed down by urban violence and the struggle to care for their community (137–38). These are the ways many Black lesbians understand the depth of their vivências amid violent macro- and microaggressions and microinsults in gynecology that burden them, thereby "picking up the pieces" from a society and economy that fragment and intensify their vulnerabilities. Erotic autonomy is an embodiment of vivência, tending to the openness and strengths of the body, mind, and spirit.

(Un)welcoming Black Lesbian Virginity

On the day I interviewed Marcia, I appreciated observing her exhaling deeply, gathering her thoughts while staring out the window at the sailboats on the blue water of Bahia Bay; our breakthrough giggles; and even her becoming frustrated during some topics. Her emotions and reactions, triggered by my questions about sexuality, race and racism, and being a Black lesbian, were heavy for both of us. Marcia had brought her pelvic ultrasound reports to the

FIG. 1.1: My apartment window in Bairro Dois de Julho overlooking the Bahia Bay.

interview, including presurgical ultrasounds for the hysterectomy performed just a year earlier for multiple large uterine fibroids (often referred to as benign uterus masses or myomas). I was deeply moved. As a physician assistant, I considered these documents private. When she invited me to make copies for my research and began to explain how they fit into her story, I knew she wanted to be recognized not only as a Black lesbian but as a patient and as someone who had undergone a hysterectomy. I understood, too, that Marcia sought my medical insight for reading and understanding the severity and enormity of her myomas and respecting the impact they had on her life and health before the surgery: anemia, fatigue, heavy menstruation that felt like hemorrhaging, and a distended abdomen that made her feel so uncomfortable and unattractive that she stopped dating and having sex. More importantly, she wanted me to know that virginity was central to her identity as a homosexual subject deserving appropriate *acolhimento* (welcoming) by the gynecologist.

At eighteen Marcia had her first sexual experience with a woman. She has been out to and affirmed by her family since her early twenties (in fact, she has a lesbian sister who is *masculinizada e casada* [masculinized and married] who also helps take care of the family). Although her mother struggled the most to accept her sexuality, her father and maternal grandmother affirmed her from the start. Marcia has only slept with women and has never been vaginally penetrated for sexual pleasure. For Marcia, now in her early forties, and others like her in this research, being a *virgem* included sex, herein broadly construed. They described virginity as representing social and sexual lifestyles, not necessarily celibacy or intentional abstinence for religious purposes or waiting for marriage, normatively speaking. Virginity meant sexual autonomy and the capacity to define their erotic pleasure and practices in nonnormative ways, such as not being sexually penetrated. Virginity becomes a social category of experiences and meaning about different expressions of erotic desire, corporeal autonomy, and freedom—even pride—in being "intact." Although I am not privy to the details of her sexual practices, Marcia is aware that talking about her sexual practices is taboo for gynecologists. These taboos, along with related stigmas and myths, are sociohistorically entrenched in societal norms that prohibit honoring lesbians' sexual practices and pleasures. For example, one myth is that nonvaginal penetrative sex among women who have sex with women assumes that the person not being penetrated must have a masculine gender presentation. Also, nonvaginal penetrative sex stigmatized by heteropatriarchal forces constructs women as "rubbers" (Wekker 2006) and "grinders" (Habib 2009) to devalue the endurance of erotic sexual play in resistance to patriarchy.[5]

I see Marcia's Black lesbian virginity embedded in her erotic political freedom. Through her lens, I understand her virginity as a site of resistance using myriad practices of sexual autonomy, such as lesbian friendships and political allyships, and as the erotic contestation of patriarchal power. For example, Gloria Wekker's (2006, 26) work on the Creole *mati* women in Suriname describes rubbing as a sexual practice to preserve the "rope" or hymen of young women waiting to give themselves to a man in marriage. However, for socioeconomic reasons, many *mati* women had sexual relations with both men and women. Wekker argues that these sexual relations deviate from heteronormative sexual expectations within a "politics of passion" by anchoring sexual pleasure in the erotic relations between women. In these instances, virginity is "not so much connected to male honor but to female pride. It is also an instrument in the negotiation with men" (27). Thus, the heteronormative way to view virginity would be to negotiate an intact hymen with men, marriage, and social respectability. In this context, the notion of virginity is inscribed by society's masculinist norms and values about the female body's function to reproduce and offspring guaranteed by the marriage rite. These widespread views about virginity erase women's valuation of sexuality, most of all for sexually active Black lesbian virgins.

Virginity is an embodied value system that grounds self-worth within gynecological spaces. My interlocutors' sexual politics, combined with their self-identification as virgins, gave them sexual agency and sexual freedom throughout their gynecological experiences. Marcia wanted to protect her sexuality and mode of being as a lesbian as she sought medical intervention for her growing and symptomatic uterine fibroids (which led to her hysterectomy in 2011). The ultrasound reports were part of this tangled narrative. Marcia sought to preserve her virginity by seeking a gynecologist who would not penetrate her for a vaginal exam or transvaginal ultrasound, which is typically done in Brazil as a routine screening or presurgical test. Marcia wanted to be respected as a lesbian and accepted as a virgin. Too often she had had negative experiences with female gynecologists who did not accept her notion of virginity, stating that she could not be a virgin as she was having sex with women:

MARCIA: I refused to go to the gynecologist, especially women. I had several problems with female gynecologists. They do not listen, are rude (*grosseira*), and do not show concern for my issues.

ME: You would tell them you are a lesbian?

MARCIA: (nodding) The medical exam approach is solely based on doing [vaginal] penetration. Their approach is very conservative and violates me. Besides insisting on how they wanted to examine me. One time it was just ridiculous. They acted toward my virginity like, "Ah, that's nonsense."

ME: Are you talking about the use of a speculum?

MARCIA: Yes. It was normal or acceptable during my early twenties to be a virgin. Now, they are disturbed by it. They say, "How is it that I am still a virgin and no man has had sex with [me]? Maybe you like a woman because you never slept with a man." This embarrasses me. It is hard for them to understand [me] as a woman that is still a virgin.

ME: But did they still want to do the speculum exam?

MARCIA: (nodding) Women gynecologists can be very mean. Once had one that gave me the ugliest facial expression. What did I do? [I told her] Girl, goodbye! I have always had a lot of autonomy in public or private health care. I have always been very self-caring. And then I found myself not wanting to go to the gynecologist.

For Marcia, this memory of her gynecological encounter exemplifies what is minimally not *acolhimento*, or not welcoming, of her and all of her parts (bodily, subjectively, and socially) in the medical space and encounter. Marcia's embodied notion of lesbian virginity guided her refusal to be physically penetrated by a speculum or metaphorically penetrated by societal rejection. She understood being penetrated as an act of social violence that would obliterate her sense of self as a lesbian virgin and negate her efforts to manage her sexuality.

For eight years, Marcia tried to find a gynecologist who would not disregard her need to be respected as a lesbian and a virgin. Her virginity was a driving force in negotiations with her clinicians. Their disregard for her unique conception of her body and sense of being exemplifies the prejudices toward lesbian sexuality held by many physicians. Marcia recounted the *vergonha* (shame) and rage she felt when gynecologists did not believe that she had not had sex with men, despite indicating that she was a lesbian and virgin. As Marcia showed me her report of an ultrasound, ordered by a male surgeon, of her abdomen and pelvis, she proudly explained that Dr. Carlos had said, "Sim, eu atendo mulheres lésbicas e virgens" ("Yes, I attend to lesbian women and virgins"). For Marcia, this response was enough to initiate a dialogue based on respect and her request not to be penetrated by transvaginal ultrasound. She explained that his care was welcoming; he demonstrated sensitivity to her needs to be respected socially and physically. He signaled protection of her vivência by affirming her medical decision-making. This was a humane connection that was absent with other gynecologists. Her request to not be penetrated vaginally and not violated in multiple ways was successful; he honored her request. She was ultimately sent for a pelvic ultrasound to evaluate the myomas and her pelvic structures. She had an abdominal hysterectomy performed in early August 2011. Marcia reported feeling relieved to find someone to end her suffering. Despite her generally good health, she had worked and maintained a good health insurance plan that would allow her to secure these medical services on her terms eventually and to receive the surgical intervention that ameliorated her health status.

At the gynecology visits, Marcia wanted her virginity to be associated with her homosexuality without denigration of her social status as a woman. As she stated, "Não e uma mulher realizada porque não tem penetração" (You are not a realized [or real] woman because you have not been penetrated). This social status is one of the many heteronormative stigmas of women's sexual identities and practices; gynecology participates (and perhaps is a central culprit) in them. In Brazil, medical institutions construct racialized women's sexual health as dangerous through "risk and blame" discourses (J. Gregg 2003, 41). For example, women in the northeast region of Brazil were held responsible for not preventing HPV infections that led to cervical cancer. Anthropologist and physician Jessica Gregg (2003) more generally affirms that medical institutions participate ideologically in public discourses to dominate women's bodies.

In Brazil, female virginity represents many complex issues, including religious conservatism and intentional chastity for social and economic gains. Some gynecologists I interviewed in Salvador attempted to be considerate and attentive to virginal patients (whether lesbian or heterosexual) and their sexual and bodily needs by not using a vaginal speculum or even performing Pap smear exams. They may use a Q-tip swab instead of a speculum (see chapter 2), but this distinctive care technique is often delivered with aggression. Marcia described her embarrassment and shame in the presence of gynecologists after comments such as, "How is it that you are still a virgin and no man has had sex with [you]? Maybe you like a woman because you never slept with a man." When Marcia explained how she turned her back on gynecologists, she referred to her recognition of autonomy over her body and consumer rights as acts of freedom. Her bodily understanding of herself and others is a nonnormative sexual and social enactment of freedom that emerges in the search for recognition in the medical setting.

My own experiences as a physician assistant performing speculum exams and as a Black lesbian who engages in penetrative sex with women (and receives speculum exams) pushed me to understand Marcia's decision-making process. A Black female lesbian body challenges the normative view that virginity is verifiable and definable in an appropriate medical approach (see Schwarz 2002). Semantically, virginity indexes the instability of patriarchal power over sexual norms and virtues. My research findings tug these perspectives in a different direction, reframing virginity as a socially functional identity and as politics of embodiment. The term *virginity* translates into the self-expressed vivências and is an affirming social status claimed by the self within the gynecological space. Virginity, then, disrupts the effacement of self-value by remaining ambiguous, undefinable, and unverifiable by the medical gaze (see Abbott 1999; Bernau 2008; Schwarz 2002). A patriarchal medical gaze deeply informed by physicians' personal beliefs and values about social and biological order is further challenged by nonnormative ideas of virginity. Not giving access to the Black lesbian virgin vagina, not because it is being preserved for a man, heteronormative marriage, or reproduction, but in an expression of political freedom to live *minha sexualidade* (my sexuality), is a powerful claim.

What does it mean to demand respect of all different positionalities at once—virgin, lesbian, Black, woman? Gloria Wekker's (2006) perspective on Black diasporic sexual subjectivities is helpful here. As she states, we should think of "sexuality as activity, not exclusive identity" (214).[6] By this she means not returning to sexuality as sex but moving beyond crystalizing sexuality as identity and opening a dialogue about sexual practice through the embodiment of Black lesbian life. Wekker's work shows us that *mati* women live their erotic subjectivity as resistance in ways J. Allen (2012a) describes as "the deployment of the erotic subjectivity of a thinking, desiring, decision-making subject, willing to transgress. Erotic subjectivity is an alternative way of knowing, looking for one's own lived experiences and one's intentions and desires and more 'authentic' pathway than ways of knowing that are imposed or imbued by others" (329). Wekker's and J. Allen's approaches to erotic subjectivity rethink the ways of knowing one's limits and boundaries and are predicated on being anchored in the embodied experiences of vivências on multiple scales. Black lesbian vivências' registers of erotic autonomy shield self-value when exerted within institutional spaces. There is no distinct shape to an architecture of resistance for self-protection. Marcia's choice to protect her virginity as vivência grounds her self-worth, as it does for other women. These small acts of resistance are rooted in self-worth, shaping her as a reflective being who resists the hierarchies of language, technology, and material tools used to disintegrate the labor of self-care. In this sense, virginity is a state of expression within the plentitude of social categories shaping vivências; it is not necessarily the physical status of biological parts.

Violent Disequilibrium in Gynecology

Marcia's pursuit of inner stability in the medical encounter echoes what another Black lesbian described by saying, "sexuality is equilibrium." This participant said that after her pelvic exam, the male gynecologist told her that her uterus was ready to conceive and recommended that she take medication to correct her *falta de apetite e estímulo para homens* (lack of sexual appetite for men). She never wanted children. She was adamant that "eles não saben como respeitar a gente como pessaos. Não preciso ser um orientador sexual!" (They [gynecologists] don't know how to respect us as people. He did not need to become my sexual advisor!). Equilibrium here means taking care of oneself in all *sentidos* (ways), including health. Too often, Black lesbians feel that the insulting and violently unwelcoming entry into the medical space disrupts that equilibrium.

My informants described gynecologists' pervasive assumption that lesbians who have had penetrative sex with men at some point in their lives should tolerate the insertion of a vaginal speculum in the same way as most sexually active heterosexual women. Such medical attitudes and approaches are a feature of the reproduction of compulsory heterosexuality, which generally functions to uphold the patriarchal structure of medical practice and control over women's reproductive care and sexual practices. These approaches, in turn, subject female patients to both social and medical discourses primarily concerned with the biopolitics of STDs and reproduction-focused sexual health. I consider these normative approaches part of the gendered and sexualized subjection of women in gynecological settings. We should avoid ascribing fixed meanings to sexual terms.[7] Being a Black lesbian and a virgin is a slippery proposition to balance in maintaining self-value when value is organized and projected through racialized sexual subjectivities in institutional spaces. In seeing Black lesbians' constant reformulations of inner equilibrium to affirm themselves, I lift the ways they know they want to be received and treated and how they insist on moving beyond medicalization by gynecologists.

Black lesbians forced to assert their value in gynecological spaces expressed the coexisting violence that targets their subjective selves and bodies. These assertions represent how their erotic autonomy threatens both social and medical hierarchies. My interlocutors describe sexuality as pleasure and sensation; it is within the self and at the same time a public mode of being. These existential reformulations resist the world's rejection of their Black bodies as hypersexualized yet undesirable, not to mention dangerously subject to social violence within the medical practice of gynecology. Medical interactions that cause disequilibrium of being are a subtle form of colonial violence. I think about how the embodiment of both struggle and freedom keeps Black women in a constant state of self-defense. As Marcia said, "It [gynecologists' behavior] violates me." These Black lesbian narratives articulate a violent disequilibrium of their erotic autonomy taking place in the clinic. As Alexander points out, "Not just (any) body can be a citizen any more for some bodies have been marked by the state as non-procreative, in pursuit of sex only for pleasure, a sex that is non-productive of babies and of no economic gain" (2005, 6).

I draw from Alexander's analysis of state violence and surveillance deployed to control the sexualization of queer bodies to point to the entrenched dysfunction of physicians' practices toward women's social identities and lived experiences. For example, tying sexual health primarily to STDs and sexual dysfunction is an infrastructural, medicalized tool that gynecology uses to control and surveil sexuality. Like Alexander, I assert that "homosexual difference is indispensable to the creation of the putative heterosexual norm" (Alexander 1994, 6). Gynecology is often complicit with the social norms (and dysfunctions) that disrupt Black lesbians' liberatory embodied autonomies. These subjective disruptions, or disequilibria, are deeply imprinted in their minds and bodies; yet these disruptions become intolerable. Marcia's recollection of her experiences produced anguish over and disdain for gynecologists' unprofessionalism as if the events had occurred just yesterday. As a physician assistant, I see the embodiment intrusion. I also see how these moments express embodied self-value in self-affirmation and quickly reformulate into self-protective resistance.

How does gynecology devalue a thirty-nine-year-old Black lesbian virgin body? Marcia's normatively construed nonreproducing body strips gynecology of its capitalist intent to crystalize patriarchal value systems. Wekker says of virginity that its "honor is less about men ultimately than indicating a woman's readiness to have babies" (2006, 27). The assumptions of *falta de apetite* for heterosexual sex and having babies are part of the ongoing colonial gaze centering reproductive bodies as the ultimate form of legitimacy. Like Marcia, other Black lesbian virgins (and nonvirgins) interpret their resistance to this normative gaze on virginity—a gaze that interferes with proper *acolhimento*—as part of an ongoing struggle to defend their humanity against gynecology's abuse of power by experimenting with desexualized or hypersexualized curiosity in the name of enacting medical expertise.

All of my medical interviewees acknowledged that sexuality and gynecology practice are related and that gynecologists should be more explicit in their approach without sexual *preconceito*. Even when questioned about whether their practices may devalue Black lesbians' experiences, they blamed a medical training system that does not prepare them to engage in such matters (see chapter 3). Human value for a Black female body has always been about its domination and erasure. Alexander Edmonds interrogates medicine as ideologically normative, reminding us that "the notion of sexual and reproductive choice is paradoxically accompanied by regimes of medical control" (2010, 32). Edmonds and others point to such power relations as driving practices to sustain medical control over their bodies.[8] Medical control itself is ideological and predicated on the social vulnerabilities of marginal patients. Thus, gynecological normativity belongs to a more extensive reproduction of social norms around gender and sexuality, such as the notion that women with putatively reproductive bodies and heteronormative sexual relations must prioritize their health to sustain such reproductive capabilities. Heteronormativity within the gynecological encounter deflects attention from the ontological expressions of Black lesbians, particularly Black lesbian virgins. These are the unseen systematic ways that power creates convergence between the biological and social realms to maintain medical authority over certain bodies.

In the normative view, reproduction sits at the center of gynecological examinations (Ginsburg and Rapp 1995; Kapsalis 1997; Sanabria 2011, 2016). But many scholars and medical practitioners (like myself) argue that if there is a center to gynecological examinations (interviews and assessments), it consists of much more: normative, systematic ways of constructing women's bodies, gender, and sexuality, all pivoting on racial relations (see Sanabria 2011; Edmonds 2010; Edmonds and Sanabria 2014). Deirdre Cooper Owens (2017) reminds us that, in the United States, gynecology has always had a complex relationship with Black women's bodies. Owens refers to how white gynecologists turned to enslaved Black women as experimental subjects and as medical workers who helped move the discipline forward. This violent complexity is woven together with racial capitalism, technological advancement, and manipulations of medical authority. In Brazil, we can apply such complex relationships to what Cooper Owens (2017) calls "medical superbodies," referring to enslaved Black women's bodies' usefulness for labor and how they were regarded as inferior to white women, lacking "beauty, humility, patience, and meekness" (109). Yet white doctors regarding white women's physical attributes and sexual prowess as less superior than those of enslaved Black women demonstrate that doctors' socialities inform their medical gaze and the construction of sexuality and gender (109). Cooper Owens helps me think about the ongoing colonial logics in how gynecologists who abuse power via their socialities treat Brazilian Black lesbians as having a different kind of modern medical superbody. As this book demonstrates, there is an expectation that Black lesbians will tolerate speculum examinations under any circumstances; they are also viewed as nonreproductive bodies and treated as such.[9] Attending this legacy of enslaved medical superbodies is the expectation that these targeted Black queer women should tolerate such insidious and blatant prejudice, a routinized expectation of dehumanization that white heterosexual women and lesbians ordinarily escape.

As medical subjects and as medical consumers, Black lesbians know that resisting the medical infrastructure's attempts to discard their subject positions is the pathway to attain agential power or resist disequilibrium of their self-worth and sense of self in their values. Yet gynecologists are unaware of how social difference is experienced across interactions. Gynecologists' lack of awareness of their orientation to patients is made possible by the ritualistic ways medical models construct women as medical subjects. As a result, Black lesbians are unseen beyond being patients and detached from their ordinary lives. Black lesbians learn to engage with normative and nonnormative systems to improve their quality of life. They seek "visibility by enunciating their homoerotic relations as a means to publicly define their sexuality" (Meinerz 2011, 46). Is Black lesbian life within a welcoming gynecological space even possible?

I personally know the impact of grandmothers affirmingly caring for our deepest inner self. Marcia talked about her grandmother all the time. She said, "She's dying soon. Her memory and physical function are slowly disappearing." At times she cried, deeply and privately. Yet her smile pushed through the tears like sunshine during a rain shower. She gives a lot of herself to others and her biological family; her dearest obligation was to care for her 107-year-old grandmother. Sra. Giselda was a quintessential part of Marcia's narrative, enabling her to strive for her erotic autonomy and, above all, her daily well-being. I learned, over time, just how much Sra. Giselda was Marcia's soul mate and source of strength and joy. Marcia and I often sat at my window overlooking the Bahia Bay in downtown Salvador and reminisced about how her grandmother almost tricked me into eating stewed stingray.

I visited Marcia's home down in the lower city for the first time to meet her grandmother, who was mostly cared for by Marcia's mother. Marcia's two younger siblings also helped occasionally, but Marcia was the only grandchild living there; she was also a caregiver. Marcia and I spent the day on Dia de Santa Barbara, then went to meet her grandmother. Like Marcia, Sra. Giselda had an infectious laugh. She held my hand tightly because she could not see well, though she was mostly coherent. On this day, Marcia's mother had already prepared fried red snapper with rice and beans. However, Sra. Giselda asked me if I would eat *raya*. Under her loving spell, I agreed to try it, though Marcia told me that Sra. Giselda was the only person other than her brother who ate *raya*. I thought it was some sort of regular fish until Marcia's mom served it to me on a separate small plate like a side dish. From my first glance, I realized something might be amiss and asked, "What sort of fish is this?" It began to dawn on me then that *raya* might translate into ray, and then I realized—stingray! I started mimicking the pointy tail of a stingray as Marcia and her mom nodded affirmatively and laughed at me. I was embarrassed and afraid of offending them, but I could not eat it. I chuckled as Sra. Giselda tried to coerce me with gentle laughter to try the *raya* next time as she chewed the heads of everyone's small red snappers.

These ethnographic moments were crucial for thinking deeply about my interlocutors' humanity and their well-being. By intimately experiencing the people and things that mattered most to my interlocutors, I soaked in the intimate vivências that shaped them racially and sexually. Marcia's grandmother profoundly influenced her and her racial understanding of the world as an elder. For example, Sra. Giselda associated me with President Barack Obama and

First Lady Michelle Obama—no ordinary *Americana*. As a Black woman, I represented that historic pride for her. Sra. Giselda challenged how Marcia learned to embody race. Marcia shared stories about how her grandmother internalized racism and "looked down upon darker-skinned people like herself." Over time, Marcia said her grandmother shifted with racial pride, but the memories of those racial struggles haunted the family. Marcia learned to disregard her grandmother when she was younger and learned to love herself as a Black woman by engaging with social movements. She believes that it is her grandmother's aura residing within her.

There is magical faith in freedom when we embody our grandmothers. It strengthens our appetite to take risks for social justice. After I had been getting to know Marcia for nearly a year through her grandmother as an enabling force in her life, I missed several calls from Marcia one night. The following day, I listened to her voicemail telling me that her grandmother had died, and I began to cry. I had not been there for Marcia. When I called back, she answered immediately and told me about the scheduled burial for the following day. (In Brazil, it is customary to bury loved ones within a day or two.) I was honored to attend. Afterward, I left Marcia at her home, curled up on her grandmother's bed, physically tired and emotionally torn. Her life anchor had passed. Still, she looked peaceful, perhaps drawing on the lingering scent of her grandmother to reenergize herself for her new life with fewer burdens of family care.

Thinking about Black lesbians as Black female bodies, women, lesbians, mothers, daughters, lovers, granddaughters, and much more should compel us to recognize that they can best tell us about their humanity and modes of being and existing. Carolyn Moxley Rouse (2009) points out that it does not matter whether the mechanisms causing suffering are recognizable to physicians; if Black women report suffering, we should believe them. Physicians' (in)ability to recognize their role in causing trauma are entangled with their socialities. Their unwillingness or inability to recognize, believe, or consider Black women's values and social conditions is the making of the unseen. Gynecologists would have to honestly believe in and appreciate Black female bodies as human beings more than reproductive organs. Under these circumstances, human conditions forge deep knowledge of how norms, codes, values, and systemic oppression maintain violent social conditions in their lives, including microaggressions and insults to their livelihood. For these critical reasons, gynecologists must be mindful of how their behavior and attitudes contribute to power structures and social conditions both in their clinical encounters and beyond. Racialized sexuality is a social condition.

The term *condições* (conditions) in Black lesbians' articulations of their medical experiences caught my attention and led me to think about these women as more than patients. For example, Marcia referred to *condições* during her interview in several contexts of attempting to create situations that would allow for her virginity to be honored by her gynecologist, such as discussing the removal of her reproductive organs, striving to afford a health care plan that would give her access to gynecologists who would welcome (*acolher*) her sexuality, and securing the education that she felt was essential to financial and social stability. In these interconnected threads, the body and the social are complexly intertwined.

When Marcia trusted me with her story about her hysterectomy, she described her uterus as not being in any salvageable condition, unlike her unremoved ovaries. She went on, "Yes, my ovaries were left in me and I don't know how this next process will be." When I clarified what she meant by "the next process," I understood that she was under the impression that she would need reconstructive surgery two years after her hysterectomy. But she could not explain what exactly needed to be reconstructed. Instead, she lifted her shirt to show me her large midline vertical surgical scar and implied that there was an incomplete condition waiting for care: an unresolved surgical area on her body. She was also not sure when she could follow up to surgically correct her scar.

Even when procedures are explained in clear terms at length, patients will often not remember everything, if they remember anything at all. It is a lot to process; I know this firsthand as a clinician in both inpatient and outpatient facilities. But, as a clinician, I also recognize that patients' affective experiences and worries about their personal lives are central to how they process their medical conditions and experiences. Marcia's adaptation of the language of conditions is tied to her virgin identity and status. When I asked her about consultations with gynecologists for virgins in general and whether it was common to be a virgin patient, she said, "How virgins are received was key for me in getting treatment [for fibroids]. Otherwise, I could not have done this surgery. I'd have worsened my situation. Why did I need to create those conditions? I needed to create concrete conditions." Here, Marcia juxtaposes several meanings of conditions: the physical condition of her health, the social conditions she contends with given her virginity, and the conditions that she creates for herself to ameliorate both her health and her social experiences with the gynecologist.

Sexuality is a social condition wrapped in all forms of necessities, desires, and resources essential for sustaining vivências or life itself. Along with race, age, class, and other social categories, sexuality drives us to think about Black lesbians as more than medical subjects and patients. Sexuality shapes our embodiment of life, waiting for expression through familiar and unfamiliar experiences. Yet, as a social condition, it also poses a profound threat to the nation's very survival or sovereignty that thrives on the conditions of Black lesbians' lives—discrimination, microaggressions, structural violence, and oppression (see Alexander 2005). Critical to how Black queer women like Marcia live is an understanding of the various social conditions that serve as limits and possibilities for a better vivência and to viver minha sexualidade with more breathing room. Below, Marcia describes the social and physical consequences of an unwelcoming gynecological encounter concerning the term *condições*:

> If you do not receive a welcoming treatment, you go out and look elsewhere until you find it. The big problem is that the public policy on health does not work on our behalf to improve our options. I had health problems, but I needed to get out of a financial situation to afford the gynecologist. I took responsibility for my choices. If I had acquired cancer, I would be the culprit. It was not the state [health service] that did not give me a chance to use those doctors even without that ability to welcome me. Ultimately, it becomes an individual attitude. I took the risk. Besides the risk, I also abandoned my sexual relations with other women during this period. Do you understand? I'll do the revision [surgery] now because I still have problems with the disease [fibroids]. But there is a price to pay: our struggles to improve my financial conditions to take care of my needs. It is better to struggle than to suffer alone for my decisions. My first hysterectomy was an expensive investment, including any taxes, to maintain this health care plan. Because I am employed and earn 2000 reais [monthly], I had to decrease quality food and resources, broaden my studies, go back to school, or start a master's degree because I could not create the necessary conditions. I had to make choices, as I told you yesterday. Today I'm in the process of applying for a job in the public sector. I'll decide to make a way to get my master's degree and leave a legacy (money) to my family in the future.

Marcia views changing the condições of her life as part of an accumulative pursuit of well-being or an intricate part of viver minha sexualidade. These are the material conditions shaping her entire lived experience, including her experiences with health care. These multiscaled conditions affect her life at various levels. Some become strivings, and as a Black woman, these strivings are intense and require emotional endurance. Black lesbians understand the material conditions undergirding and dominating their sexual subjectivities and sexual practices as Black women. I question how we might reinterpret the relationship between social and medical norms to support the emergence of medical subjects' human values and practices. Expressed sexual subjectivities within the gynecological encounter are also sites of negotiation of and resistance to trauma triggers. These women's layered decisions (socioeconomic, sexual, transformative) to improve their condições include both their struggles and their expectations as medical consumers.

Lesbofobia

One discursive sign of sexuality as a social condition is the term *lesbofobia*, used by lesbians regardless of race. Lesbofobia translates to lesbian phobia, or homophobia of lesbians. As Nanda (a participant) stated, "Since I cannot change my skin color, institutional racism is premised on what is seen—a Black body. Institutional racism is premised upon the color of my skin being constant. But homophobia, on the other hand, can be fought with much more optimism by those who wish to hide it because you can't see sexuality and can be undisclosed." Her perspective—that racial difference is a constant while sexual difference is variable—was common. Some of the approaches that gynecologists take might be the same for all women, heterosexual or gay, white or Black. In Brazil, many white lesbians, or *lésbicas brancas*, encounter lesbofobia, injustices, and inequities connected with their nonnormative sexual subjectivities in health care, education, and all areas of life. The lésbicas Negras who speak out, whether in public or private spaces, are racialized sexual subjects targeted more heavily by lesbofobia. Many lesbians, in general, strive to protect themselves—to confront, rally against, and fight against lesbophobia. Black lesbians that I knew were usually not interested in white lesbians' activism because it rarely centered Black women's issues and more often cast them as even more marginal or as a side note to the real struggle.

For decades, Black feminists have acknowledged Black women's speaking out as a necessary defense of themselves and their communities against social injustice, an ontological way in which Black female bodies hold and produce self-worth amid all forms of violence (see Brown, King, and Ransby 1991). Black lesbians specifically defend their *vivência Negra* (Falu 2019); this praxis deserves critical analysis. To resist lesbofobia is to claim lesbianism as an act of resistance (Clarke 1981). For Black lesbians, viver minha sexualidade means that they see themselves as part of a greater struggle against racial violence and anti-lesbianism.

Thinking about Black lesbians beyond their identities as patients means centering their human (and social) condições, including how these are disavowed by insult. Neferti Tadiar proposes "the notion of 'life-times' as a concept for reckoning with the diverse array of acts, capacities, associations, aspirations in practice, and sensibilities that people engage in and draw upon in the effort to make and remake social life in situations of life-threatening hardship, deprivation, and precariousness" (2012, 1). The "life-times" of the Black "assumida" or "out" lesbian subject position are grounded in intersubjective experience and informed by the precarious and singular project of making a human life as a Black woman in Salvador. Being a Black lesbian carries a triple weight: being Black, a woman, and queer. Yet it is a weight freely assumed by my interlocutors as it becomes the way to a life full of happiness, freedom, self-love, and self-care. In large part, well-being for these Black queer women means freedom to achieve the quality of quotidian life produced in time and space and through interactions—including with the gynecologist.

How might we think through the beliefs and ritualized systems that Black lesbians, as marginalized women, use to shift inner space to express and legitimize their sexual liberties as self-care? Many of my *lésbica Negra* interlocutors frame undesired interactions with their gynecologists with the idiom of preconceito as part of social condições antagonistic to their well-being. Their material and bodily conditions drive how they "make sense of the world or interpret what counts as 'reality' through the assumptions it [reality] valorizes and the subjects it [reality] produces" (Hennessy 1993, xiii). They see themselves primarily as racially *Negras* because of their brown skin. They all believe that their white doctors always see race first, via their skin color or other markers such as hair locks or Candomblé neck beads. To them, their skin color is most subject to preconceito; their sexual orientation is secondary because the heteronormative assumptions of most gynecologists render their sexuality invisible. "Sou Negra, mulher, depois lésbica" (I am Black, woman, then lesbian) is how intersecting preconceitos (racial, gendered, sexual) are experienced.

This ethnography is an opportunity to see gynecology as not just a practice instantiating a "compulsory heteronormativity" (Rich 1993, 227) but also as a systematized medical field reproducing the "natural" in gender and sexual subordination alongside anti-Blackness in sharply painful ways. There are deeper social structures, beyond mere individual callousness, that prevent an effortless sense of belonging in the gynecologist's office for Black lesbians. Emily Martin suggests that women often "represent themselves as fragmented—lacking a sense of autonomy in the world and feeling carried along by forces beyond their control" (1987, 194). She attributes "this fragmentation to the effect of social hierarchy and the implicit scientific metaphors that assume women's bodies are engaged in production" (194). Fragmentation of sexual subjectivity and embodied experience are ongoing social processes in these women's lives. The resulting socially complex experiences leave many women torn but not destroyed. I follow Martin to rethink how an "embodiment of opposition" can lead us to a more sophisticated understanding of Black lesbians' subjective strivings and reproductive and sexual health and how "fragmented images" of the self might arise through efforts to resist internalizing the effects of the too often white, male, elite dominance typical of the medical domain (194).

This chapter has argued for the ways erotic power makes self-worth for Brazilian Black lesbians who seek to reposition and reformulate their subject positions in gynecology spaces. These reorientations of embodiment and the body itself to self-define vivências are the loci for illuminating the stakes of intersectional experiences in those medical spaces. Most importantly, this chapter places deep value in who Black lesbians are beyond being patients. In summary, this chapter delved into a broader scope of sexual health redefined by my interlocutors as liberatory and well-being. It explored under what conditions sexual health is expressed and embodied (for example, in sex, relationships, spirituality, forms of freedom, and even institutional spaces). What happens in the gynecological exam room is a moment that is tied to other people's lives, as in Marcia's grandmother's care. Black queer freedom is worth-making. This comprehension inflects our practice in an institutional arena or a specific place, such as the gynecologist's office, we anthropologists happen to be observing. The quality of interaction with gynecologists, of practitioners' (in)ability to integrate their patients' sexuality and identity, may be among the chief complaints about unwelcoming medical practices. However, interrogation of worth and worth-making takes us into deeper layers of self-making against subjects' unseen layered traumas.

2
_____

UNSEEN FLESH

Gynecological Trauma, Emotional Power, and Intimate
Sociomedical Violence

We might concede, at the very least, that sticks and bricks might break our bones, but
words will most certainly kill us.

—Hortense J. Spillers

Black women's living is itself radical. Naming our emotional trauma from oppressive interactions and spaces is an act of rebuke and rebellion. Hortense J.
Spillers' distinction between "captive bodies and captive flesh" is appropriate
for rethinking how gynecological encounters "adopted for the captive flesh demarcate a total objectification, as the entire captive community becomes a living laboratory" (1987, 68). This chapter is concerned with intimate forms of
Black captivity within medical spaces. When a Black lesbian enters a gynecology office, she is seen not as an individual but as part of a larger disposable
collective of body and flesh—as Spillers argues, a living laboratory. The gynecological procedure (both interaction and examination) also holds the Black female body in confinement to medical strategies driven by the abuse of medical
power; these abusive relations penetrate the Black lesbian flesh. With Spillers,
I reenvision these fleshy penetrations as embodied and released emotions that
signal oppressive, harmful experiences. These archives and structures of emotions

represent what Brazilian Black feminist Sueli Carneiro referred to as "a dor da cor" (pain of [our skin] color), deeply seated in Black flesh by the entrenched racial "miscegenation or mestizaje as a letter of freedom from the stigma of black-ness" from slavery (2011, 64). In other words, the manipulation of racial differ-ence in Brazil shows how being a lesbian is yet another entry point for Black female bodies to be targeted with insult and dehumanization, and how being Black and queer continue to cause institutional injury.

Black lesbians' embodiment of physical pain and negative emotional dimen-sions such as rage and fear must stand as critical evidence to interrogate power relations and spaces of power. Indeed, the interpretation of pain and negative affect is Brazilian Black lesbians' grammar for naming their racial inferiority within medical relations. Emotional trauma breeds these interpretations as critical sources of knowledge about how gynecologists receive and treat Black lesbians. Spaces of power compel us to question what freedom looks like. In this chapter I capture what gynecologists and the medical system ignore about the affective experiences of Black lesbians during medical interactions. For example, how does it feel to be insulted or belittled just before or after taking one's clothes off for a speculum or breast exam? What layers of emotional work are undertaken by Black lesbians during and after such interactions? How does emotional work coexist with resistance against trauma? What attitudes of survival and resistance emerge from these experiences in response to their emotional and bodily traumas?

This chapter disrupts the normative definition of gynecological trauma in medicine and society: genital injury resulting from surgical procedure or sexual trauma (see Mulla 2014). My participants reported genital trauma (not just dis-comfort) caused by gynecologists. Nevertheless, we often do not attend to the emotional and social trauma emerging from these spaces of power. Here, I chart a pathway to rethink gynecological trauma, or what I refer to as *gyno-trauma*, to en-compass the affective injuries and social burdens from intersectional prejudices and other abuses of power. I argue that gyno-trauma carries a wide range of bodily and subjective experiences related—but not limited—to genital injury, resulting in the body being a site of survival and resistance. A reformulation of gynecological trauma is grounded in Black lesbians' affective experiences, which remind us that the words and attitudes we breathe can kill us slowly if we do not exhale, resist, and denounce them. This theoretical framework of emotions takes seriously the depth of intersectional emotional trauma and emotionally driven praxes breathing life into Black lesbians' corporeal archives of fear, an-guish, anger, shame, and rage.

We deepen our understanding of Black lesbians' vivências by illuminating their critiques of the intimate violence of the gynecological encounter. I recognize through my clinical lens that emotional trauma and embodiment of pain fester in the body, leading to cancers, strokes, and other stress-related medical conditions among the Brazilian Black population. This chapter highlights pain that is all too rampant in Brazil's medical spaces. These Black queer women learn from bitter experiences to protect their vivências by being alert and critical of the gynecological encounter. I expand the notion of gynecological trauma to address the following: (1) the viability of an archive of emotions that theorizes about emotional and social trauma, (2) a Brazilian Black feminist view of intersectional prejudice and intimate social violence in medical spaces, and (3) a Black queer feminist panoramic view of awareness and countersurveillance practices for reinterpreting Black lesbians' "sousveillance" (Browne 2015, 21) and their own "politics of location" (Rich 1986, 215) within the gynecological encounter. First, I discuss Dora's narrative as an exemplary interaction between Black lesbians and gynecologists to sort these dynamics.

Troubling Speculum—Dora's Story

I first met Dora, Marcia's lesbian sister, during Sra. Giselda's 107th birthday celebration in March 2013. Dora is a couple of years younger than Marcia and came out as a lesbian later than Marcia. She identifies as a masculine-presenting woman, in contrast to her sister's femininity. My first interview with Dora was alongside her girlfriend, Sarah. I construed their eagerness to speak with me as a special courtesy given my participation in her grandmother's birthday. Dora was disgruntled about her experiences with the gynecological services in Salvador (both the Sistema Único da Saúde and private health care services). At the same time, Sarah wanted to speak to the importance of gynecologists developing better ways of approaching lesbians during consultations and examinations.

Dora's life was very different from Marcia's. She worked full-time as a supervisor for a call center that was full of *sapatonas* (butches, dykes, or lesbians) who chose the job because they could be "hidden" from the public, according to Dora. She attended college part-time. She was not as engaged in activism and public discourse as Marcia, but she volunteered in community programs. Dora also frequented *terreiros* (Candomblé temples), though she did not feel called to become initiated. In the past she had been in a publicly open relationship with a Candomblé priestess; openly lesbian priestesses were not common in Salvador.

After the party, Dora pulled me aside and said, "Vamos encima pra fazer a entrevista" (Let's go upstairs for the interview). Interviewing on this topic after such a lovely family gathering felt strange. However, Dora insisted on not postponing it. She also insisted that I return to eat her baked *pudim*. So we headed up a narrow staircase to a room on the second level, and her partner followed us. I was not prepared to conduct two interviews, but, as it turned out, Sarah played an intimate role in Dora's stories of gynecological experiences. During our interview, Dora associated her sexuality with her sexual organs, erotic desires, and sexual relations with women. When I asked if sexual health could affect how sexuality is experienced or expressed, she and Sarah responded simultaneously, "Vai" (It will). Dora added that the negative impact on sexual health is the vivência of when a family does not accept a person's sexuality and relationships. Unlike Dora's family, Sarah's family did not accept her sexuality and did not accept Dora when they began their relationship. This rejection gave them deep sadness, depression, and feelings of isolation. Such psychological and emotional pain limited their subjective ability to feel, they said, "free[dom], desire, and belonging."

Like others in this study, Dora felt anguished about being targeted as a Black female body seen as masculine and lesbian by gynecologists. Dora likened being Black and experiencing her Blackness to being a lesbian and doubly targeted: "Ser Negro sofre mesma discriminação do homosexual. E ser discriminado, e ser inferior, e ser uma classe mais baixa" (Being Black you suffer same discrimination as homosexual. It is to be discriminated, to be inferior, to be a lower class). Compared to *brancas* (white women), in her view, to be a Black lesbian means to suffer discrimination. Dora's awareness about a medical system fraught with systemic racism helped her interpret the doctors as "unprepared when it comes to homosexuals." She told her doctors that she is "gay" to avoid heteronormative questioning about her sexual practices. Most of the time, doctors treated her in a cold, dismissive, objectifying manner. Her facilitation of the interaction was difficult, she lamented, because "it still seems that gynecologists do not listen, do not realize what is at stake for me. I do not know if they don't listen because of my sexuality. If I have already said I am gay, there are some questions that I think no longer apply to me, but they still asked them." Dora wondered if she was ignored because doctors did not want to acknowledge her sexuality or her gender as a masculine-presenting Black woman. She felt it was the latter. These negotiations left her feeling unheard, frustrated, and unable to express her fear of the speculum exam.[1] As a result of doctors' dismissive or insensitive approach to her disclosure of her sexuality (despite her deep fear, as she expressed to me), she had to muster the courage to warn them that the speculum exam caused her much pain. Still, gynecologists usually proceeded without discussion to what always felt like a brutal examination. Dora's main reason for eagerly sharing her story was to tell me that she was horrified by painful speculum exams and gynecologists who never made her feel heard.

Dora reported that she has never had sexual relations with men. Unlike Marcia, she did not identify as a lesbian virgin because she engaged, albeit infrequently, in other penetrative sexual acts with her partners. She believed that because of her sexual practices, she could withstand a speculum exam. Dora learned not to absorb either the experience of the exam or the gynecologist's disregard. Many Black lesbians believed that sometimes it was best to not share too much about their sexuality, even if they self-disclosed, for fear of worse aggression during the speculum exam. Black lesbians also felt that gynecologists do not often engage in "appropriate" conversation during the transition to the pelvic examination. For example, many gynecologists do not consider that a woman saying that she is gay or lesbian is an attempt to open conversation about their speculum exam needs. Dora told the gynecologists, "I'm a lesbian," as a prompt for them to ask more questions about her examination needs. The gynecologist ignoring her and proceeding with the exam caused undue distress over being unheard, physically and emotionally hurt, and even violated. This mistreatment led Dora to believe that being respected and listened to is a fundamental human right. At times, though, Dora reported being too timid to speak up at all—especially with male gynecologists—and she never returned to that first gynecologist for a repeat Pap smear. Both Dora and Sarah reported that Dora's anguish about going to the gynecologist affected their relationship. Sarah said she needed to keep Dora calm for days before and after the appointment. Dora said, "I need Sarah with me. I get very nervous."

Dora became angry and uneasy when we shifted to talking about the gynecological examination. She said unequivocally that she did not like going to the gynecologist because of her ill-treatment and how that treatment makes her feel:

> I go because I have to go. I could even go more often, but I will not because I do not feel right. The exam hurts me and causes embarrassment. By the time of the examination, I was even more scared because now, the moment they touch me lacks delicacy. The material and size [of the speculum] always still hurts me. I always have vaginal pain when I get out of seeing a gynecologist. My fear of gynecologists is much like the fear that people must go to the dentist! Some people say, 'Oh, no, not the dentist!' For me is like: 'Oh, no, not the gynecologist!'

Dora experiences physicians' heteronormative medical practices and instruments (e.g., the speculum) and how they disregard what nonnormative or nonbinary

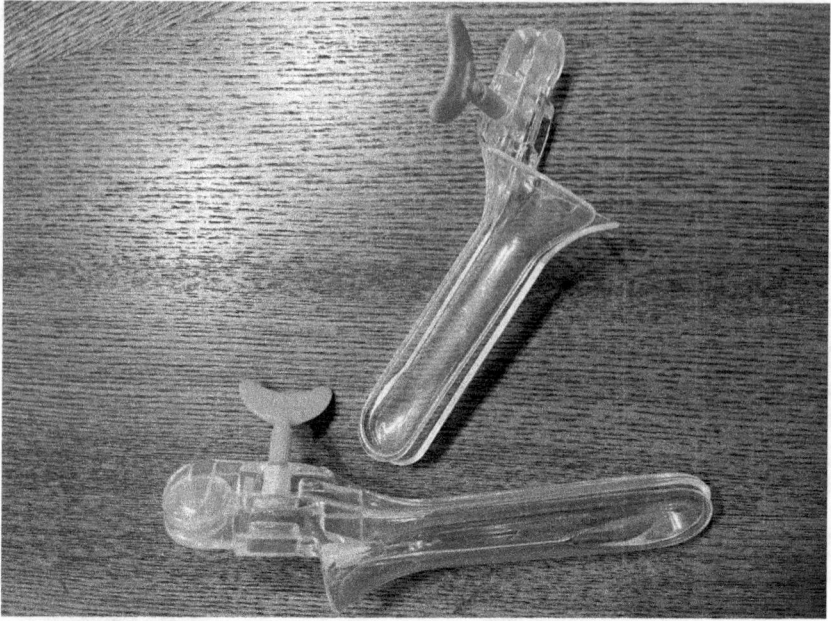

FIG. 2.1: Plastic speculums from a private doctor's office. Photo by author.

bodies need during an exam. Dora said to me that she only goes to gynecologists because "there is no other way." She meant that she needs the medical care
that only gynecologists offer, though none of them tend to her emotional and
physical states during consultations.

In these cases, Black queer women are thrust into a medical process that
subjects them to an aggressive experience of vaginal penetration. Figure 2.1
shows plastic speculums given to me by a gynecologist in a private office. However, Black lesbians reported experiencing large metal specula at their doctors'
offices. These plastic specula exemplify the different experiences in some private and most public clinics. Black lesbians, in particular, walk in anticipating
that their Blackness will elicit first a predisposition to inhumane examination.
When they then disclose their sexuality, they immediately recognize physicians'
lack of acceptance in their behavior and attitudes. Dora described her intense
anguish during the speculum exam and gynecologists' aggression toward her
masculinity and lack of recognition of her homosexuality. She said, "There is a
preconceito to say, 'I am homosexual, and therefore the treatment toward us is
different.'" I barely knew Dora, but she trusted me enough to share her subjective sensibilities. I began to rethink how to interpret her and others' affective
experiences during these encounters. Dora told me that she often needed Sarah

to accompany her to the gynecology visit as support. Such companionship is an act of resistance and care in the aftermath of trauma or in reliving past trauma. It is also witness work. Sarah witnessed Dora's affective experiences after each visit. She learned of gynecologists' inability to tune in to Dora and her need for, perhaps, a smaller speculum or a gentler exam. She emphasized that a gynecologist could choose a smaller speculum or a different way of performing a Pap smear. Sarah said, "Dora vivenciado (experienced) suffering postexamination because she would get there nervous, the doctors would disregard her, she would still have an invasive examination, and then leave there with post-trauma. I would often have to soothe her for days." Sarah used the term *por cima* to describe how doctors took Dora's concerns and threw them to the curb. We agreed that a gynecologist should always choose the option that eases discomfort. Gynecologists' lack of attention and failure to use inclusion to guide their practices within the relational experience were the most substantive concerns. They had a mental impact so profound as to cause a long-lasting post-traumatic reaction. It was clear that many gynecologists do not prioritize Black lesbians' subjective or bodily experiences; otherwise, they would have to pay attention to how they harm Black queer women.

When, in conversation with gynecologists, Dora attempts to establish the connection between her sexual identity as a lesbian (representative of her sexual practices in this context) and the pain a vaginal speculum exam causes, she invites gynecologists to listen and tune in to her subjective space and affective experience. Black lesbians who demand recognition as agents of their own affective experiences in this setting know that they have the human right to a whole, unfractured sexual subjectivity, even when it does not seem directly relevant to their care.[2] Black lesbians' sense of alienation related to pelvic speculum insertion is nearly universal (see Sanabria 2016; Martin 1987). However, Black women, particularly Black lesbians, are subjectively traumatized through a corporeal alienation beyond the technology. Black women already enter the gynecological exam room embodying high levels of vulnerability through the "weathering hypothesis" (Geronimus 1992), also known as bodily fatigue and injury from racism and other power structures. Brazilian Black women scholars have well documented the double vulnerability of Black women in health care due to racism and sexism (see Goes, 2021; Goes and Santos 2014; A. Nascimento 2016). A Brazilian Black lesbian who embodies queerness, nonnormative sexuality, and gender expressions walks into a gynecology office designed to hold heteronormative structures firmly. That Black/queer alienation is felt through layers of pain created by the depth of preconceito from gynecologists and a system designed to undermine the value of Black female bodies. Black lesbians' gynecological negotiations are grounded in their awareness of their subject position as Black female bodies up against the too-common experience of gynecologists not hearing or respecting them.

Gynecological Trauma: Intersectional Formations

Dora's affective and bodily experiences signal that gynecologists disregard the emotional work done by Black lesbians during the gynecological encounter and the deep emotional and bodily injuries that they endure. The imposed emotional burden imprints on their memories. Like Dora, participants recreated their gynecological experiences through potent emotional energy, giving voice to their pain and disgruntlement. The emotional intensity of their gynecological interactions embodies the "social pain" that reveals traumatizing effects beyond the genital pain from speculums (Sturgeon and Zautra 2016). For Dora, her postexamination vaginal pain gives her a voice to tell a profound story about her layered emotional ill-being. Her emotional and bodily trauma narrative mirrors the deep-seated social gyno-traumas that inform how Black queer women reinsert themselves into their quotidian lives and the subsequent gynecological encounter.

Gynecological trauma represents what Elaine Scarry calls the "inexpressibility of physical pain" (1987, 3). The inexpressibility of physical pain in gyno-trauma also carries the inexpressibility of its unseen social and emotional pain. Inexpressibility is itself an unseen expression of layered or simultaneous forms of pain. Inexpressibility is constituted by the injustice of inequitable social relations. Buried emotional pain linked to social relations within institutional spaces is often the root of varied difficulties in "expressing physical pain, in the political and perceptual complications that arise as a result of that difficulty, and the nature of both material and verbal expressivity, or, more simply, the nature of human creation" (3). Dora's story demonstrates the inseparability of these points about physical pain from the "embeddedness in one another" that also exists in gynecology. These intersectional formations of gyno-trauma, including Black/queer formations, carry pain through these multiple social relations in gynecological interactions. During interviews and casual conversations, I often had difficulty focusing on the medical details of my interviewees' experiences as I watched them push through their many emotions. The emotional work in telling their stories was enough to rethink what is unsafe and harmful within these spaces. Black lesbians' capacity for and willingness to express the holistic pain emerging from these experiences does the work of redefining and reframing gynecological trauma within gynecology.

In the biomedical sense, gynecological trauma is any injury to the female genital area. It is usually attributed to pelvic organs or pelvic trauma from sexual abuse or rape, penetrating injuries, straddle fall injuries, or even surgery. The range of symptoms includes pain in the genital area, vaginal bleeding, bruising, swelling, abrasions, and others. Pelvic trauma is typically attributed to "blunt mechanisms" causing a forceful impact on the pelvic area. The field of gynecology is oriented toward treating pathological and traumatic medical issues of reproductive organs. Like other medical disciplines, gynecology depends on a narrow field of vision. As Sameena Mulla says, "Gynecological professionalism demands that during the examination, practitioners orient toward their patient solely as a pelvis" (2014, 140). It is well established that the gynecologic trauma caused by a routine speculum pelvic examination encompasses varying degrees of physical and mental injury for women.[3] However, the need to hold physicians accountable for medical negligence is not widely discussed.

Black queer women's emotional and bodily traumatic experiences in gynecology should not be presumed universal. To collapse together all women's disembodied experiences in these spaces ignores the more profound social pain and trauma imposed by entangled forms of structural power such as racism, heterosexism, homophobia, sexism, and classism. It is also important to note that not all speculum-derived pain should be reduced to physical pain. For example, neuroscience and pain management research show that physical pain and social pain overlap in neural pathways, exacerbating bodily pain (Sturgeon and Zautra 2016, 63). Social pain is attributed to experiences of "ostracism, loss and interpersonal conflict, or social exclusion circumstances" (65). I point to this medical discourse to consider how Dora's deep fear of the speculum exam is intertwined with physical and social pain. She anticipates a dehumanizing response to her presence in the exam room based on past experiences. Social pain can also result from dehumanization, which occurs concurrently with the physical pain of a rough speculum examination. In Brazil, it is common to interrogate reproductive and healthcare inequity toward women, particularly Black and Indigenous women, through the notion of *desumanização* (dehumanization). Gyno-trauma expresses those forms of dehumanization relationally. It is a pathway to reexamine what constitutes dehumanization. However, the term *dehumanization* has also served to implement colorblindness and heteronormative ideologies in Brazilian health care. The notion of gyno-trauma encompasses other "blunt mechanisms" such as racist, homophobic, and sexist attitudes and interactions. The oppressive relations causing long-lasting harm to Black lesbians during the gynecological examination sit at the center of gyno-trauma.

Gyno-trauma loudly articulates the invisibility of Black lesbians' intersectional power relations within gynecology. It is the social pain, or *dor da cor*, that communicates to the social world how gynecologists manifest intimate intersectional violence. This ease is more than unprofessionalism; it reflects the anti-Blackness entrenched in a system that devalues Black women, particularly lesbians, bisexual women, trans folk, and working-class cis women. One main blunt traumatic social mechanism is the pervasive practice of insult in gynecology. It is a way to perform hypermasculinity and heterosexuality, make race, and construct other social differences and authoritative power relations. In Brazil, racial and sexual stigmas are pervasive in the medical context, and specifically in the gynecological setting. It is evidenced by how intersectional stigmas transform into "*micro-assaults, micro-insults, and micro-invalidations*" (Moreira 2019, 52). For me, these terms, including *microaggression*, do not sufficiently elucidate the gyno-trauma and racial fatigue caused in these contexts. Instead, they are iterative aggressions, insults, and invalidations anchored by anti-Black, anti-queer logics. Black lesbians report gynecologists' willingness to insult their sexuality and sexual practices through facial expressions of puzzlement, disapproval, disgust, and aversion upon learning of their sexuality.

Insult pervades the gynecological encounter. I heard reports of gynecologists addressing Black lesbians as *sapatonas* (which can be a pejorative term depending on how it is deployed, along the lines of "dyke"), the sort of pathological, stigmatizing, and often traumatic appellation that some Black lesbians already experience at home or in the streets. Didier Eribon's (2004) work on the multidimensionality of insult in making gay subjects helps me think about how Black lesbians are thrust into inequitable relations and intersectional subject formations. The primary consequence of insult is to shape Black lesbians' relations to others, and the world, thereby shaping their subjectivities and ways of being in the world. Black lesbians experience (or *enfrentar*, "face up to and deal with," as they said to me) preconceito against their sexuality from their gynecologists in sexual verbal insults directed at whom they are trying to be and at their ability to live as proud and self-caring individuals.

Emotional Exploitation—Luciana's Story

In my conversations I did not ignore how I navigated deep emotional terrain linked to gynecology. This ethnographic tension revealed the existence of chronic emotional exploitation in medical spaces. Indeed, Black lesbians were disgruntled. However, there was more to their agitated critiques—their body language unleashed archived feelings evident in their rageful facial expressions, restless or tense bodies, and at times tears. I began to pay attention to how their memories were not distant from their daily existence. Instead, it was as if their gynecological encounters had occurred just yesterday. Their memories elicited all sorts of heavy emotions that wrapped their minds, bodies, and spirits like a blanket of injustice. Their memories projected emotional exploitation awaiting recognition and understanding far beyond the discomfort that pelvic exams can cause for many women. Ultimately, I understood their emotional pain to sit at the deepest level of mistrust in a medical system that disparages their presence in the room. I read their emotions—anger, fear, anguish, and resentment—as the expression of gynecology's harm to their well-being. This emotional expressivity signals the tug between striving for *bem-estar* (well-being) while grappling with *mal-estar* (malaise). Gyno-trauma is an essential analytic for paying serious attention to the weight of multiple negative emotions for Black lesbians.

I first met Luciana in 2007 at Sankofa bar in Pelourinho, the old historic center of Salvador. It was a brief introduction to Afro-Brazilian music and lots of sambas. Since our first meeting, Luciana has been authentic to her sense of self in her most flirtatious, supportive way. She also demanded respect and made her opinions known. By the time we began spending significant time together, after 2011, I had begun to understand her venting about social injustices as part of her everyday analysis of the world around her and how she occupied institutional spaces, including her workplace. She analyzed power relations bluntly. Luciana's discontent was palpable through an emotional expressivity about the intertwined anti-Blackness and heteronormative affect during gynecological encounters. Luciana was aware that being a masculine-presenting Black woman with locked hair made most doctors uncomfortable. She was acutely attentive to how her racial and sexual vivências intersected. Like Marcia, she wore her erotic power and autonomy on her sleeve. We talked for hours about her long-term same-sex relationship and her wandering admiration for beautiful women. These conversations quickly transitioned into discussing gynecology as we prepared for a series of filmed interviews at the end of my fieldwork. Aside from her own experiences, she had cared for her partner, who had had a hysterectomy. Also, her sister was a breast cancer survivor. Luciana was closely attuned to the injustices in healthcare, in SUS in particular. Like many others, Luciana observed gynecologists' heteronormative strategies to deny lesbians a safe sense of belonging. Still, she did not hold back. She said the following about gynecologists in private care:

When I started going to the gynecologist, I already had a sexual relation with a man. So, I was not surprised by [gynecologists'] routine cold
questions and examination practice. At first, I did not bother saying it hurt,
though it was terrible and everything. And when I started relationships
with women, I would always prefer to talk to a female gynecologist. If they
[male or female] insisted on questions like, "Do you have children? Do you
use any contraceptive method? Use condoms?" it is easier to reply no to
everything. Once, they pushed other questions, like, "How come you do
not use a condom? You must use it! Do you use any contraceptives? So
how do you prevent [pregnancy, STDs]"? I would reply with: "I often wear
gloves. I have a relationship with a woman." But they do not care that I
can use a condom at the time of oral sex, or if I do not have an oral condom, I limit my direct physical contact. So, if I am going to use a penis
dildo, I will put on a condom. They only care about heterosexual sex.

Luciana's divulgence of her nonnormative sexual practices was also her tactic for breaking down heteronormative relations. Unfortunately, Black lesbians
do not always feel comfortable or willing to describe their nonnormative sexual
practices to gynecologists, even if they want to. Luciana recalled, "I went back
to the gynecologist after getting work and a healthcare plan. When I found a
gynecologist, they first asked, 'Do you use a condom?' I reply, 'No' They ask,
'Do you use contraception?' I reply, 'No.' They ask, 'Do you use what?' And I
say, 'I do not use anything. I do not mess with men, I'm a lesbian.'"

Luciana and many other participants see that gynecologists insist on applying history-taking strategies that disregard their nonnormative sexual practices
and sexualities. Luciana mostly recognized that, during these conversations,
being Black subjected her to aggressive behavior from the gynecologist. Her
truth-telling about her reality and these "abhorrent" practices is itself an act of
resistance. The emotional exploitation is evident by the obliteration of Black
lesbians' subjective positions and the intrusive and violent question-and-
answer moments. Emotional exploitation, or maltreating someone to benefit
from their work, is, then, an appropriate entry point to situate the disregard
of Black queer women's affective experiences during medical questioning. This
call-and-response ritual of medical encounters is where my participants experienced egregious insult, erasure, and belittlement. The effects of emotional
exploitation are the basis on which the totality of the gynecological encounter
constitutes intimate violence. Black lesbians' emotional exploitation as intimate violence is illustrated by Luciana: "They [gynecologists] would not ask
me many questions. When I would say that I did not have relations with men,

they would stop questioning me as if I did not have an active sexual life. And at the time of the [pelvic] exams, it was total brutality. So, they would not ask anything." My interviewees interpreted their gynecologists' silences as abandonment and neglect and as avoiding, undermining, or erasing their sexual subjectivities. They understood the lack of engagement and silence as forceful, aggressive, or repulsive. Black lesbians must engage emotionally on multiple scales to decipher what their gynecologists think and anticipate how gynecologists will respond to them (silently or with insult). Ultimately, Black queer women must decide whether they will experience a "brutal" examination.

Luciana delayed her visit back to the gynecologist for ten years. Still, she remembered her visit as if it was yesterday. The intensity of these deep-seated memories and their interpretive labor crystalizes these traumatic experiences into a silent, long-term mal-estar. Brazilian psychologists and scholars Marco Antonio Chagas Guimarães and Angela Baraf Podkameni (2012) argue that racism and the negation of rights for the Brazilian Black population cause mal-estar. They point to an *adoecimento psíquico* (psychological sickness) that not only impacts subjectivity but also carries long-life effects (211). M. Guimarães and Podkameni aim to "deepen an understanding of the lived feeling of discomfort" (212). Here, the Portuguese translation is vital to capture the vivências of being Black and subject to the psychological effects of racism (insidious or blatant) in Brazil. *Mal-estar* carries more layered meanings than the translation *malaise*. According to the New Oxford American dictionary online, malaise means a "general feeling of discomfort, illness, or uneasiness whose exact cause is difficult to identify." M. Guimarães and Podkameni ground mal-estar in memories of various life areas (work, education, and home) to expose the extreme "danger of racism upon subjectivity" (220). In this sense, gynecology contributes to such vulnerable material realities of poor social conditions as elaborated by Marcia. Dora and Luciana reveal a mal-estar lingering within themselves. We cannot say it is always dormant or without impact on well-being and health. Our conversations elicited its presence and the impact on their vivências point to the imminent and transient absence of well-being. If bem-estar situates the most valued quality of life in this book, then mal-estar is an undesired human condition under violent institutional circumstances. Mal-estar can be more than a temporary psychological state. It is also an embodiment of violent social relations, sort of like if you ask, "Irmã, você esta bem?" (Sistah, are you good?) "Não estou bem, não." (Nah, I am not good.) That is the sentiment of being in mal-estar.

When Luciana described her gynecological affective experiences as "I have always felt violated and need to feel safe, feel respected," she was not just denouncing states of mal-estar but recognizing that gynecology is a limitless source of oppressive experiences. Black lesbians' mal-estar exposes gynecological encounters in what Angela Garcia (2010) refers to as "landscapes of affect" mapping gynecology as "geographies of land, people, events, and other elements" (30)—here, a circuit of trauma from the behaviors, language, and symbols of gynecology. Gynecology, then, is part of an affective landscape of society and the people, events, and other elements that manifest mal-estar anywhere, anytime, by any gynecologist. Garcia's work is helpful for imagining how Black lesbians' clusters of emotions are tied to and splattered across wide landscapes of affect, inducing social vulnerabilities through their exhausting emotional labor. We understand the relationship between these gynecological landscapes of affect and women's clusters of emotions by interpreting emotion, according to Brazilian Black feminist scholar Ana Claudia Lemos Pacheco, as "a cultural code that is negotiated through social relationships, intentions and actions produced between individuals in specific contexts" (2013, 44). In other words, how we may value Black lesbians' "emotional and affective lives as individuals in relation to the social connections cultural codes" (44). Pacheco's work examines emotions and solidarity among Brazilian Black women activists and community organizers to demonstrate the critical significance of valuing strong affective ties and exchanges of knowledge production about social conditions and normative structures.

Black feminists have long established the utility of emotional knowledge, such as anger and rage, to survive and defend themselves against institutional violence (Collins 1989; Lorde 1984; hooks 1995). Across the African diaspora, emotional knowledge is not respected, particularly not in health care. For these reasons, Black lesbians' cultural codes are critical for self-grounding and acting upon emotional knowledge for self-care and self-defense. Cultural codes in gynecology flood these channels from different directions and circumstances, informing the inestimable value of Black queer women's "communicative forces" (Spillers 1987, 69) and pertaining to the ways nonnormative Black female bodies respond to medical language and signs. For example, Black lesbians relate that their gynecologists did not generally follow their inappropriate questions about sexual relations with men with pertinent questions about their patients' actual sexuality and sexual relations. Luciana and others consistently described gynecologists changing their tone, posture, and ways of handling women's bodies in a "harsh, dry, and brutal" manner that felt demoralizing and dehumanizing. *Brutal* is a problematic term here, as it connotes violent impact. *Brutal* also represents the mental and spiritual impact that any tormenting violent experience has.

Sometimes my participants' facial expressions were enough to convey the crass, aggressive feelings of the speculum exams they experienced and remembered and even disremembered themselves. Luciana said, "You realize the negative change in the professionals' posture. Once I asked for the exam to stop, got up from the table, and left and never came back." First, routine heteronormative questions (e.g., do you use condoms?) generate fear, anger, and uncertainty about the physicians' response to their sexuality disclosure. Still, many Black queer women push through, knowing that they are targeted in amusement or repulsion as Black female bodies. That is, if they do not answer this question correctly, heteronormatively speaking, then the doctor might react in racist and homophobic ways. Mal-estar is their communicative force about the mental anguish of the embodied emotions elicited by these medical relations. Mal-estar is not a silent state of being; it is inner energy, or unseen flesh, seeding mistrust but raising protective consciousness of social injustices.

Como Chega Esse Preconceito: How Prejudice Hits Us

Thus far I have focused on emotional trauma and how it reveals intersectional subjective exploitation in gynecology. Now I ask, following Ana Claudia Pacheco, "How are norms [and normative codes] redefined and defied" in Black Brazilian women's affective experiences (2013, 45)? My participants' racialized, heteronormative, anti-lesbian, gendered experiences are central to understanding emotional knowledge as a critical source of social and political striving and knowing. Affective experiences in these medical spaces reinforce how emotions—along with knowledge production—as Sara Amhed argued in her extensive work about emotions, are produced in relation, passing, or contact with subjects, objects, and signs (2015, 2010). My participants' negative emotions are responses to the sociality within medical spaces toward anti-Blackness and anti-queerness. I agree with Bianca C. Williams that emotions are "not simply private things but are constructed in publics, with technologies, and in the context of social conditions, and are therefore political" (2018, 37; Ahmed 2010) I understand emotions through Williams's interpretation of Ahmed to shape Black women's affective lives in life-changing sociopolitical ways.[4] Williams reminds us that it is common to think about affect being both social and political. However, Williams says, "if affect is social, then it must also be a process and one that is undoubtedly influenced by historical and contemporary processes of racialization. Furthermore, if affect is social and racialized, then I consider how racism influences affect" (36–37). Black lesbians' emotional knowledge, engaged in these medical contexts, is a critical expression of the relational power to those who abuse their social and medical privilege in institutional spaces.

Como chega esse preconceito is a commonly used expression among Brazilian Blacks that is useful for rethinking emotional knowledge as part of the sociopolitical fabric of justice. I heard this expression a lot from my participants. *Como esse preconceito chega a nós/até nós/para nós* signifies a few views: how that prejudice hits us, how that prejudice comes at us, or how that prejudice comes to us (or arrives). These translations carry different meanings linguistically but strongly suggest how local knowledge visualizes an imminent oppressive force, usually that of racist behavior. This Brazilian expression—not a question but an interrogative statement—connotes recognition of broader entrenched systems of power. This interrogation taps into the quotidian language of resistance to shape knowledge about medical injustice. It is challenging to communicate bodily pain (as experienced by Dora) and emotional pain to the person who is causing it, especially when that person casts doubt on your account (see Scarry 1987). Black lesbians' recognition of gynecology as racially, gendered, and sexually hierarchical sets them in position as deeply evaluative beings by drawing on their affective experiences and intersubjective positionalities. For example, *afetividade* (affectivity) is also commonly used not just in Brazilian scholarship but also among the public when reflecting on sexual and other subjectivities and vivências.

Como chega esse preconceito suggests a critical, rebuking *olhar* (gaze) shaped by the emotional knowledge channeled through affective experiences from deep prejudice in institutional or other public spaces. It is an embodied outlook on anticipated oppressive forces lurking in society. More importantly, it is a highly sentimental expression of anger and lament of experienced injustice. When the prejudice is intersectional, these affective experiences are external mechanisms to detect and evaluate the processes for the very "verbal objectification" they are resisting through their affectivity—in these cases, social pain and discomfort (see Scarry 1987, 13). These articulations represent anti-racist evaluations that constitute what Bianca Williams refers to as *productive analytics* about the emotional transnationalism of African American female tourists who travel to Jamaica. Williams notes that "feeling, emotion, and affect are forms of knowledge. They provide ways of knowing the world and figuring out how to navigate it" (2018, 37). I understand Williams's intervention about Black women's emotions crossing borders. The idea of productive analytics also helps me think about how Brazilian Black lesbians' evaluative practices about their gynecological experiences travel in local and critical sites of emotional knowledge production.

As Audre Lorde states, Black women's response to racism is anger. Black lesbians' response to racism is clustered anger, resentment, and fear. This emotional intensity is palpable in expressions such as *como chega esse preconceito*. Who are these Black queer women after they experience intersectional preconceito and a medical interaction designed to obliterate their senses of well-being and freedom? Black women are reflective beings—or, rather, they engage with reflective modes constantly, exhaustively, about social violence. Their reflective selves are a mode of survival and transformation to evaluate power relations and their environments. As Black lesbians willing to "transform silence into language and action," they understand their affective labor in the face of fear and pain in the ways Lorde projects as "our labor has become more important than our silence" (1980, 17). As Black women, their value systems, shaped by their emotional knowledge, are anchored by the belief that neither bodily nor social death should be caused by violence. I follow Lorde (1984, 19) in her questioning: "What are the tyrannies you swallow day by day and attempt to make your own, until you will sicken and die of them, still in silence?" First, I find affirmation for this in knowing that Lorde published her 1977 speech "The Transformation of Silence into Language and Action" in her book *The Cancer Journals*. Alongside her critical reflections on being a Black lesbian with cancer in gynecological and oncological medical spaces, she urged women to contemplate the words that they may not yet have in the face of fear and rage. Her concerns about swallowing tyrannies are not directed toward all women; rather, it is "because I am black, because I am lesbian, because I am myself, a black woman warrior power doing my work" that she comes to "ask you, are you doing yours?" (Lorde 1980, 19). Black lesbians' affective knowledge about intolerance on specific issues—virginity, painful pelvic exams, or something else—inform their insistence to be heard and handled with care. The force of affect poses possibilities that only some bodies hold dear as critical steps for liberation (see chapter 4). In this study, Black lesbians highly value their nonnormative Black bodies in all sense. One critical step toward (sexual) liberation is their evaluative mode of being.

Affect and Preconceito

The term *preconceito* captures the intersectional effect of all prejudices in the singular form. My analysis of intersectional prejudice is rooted in how Black lesbians communicate their *afetividade* (affectivity) of intimate violence in medical spaces. We cannot disregard the sequelae of Black lesbians' emotions from institutional violence. Their afetividade as Black lesbians unveils the injustice they experience. For example, Dora believes that gynecologists are more aggressive toward her than toward her partner, Sarah, because Sarah has lighter skin, straight hair, and a feminine cisgender presentation. Given these racialized and gendered dynamics, we understand how preconceito is encountered and interpreted by my interlocutors. The recognition and experience of preconceito through intersectionality produces multiple subject positions within power relations. The term also allows people to hold others accountable for seeing systematic ways of producing inequality.

A thoroughgoing qualitative analysis must recognize institutional practices that are *preconceituoso/as* (prejudicial). *Práticas preconceituosas* are subtle, discriminatory materializations of embodied experiences and ideological beliefs about social differences. Recognizing a preconceituoso act might be difficult for those with more power and privileges of class, race, gender, and sexuality—but it is undoubtedly easier for those chronically subjected to these mechanisms. Black lesbians' interpretations of physicians who are preconceituoso point to the capacity of "force-relations" (M. Gregg and Seigworth 2010, 2) to affect the body cumulatively. M. Gregg and Seigworth argue that "affect accumulates across both relatedness and interruptions in relatedness, becoming a palimpsest of force-encounters traversing the ebbs and swells of intensities that pass between 'bodies' (bodies defined not by an outer skin-envelope or other surface boundary but by their potential to reciprocate or co-participate in the passages of affect)" (2). However, Brazilian Black bodies are defined by their *negritude* (Blackness) and relegated to an inferior sense of relational belonging. We cannot ignore or overshadow in our analysis of race and ethnicity the systemic ways that anti-Blackness seeps into the everyday lives of Brazilians Blacks. This critical point applied to *negritude* helps me understand how Black lesbians' afetividade is expressed within preconceituoso moments signaling gyno-trauma.

Black lesbians collectively reinforce their emotional knowledge through the expression *como chega esse preconceito*. I also interpret the notion of subjectivation in the gynecological setting as subject formation tied not just to the individual but to a collective of other beings, ideas, social issues, systems, and norms. Foucault's notion of subjectivation (*asujettisement*) refers to "how subjects are formed in power relations, including how the self acts on and shapes it" (Laidlaw 2014, 101; see also Laidlaw 2010). Like James Laidlaw and other anthropologists of ethics, I take subjectivation to be a process of self-formation that allows people to have "active, reflective freedom" about power (2014, 102). Subjectivation allows me to consider the shaping of Black lesbians' subject positions and their realities. Let us not underestimate the active, reflective freedom experienced through emotional labor during violent moments for Black lesbians. Subjectivation is also useful in illuminating the liberatory practices forged in survival and transformative modes, both within and outside the medical domain.

Subjectivation, unlike subjection and subjugation, includes the myriad ways in which some subjects hold, experience, and are constituted in any subject position. It also moves us to rethink modes of freedom beyond focusing on the normatively female status of my interlocutors' bodies and toward a greater awareness of cross-cutting intersectional identifications. After all, the more subject positions that any given medical subject holds at any given time in an expressed, aware manner, the more remarkable that subject's intersubjective domain of being, or vivência. For Black lesbians, subjectivation is part of a process to relate to and negotiate the coded terms tied to their subject positions in the gynecologist's office. Black lesbians are not, in the Foucauldian sense, individuals establishing relations to a set of rules they are obliged to carry into practice (Foucault 1985, 7). But subjectivation is key to examining the gynecological encounter as a locus of Brazilian Black female homosexuality to unveil Black lesbians as more than medical subjects in transformed subjectivities. Above all, I am interested in transforming the "medical subject" designation as they exercise accountability first to themselves in unseen relations. They remind us that they deliberately track their sensibilities and awareness about their social conditions in the gynecological encounter as *como chega esse preconceito*.

Black Lesbian Body Scanning—Taina's Story

Anywhere and on any day, I gawked at Taina as she smoked her cigarettes, admiring her inner and outer beauty and strength. Her dark skin, locked hair, and flirty smile and eyes made her glow. In my June 2013 field notes, I wrote, "I am drawn to her. Don't know why . . . She has a fire within her. She wants to fight back the resistance against her from family and other social issues." Luciana introduced me to Taina in September 2012, and we spent much time together at social events. When I first read Brazilian Black feminist Sueli Carneiro's essay on *dor da cor* (pain of my skin color) during my fieldwork, Taina's interlocking racial and sexual vivências first came to mind. She was a young mother with a small child. She was also dating a woman who was in love with her. Unfortunately, her love for this woman brought much disdain from her family. Taina's family had recently learned of her homosexuality. In our private conversations she agonized over her family's rejection. She was very close to her mother and immediate family, and she depended on her mother for childcare. In Taina's view, her family had endured profound racial violence and inequity as a Black family in Salvador. According to her family, her sexuality was a more significant burden on the family. Taina resented feeling like her sexuality caused more pain to the family. Nevertheless, she refused to deny herself her happiness and liberty to express her love and life, despite the emotional cost.

Her mother was also a reproductive cancer survivor. Taina, who was in her early thirties, was anxiously committed to going to the gynecologist at least annually. Hyperawareness about familial risks of reproductive cancer is emotionally taxing, especially when one has a young child to raise and live for. Taina had become guarded because of her family's and her own experiences of insidious racism in nonmedical institutional spaces. She was skeptical about medical spaces, so she sought treatment from her family's doctor even at the expense of silencing her sexuality. Taina's perspectives on differential racial and sexual experiences in institutional spaces are a window into how she automatically scans environments for interlocking prejudicial forces directed toward her. She said:

> When they [whites] come to talk to you, they will think, reconsider, think again until you get closer to them, especially given your [homo]sexuality! I know I am differentiated (*diferenciada*) in the room. *Preconceito* exists there. People are *preconceituosas, racistas*! They look at me and take issue with me being a lesbian, belonging to Candomblé, being Black, being already different to them when they entered the room, looking at me with another view as not belonging. It feels as if they [whites] think we [Blacks] are not people. Even without the masculine stereotype that's already placed upon you, if you are not feminine like others, you know? It is assumed that because you are a lesbian, you have masculinity traits because you like another woman. Racism and sexism are extreme here.

Taina's strong views on how to transcend inferior treatment and social stigma, like those of other Black lesbian interlocutors, shape how she scans for her presence amid power relations. Intersectional preconceito also creates these inequitable encounters through gynecologists' unspoken social differentiation of Black female patients. These classed, racializing perceptions and attitudes were confirmed by Dr. Rosa, a Black female heterosexual gynecologist. When I asked her about preconceito from gynecologists, she animatedly told me how at both the private and public clinics where she worked, some Black women were called *diferenciada* (differentiated) if they dressed and spoke "well." Dr. Rosa's view that the "'differentiated patient' is the patient better" suggests that constructing social difference is primarily about race, not just class, since only Black women were targeted. *Diferenciada*, among racializing terms for Black female bodies, is a mechanism used in the gynecological encounter to produce social difference. It indexes the social complexities I am describing here and is a social symptom of raced, classed, sexualizing preconceito and of "racialidade das relações sociais," or the racialization of social relations (dos Santos 2012, 31). Black women notice how they become viewed as socially inferior when they do not fit a diferenciada construct. Kia Lily Caldwell's work recognizes these racializing social relations in *boa aparência* (good appearance): Black women too often must perform a "good look" with clothing, hair, and other aesthetic efforts in order not to be dismissed as working class regardless of actual class or socioeconomic status (Caldwell 2007, 65). But many Black women do not have the means to construct such a boa aparência and step out knowing the risks of being targeted as inferior. Regardless of how they dress, Black lesbians still experience inferior treatment at medical clinics. Even a boa aparência might not protect a Black lesbian in institutional spaces if she is called diferenciada. A Black lesbian body is never synonymous with a lesbian body. These racially coded affective experiences will never apply to white lesbian bodies.

The term *diferenciada* mirrors whiteness as a symbol of wealth, class, and access to higher education. Diferenciada is a marker for the white privilege constituted by a social status image for Black bodies. Diferenciada, as Dr. Rosa described it, was her colleagues' deep, elitist, entitled sociocultural bias that ultimately stigmatized working-class Black patients regardless of their sexuality. As I listened to Dr. Rosa, I remembered a few Black lesbians telling me that they always "dressed nicely" to go to the doctor so as to be received and treated with respect. Some Black lesbians complained to me that reporting their highest level of education raised eyebrows at doctors' offices. These jarring experiences elucidate social expectations that Black women are not likely to have higher education. The eyebrow-raising also signifies a shift of their social gaze into a diferenciada view of the patient. How can we deepen our view of Black women's existence being adversely framed as diferenciada *in* gynecology and society at large?

Taina's mental survey of white Brazilians' unwelcoming postures is a way of scanning institutional spaces. There is a need to scan the room at the onset of experiencing prejudice and being marginalized, as Taina also said. These Black queer women are not striving to conform to white heterosexual norms and codes to be perceived as equal citizens. Black lesbians move against the normative social grain, accentuating their Blackness by keeping their hair natural, adhering to Candomblé dress codes and wearing neck beads, and often by avoiding the extreme femininity of the ideal image of Brazilian womanhood. The instant anti-Blackness and desexualization experienced by Black lesbians is provoked by their nonheteronormative and nonbinary sexual codes from dress to natural hair.[5] These societal perceptions heighten Black lesbians' self-awakenings by their racializing dynamics.

The channeling of gyno-trauma in a gynecological space transforms "silence into language and action" (Lorde 1984) through what I interpret as body scanning. Body scanning is a powerful, knowledge-producing mindfulness tool with which to find clarity in conflict and feelings of unsafety. It is an embodied form of assessment about affective experiences in spaces. By scanning, I refer to how Black queer women turn to visual observation and sensory praxis to assess their environment, the behavior of others, and how their bodies exist in relation to people and objects. These visual pathways forge possibilities for Black lesbians to use corporeal and subjective countersurveillance practices to counter gyno-trauma. Black lesbians may be sitting on the examination table with breast/chest or reproductive cancer, fibroids, an STD, or one of many bodily health concerns. Black queer women who choose to exercise their right not to identify as a lesbian do not ask any health-related or medical questions that might reveal their homosexuality.

The silencing of Black lesbians does not necessarily indicate that they do not belong at all. Instead, it indicates that they can belong only through heteronormative, gendered, white, classed norms. Most Black lesbians I spoke to continually tried to redirect their gynecological conversations, interactions, and outcomes toward their understandings of their sexuality. When Black queer women like Dora, Marcia, and Luciana recalled sitting on the examination table, I interpreted those body-scanning moments as "moral breakdown" (Zigon 2007), where self-revelation is critical for survival.[6] Moral breakdown are moments of evaluation and deep awareness in a space that has caused gyno-trauma. This moral breakdown is not external to the women, nor is it a sign of weakness.

Jarrett Zigon (2007) uses ethnographic data and people's spontaneous reflections as loci for assessing their moral codes in moments of conflict. A suddenly compelled moral assessment about what is faced is a moral breakdown that clarifies what may not otherwise be elicited from one's moral archives—for example, Black queer women tuning in to their own abilities to evaluate and respond to mistrust and discomfort during the pelvic exam. Zigon argues that moral breakdown is the "moment of problematization or ethical moment in which ethics must be performed" (137). Furthermore, Zigon makes the "distinction between morality as the unreflective mode of being-in-the-world and ethics as a tactic performed in the moment of the breakdown of the ethical dilemma" (137). We can also rethink moral breakdowns as moments of heightened anti-racist awareness, of imminent social violence. For example, we can read as a moral breakdown Luciana's experience of being confronted by a gynecologist being "harsh and brutal" and her decision to end her consultation midway through. In this sense, a moral breakdown is not a fracturing of moral codes and beliefs but a suspension of the self in order to spontaneously reflect on those moral codes as they quickly (or slowly) decipher unsafe circumstances.

Body scanning, which we may consider a technique of countersurveillance after moral breakdown (or registering such moral breakdowns from past experiences) in power relations, is one way Black lesbians have engaged in conscious assessment of how their own racialized, sexualized, or desexualized bodies are positioned in the medical space. It is praxis against objectification and violent experience; an awareness about their connection to what they feel, internalize, react to, and then evaluate about their environments. Body scanning is necessary praxis for surveilling power relations and the sociomedical gaze. It creates the knowledge necessary for Black lesbian interlocutors to identify derogatory physical and linguistic contact with a gynecologist, a critical optic that interprets power relations. Luciana said to me, "Physicians' bodies talk [communicate messages]. I remain comfortable/calm. They are the ones that remain uncomfortable. In those moments, it appears as if they no longer even want to listen to you or look at you." Here, she is scanning not just her bodily affect and movement but also the physicians'. Black lesbians' agential and evaluative gaze on medical violence is grounded in critical knowledge about, and their relationality to, social power.

Simone Browne's notion of dark sousveillance helps me think about how body scanning in these situations also "plots imaginaries that are oppositional and that are hopeful for another way of being" (2015, 21). In other words, if, as Browne argues, dark sousveillance is "a site of critique, as it speaks to black epistemologies of contending with anti-black surveillance," then Black lesbians' body scanning for gyno-trauma is a pathway to recognizing that they will die from social stress caused by denigration, melancholy, and mental trauma faster than, for example, traditionally defined medical malpractice (21). Browne reminds us that Steve Mann coined *sousveillance* to identify "an active inversion of the power relations that surveillance entails" (21). Like Browne, I consider Black lesbians' attentiveness to the power relations and to their corporeal orientations in the gynecological space to detect the social surveillance on them and unfold, even in silence, epistemologies countering the normative and oppressive coded behavior and language against them. Acts of body scanning, or dark sousveillance, are rooted in their critiques of gynecological practice. Such gynecological practices are not medical surveillance techniques but rather close observations of their otherness—that is, their criminality, deviance, immorality, and subservience. Black lesbians' radical countersurveillances change their subject positions in relation to the clinical gaze through intertwined acts of establishing self-worth and awareness of a social gaze.

Black feminists have long reminded us how such objectifying experiences disembody Black women in oppressive and exploitative ways (see Bailey and Peoples 2017; Cohen 1999; M. Moore 2011; Mohanty 2003). Zora Neale Hurston, in her essay "My Most Humiliating Jim Crow Experience," shares her objectifying, denigrating experience of seeing a physician who relegated her to a closet for a medical examination "in a desultory manner to ask about symptoms" (as quoted in Walker 2011, 163). In this account, she says, "I went away feeling the pathos of Anglo-Saxon civilization. And, I still mean pathos, for I know that anything with such a false foundation cannot last. Whom the gods would destroy, they first made mad" (163). In her body-scanning praxis, Hurston demonstrates her knowledge about both institutional and societal white supremacy. Alongside an anti-racist lens, the heteronormative entanglement of culturally specific versions of femininity and heterosexual desire at the core of much gynecological practice is a crucial provocation for Black lesbians' resistance, leading to their orientation to their bodies. The expression of Black lesbian life is active in institutional spaces such as the gynecology clinic, a means by which to check in with the self and its subjective space and bodily presence in the face of power relations. Black lesbians learn to recognize preconceito primarily by what it always feels like, which ultimately directs them to scan their bodies and their environment for safety and prepare to defend their well-being and bodies.

In conclusion, I have argued for more attention to body and flesh in pain and trauma—gyno-trauma—intersected by various prejudices and abuses of power. If the Black lesbian body has such autopoietic character, then the body-as-organism is available energy to itself and not its environment (Clough 2010, 207). A Black lesbian who body scans her emotions and energy in any given environment has autogenerated knowledge about her afetividade in response to all stimuli (bodily, social, affective, technological) in the contact zone of colonial power. The Black body is sensorially informational and can self-organize to defend and strategize as a thriving organism in these affective turns. Body scanning is thus also an evaluative optic locating the self in social conditions and in relation to the gynecological encounter: a Black lesbian counter-gazing at the power gazing upon them.

Brazilian Black feminist Joice Berth's work on Black women's empowerment reminds us how Brazilian Black feminist anthropologist Lélia Gonzales affirmed that Black women share an oppressive history and familiar pathways in their struggles against oppressions (Berth 2019, 92). Body scanning is an ontological production of mindfulness, presence, and aliveness (Quashie 2021) about Black/queerness. It is praxis, then, to hold steady a nonheteronormative, anti-racist gaze situated in resistance. It is energy scouting its surroundings for danger and safety. Black lesbians are keenly aware of the many mechanisms contributing to all forms of social violence, including intimate sociomedical violence. Luciana's description of an exam as brutal points beyond the handling of a speculum to the ghosts of history in Brazil that permeate the field of medicine and tie it tightly to society and the social world at large. What are Black lesbians crossing when they step into and out of gynecological spaces in Brazil? What is that terrain made of, tied to past and present in contact zones?

Let us now cross into Brazilian gynecology as a contact zone.

Angela

Angela signed the consent form for me to escort her, but we did not want to alert the physician that I was a researcher. Angela and I had grown closer as friends since 2008. She was playful, smart, and led a lesbian collective for social justice. She would always say, "When I go to the gynecologist, it is like being raped," then laugh, and I knew it was not literal. Being raped was her perception of the intrusiveness of the speculum exam or transvaginal ultrasound performed by a gynecologist.[1] When she suggested that I keep my identity undisclosed and play as if I were her "friend," I followed her lead. I knew that I would witness only the conversation between her and the physician, not the examination. I was fine with the secret plan.

When we were called into his office, she gestured to me to walk in with her, which signaled to the physician that those were her wishes. She told him that I was her "amiga." My guess is that *amiga* could also be perceived as partner or lover by the physician. Who would come into a consultation office and hear a private conversation for a routine examination? It's not like she was awaiting test results and concerned for cancer. I was humbled and excited to be witnessing a gynecological visit. This was an opportunity to see how Angela was received and questioned by the gynecologist.

Angela and I sat across her gynecologist's desk in a narrow space, squeezed up against a wall. His consultation area was very small. I could see the unlit examination room a few feet away. There was a curtain hanging from the doorway. The gynecologist was known to Angela. She was not completely fond of his demeanor, but she continued to see him out of convenience. He was a white man, likely in his sixties. I was not able to write notes until that evening and could not remember the questions he asked her before taking her into the examination room. The questioning was very brief—five minutes at most.

The longest five minutes . . .

That brief time felt long to me because he never looked up to give Angela eye contact. He had given me a soft smile when I walked in. Our eyes did not meet again, not even for a goodbye. I looked over at Angela as he spoke to assess her comfort. Her gaze was downward on the paper he was writing.

When we left, I asked her what she thought about his lack of eye contact. She said he rarely looks at her and likely was uncomfortable with my presence. I had heard reports of many Brazilian gynecologists never looking at their patients. I witnessed it for myself. How do you establish trust if you never make eye contact?

Establishing trust must not be at stake.

3

THE SOCIAL CLINIC

Mapping the Social and Colonial World of Gynecology

16. Whoever would like to buy a black woman with milk, who can also cook and wash, should go to Rua do Senhor dos Passos, No. 35, opposite [the statue] of the same Senhor dos Passos . . .
 —Newspaper advertisement in *O Diário do Rio de Janeiro*,
 December 17, 1821 (Conrad 1983, 112)

Law of the Free Womb,
legislature to free children born
to enslaved women in Brazil.
—September 28, 1871

It is an era of when a woman's life enchants the poets and awakens the
attention of gynecologists.
—Dr. Francisco Carvalho, Bahia, 1914

Gynecology Is a Contact Zone

I open this chapter with a provocation about hegemonic colonial power and the zoning of power structures in society and through medical spaces. I move us toward rethinking Brazilian gynecological spaces through multiple lenses (anticolonial, anti-racist, anti-LGBTQ+, and antipatriarchal) to envision hegemonic power at work through language, interactions, symbolism, and the socialities of physicians. This multilens analytic is critical for uprooting the interlocking sociohistorical conditions producing Black lesbians' gyno-trauma and how gynecology is woven into the fabric of sociohistorical hegemonic power.

To examine European travelers' writings about Latin America during the nineteenth century, Mary Louise Pratt coined the term *contact zone* to interpret the "colonial frontier" of conquest and domination between colonizers and the colonized as well as to understand imperial encounters suppressed through narratives that have only been told from the invader's perspective (1992, 8). We don't often think about gynecology as a contact zone or interrogate it as "a space of imperial encounters, the space in which peoples geographically and historically separated come into contact with each other and establish ongoing relations, usually involving conditions of coercion, radical inequality, and intractable conflict" (8). I examine the contact zone and colonial frontier that Pratt has identified and look at its application to gynecology "not in terms of separateness, but in terms of co-presence, interaction, interlocking understandings and practices, and often within radically asymmetrical relations of power" (8). Given Brazilian gynecology's history steeped in gender and familial construction and domination, it is important to point out how race, gender, class, and heteronormativity continue to privilege a medical authority that devalues the Black lesbian presence spatially, institutionally, and through the hauntings of sociohistorical colonial power.

During fieldwork, I began thinking about gynecology as a social context. At that time, the idea of social context helped me understand these Brazilian gynecological spaces to be fraught with particular social processes and unseen dimensional, interactional power. Nearly all physicians interviewed positioned themselves defensively by claiming that they had received no training in medical school to *lidar* (to handle or deal with) or *abordar* (approach) patients with gender, sexuality, or racial "issues." The physicians also proclaimed that they must learn to be human with a different consciousness. In response to my interview questions, these perspectives reflected even more widespread epistemological opposition to reposition—even negate—their professional accountability within power relations.

Watching a 2013 short documentary *O Fio das Masculinidades: Uma Reflexão das Masculinidades em Mulheres* deepened my understanding of gynecology as a social context.[1] Marcia, whom I introduced in chapter 1, had given me a DVD. The film centers on the narratives of three characters, two Black and one white, who identify as women and who strongly identify with their masculine embodied gender expression. The characters share stories about the deep prejudice and discrimination they experienced at work and from their families. The film also elicits their liberatory views on their gender, race, and sexuality. The film interweaves appearances by a social worker and, to my surprise, the brief appearance of a white woman gynecologist; she provides insight about the medical experiences of health issues since the main characters do not speak about them. Notably, the gynecologist ascribed gynecology's limitations in providing humane experiences to this population to more than a "lack of training [doctors] to be people, and only training [them] to be a gynecologist, obstetrician, etc." Instead, her perspective confirmed that relational tensions pivot through a social gaze. She says, "If you [a physician] become more flexible to be humane, when someone arrives that appears to have a different, or same, sexual orientation than you, if your *olhar* [gaze] of this person is humane, you will better approach the other." She also presents her views of patients who bring their *preconceito* with them; they arrive full of shame and fear speaking about their homosexuality. Significantly, she describes women's feelings of fear and shame as "arriving" into the gynecological space; it is as if these feelings have not also resulted from the particular gynecological space they have entered or have not been carried from other gynecological spaces they have previously visited. This physician emphasizes her approach as one that invites patients to express their concerns and exhibits care in recognizing her patients' vulnerability. But we can interpret her film appearance and perspectives to incidentally shed light on gynecology as more than a social context; we can also see it as a contact zone of the social world.

This chapter maps out the gynecological domain's deep ties to a colonial past that haunts its present. I also show how this haunting signals socially toxic spaces of abusive power relations and hierarchical socialities. I reimagine Black lesbians' encounters with social power in gynecology: a crossing of time and space through gynecology encounters. I do not mean to suggest that all gynecological offices are toxic. I wrestle with both the rigidity and flexibility of the gynecological domain in valuing Black lesbians' bodies and subjectivities. I argue that Brazilian gynecology continues to be a microcosm of society and a reproduction of the dark sociohistorical past of society and medicine. To understand why gyno-trauma is pervasive, we must scrutinize its inherited ideological and sociopolitical legacies. I look at gynecology in ways that are similar to how Julian Peard examines the earlier history of medicine in Bahia as "a site of complex social interactions rather than one of universal biological truths" (1999, 2). We understand gynecology as a contact zone when we do not ignore that the clinic and its inherited clinical gaze manipulate medical knowledge (Foucault 1973). In particular, in its constant constructions of what it means to be human and exist in these medical spaces, gynecology manipulates medical knowledge through its objectivity as well as its subjectivity. The perpetual making of the gynecological clinic and its gaze, or *olhar*, hinges on how "difference in medicine" is distributed "in the everyday relationships between persons, bureaucracies, technologies and spaces that transform the body and the person into recognizable entities" (Street 2014, 14). Here, Alice Street's work on biomedicine in an unstable place and her careful examination of infrastructure and personhood in a Papua New Guinean hospital help me think about biomedicine's investments in the pursuit of scientific truth. As Annemarie Mol (2002) suggests, biomedicine's investments operate through different relationships to technology and the enactment of different biological bodies in clinical spaces. In other words, Black lesbian flesh is rendered visible in these biomedical relations only to enact a social world steeped in specters of Brazil's history of medicine and society as we may imagine.

Like Street, I turn to Michel Foucault's work in *The Birth of the Clinic* to contemplate the constructions and contingencies of clinical gazes and spaces. In particular, I use it to highlight the continued relevance of differentiating observation from experience, distinguishing acts of seeing from acts of knowing, and understanding the performance of medical knowledge in relation to its object. Through this lens of power and space, I reframe gynecology's clinical space and gaze by teasing out the social (racial, gendered, heteronormative) logics shaping forms of social observation and experience that derive not only from physicians but also from ties to the social world. I refer to this gynecological contact zone as a *social clinic*. This framing allows me to rethink gynecological operations in these social terms of engagement. Gynecology is a continuation of the outside social world: it may often be violent, yet it can change how marginal bodies are received in institutional spaces.

Evidence from gyno-trauma shows that gynecology is a contact zone for simultaneous forms of domination. I lay out a sociohistorical analysis and discussion of Brazilian gynecology concerning four principles: (1) Brazilian gynecology as a "science of women"; (2) the ties of the gynecological gaze to anti-Blackness and *epistemicídio* (Carneiro 2005); (3) gynecology as the invention of heteronormativity; and (4) the emergence, from intersections of these social realms, of ideas about good care in ways that are fraught with social power. These four interlocking tenets are critical for reimagining gynecology as a microcosm of a broader social laboratory, a continuum of aggressions, insults, established personal belief systems, and too often raw ignorance expressed by physicians. In addition to drawing on anthropological approaches, I offer a dynamic analysis through my clinical gaze as a physician assistant. This professional experience allows me to grasp, connect, and decide what is relevant, interconnected, and threatening in these spaces. The combination of anthropological and clinical expertise for doing, analyzing, and writing ethnography provides a guiding force for visualizing gynecology's power relations and ideological apparatus. I also draw on textual sources of the history of gynecology in Brazil and other documents, such as patients' medical histories and medical school dissertations, to trace social ideologies of medicine. My interviews with gynecologists and my experiences working with physicians further reveal these intricacies. First, I return to how Luciana's narrative is an intersectional window into the experience of Black queer being in a social clinic.

Gynecology as a Social Clinic

Whenever I listened to Luciana talk about her experiences of injustice in gynecology as well as beyond it, I sank deeper into my own conflict and anguish about the practice of medicine. I could feel her gyno-trauma in and out of her presence before I had the conceptual language to articulate it. It was impossible to turn off or separate my clinical gaze from my performance as an anthropologist and sensibilities as a Black queer woman. I knew my clinical experience was a valuable instrument. I used it to engage both medically and anthropologically with physicians, but I mostly channeled it into imagining and connecting with my participants about their vulnerability in medical spaces. Brazilian Black women turned to me with questions about gynecological health issues such as uterine fibroids and HPV (human papillomavirus) and cervical and breast cancer. I imagined the anguish, anger, and dismay that my participants must have felt during their visits as they sat across from a white provider from a specific social class, whether male or female. The anticipation based on their experiences of abuses of power or the experiences of others is not their preconceito, as the gynecologist in the film discussed above proclaimed it to be. Rather, it is the profound awareness of Blackness in flesh and spirit. Luciana's experiences with gynecologists describe this wakefulness in its most total sense. Her storytelling also illustrates the strivings of a Black lesbian to stay in her body despite social violence aiming to dislodge her spirit, soul, and mind from it.

An example is Luciana's memory of jumping off the exam table midway through her exam. As a result, she did not seek a gynecologist for ten years. Luciana tells her story about experiences in both private and public health care. Before the age of twenty-one, she experienced a brief sexual relationship with a man. She said, "I knew that I was trying sex with a man just to see what it was like though I liked women." She laughed uncomfortably and shared her horrific story of a gynecology visit. Luciana was taken by her mother to a gynecologist when she was still a virgin to address any pain or secretions. This is her recollection:

LUCIANA: When I got my menses, we [family] could still only see a public doctor. We had no money, no insurance, and SUS was the only option, but getting an appointment was always difficult. I suspected then that SUS was not a good place, although free. Then, my first [sexual] relations were with a man. I tried it and regretted it because I did not like it or him. I was curious [laughs]. I still did not have health insurance, but I went to the gynecologist. I was twenty-one years old. The first doctor's examination that I had was horrible. The exam felt like it was ripping everything out of me. It was with SUS. I did not go to the doctor for some years. When I returned to the gynecologist a few times after age twenty-five, I had health insurance for a private doctor. They asked, "Do you use a condom?" No. "Do you use contraception?" No. "What do you use?" Nothing. I do not sleep with men. I am a lesbian, I told them. Then, their facial expressions changed. They acted harshly, dry, and brutally toward me. One time, I got up from the exam table midway into the exam and never went back for ten years.

ME: You waited ten years?

LUCIANA: Yes, I felt violated, understand? I felt like they did not treat me with respect for my humanity, responding to my [sexual] orientation with aggression. I was afraid, I guess. I returned last year. I am thirty-five years old.

I return to Luciana's story because whenever she reflected on the injustices of gynecology, she recounted her experiences and interpretations from varied angles. The iterative nature of Luciana's storytelling brings her out of the shadows of colonial power in medicine and society. Luciana's decision to interrupt her speculum exam and not visit a gynecologist for ten years reflects how the social—at least the medical—emerges in contact with and in response to her sexuality and gender expression in a broader context of deploying Black lesbian bodies. It also shows how this violence is permissible, even in a private clinic, especially with her Black body. It is not possible to isolate Luciana's interpretation of the gynecologist's "brutal" reactions after she disclosed her sexuality from physicians' ill reactions toward her sexuality.

Luciana's other experiences assembled an array of social issues and symbolisms that provoked intimate intersectional violence and the negation of humanity toward her masculine gender expression, Black body with long hair locks, and religious affiliation as an initiated member of Candomblé (the largest historic religion with African roots in Brazil). She was very devoted to her religion as an initiated member for over eight years. I visited her *terreiro* (Candomblé temple) many times and met her priestess leader; Luciana also invited me to other highly recognized terreiros, where her partner and closest friends were active members. Luciana often wore her orixá beads and white or light clothing on most days as part of her religiosity. It would not be unusual for Black women to be dressed all in white for a medical appointment on any given Friday to honor the orixá Oxalá. Luciana said to me, about a gynecologist, "When you touch someone's body, if someone touched my body, they are touching my spirituality. If they are violent toward me, they are violent toward my inner spirit. Too often, gynecologists would see my beads and hesitate to touch me. I can see their facial expressions change to disgust and fright toward me. They never change to help me feel comfortable." Religious intolerance against Candomblé runs deep in Brazil; its expression ranges from microaggressions to state violence to eradicate and demonize the religion. One of two Black women gynecologists I interviewed affirmed Luciana's story. The gynecologist linked racism to her colleagues' views about touching women who appear or identify as Candomblé members. She said, "Some of my colleagues believed that if they touch these women, something will happen to them or a spirit will do them harm. And they will not touch them. It is deplorable!" I was left wondering whether Black queer women were not examined when they may have had a real need.

Gynecology is a medical space that breaches the trust of Black women due to how their bodies and subjectivities are approached and handled in gynecological contexts. As Dána-Ain Davis reminds us, Black women's bodies are "worthy enough for labor and experimentation—such as gynecological experiments to address vesicovaginal fistula—but the woman herself is not worthy of being treated humanely" (2018, 2). For centuries, Black female bodies across the African diaspora have objectified medical knowledge production and medical curiosity in gynecology (see Snorton 2017; Cooper Owens 2017; McGregor 1998; Kapsalis 1997). Specifically, the gynecological encounter of Black lesbians is a particular medical and social realm of dynamics, interaction, exchanges, and confrontations between a female patient and the gynecologist. The gynecological encounter frames gynecology as a "biosocial space" to "make sense of life" at the expense of Black lesbians' lives, or what I refer to as a social clinic (see Franklin 2013; see also Keller 2003, 2016). I understand a social clinic as a realm of professionalization and institutionalization with repetitive normative medical strategies, tactics, schematics, and technological tools—not only material objects and visuals but also linguistic expressions—to deploy and legitimize gynecology as medical science. However, gynecology's systemized network of medical norms, values, language, and gestures is never divorced from the social world. In Brazil, the history of gynecology is entangled with social norms to institutionalize sexual and gender differences and regulate women's bodies (see Edu 2018; J. Gregg 2003; McCallum 1998; McCallum and do Reis 2005; Rohden 2001; Sanabria 2011, 2016; Velazquez de Souza 2018).[2] These tensions enable gynecologists to use their socialities and personal beliefs about the world to guide their expertise and patient management. Thus, my notion of the social clinic provides a framework to examine Brazilian gynecology as a site of power relations that implicate past and present social inequities and human devaluation.

The literature of medical anthropology and the anthropology of reproduction provide critical lenses for understanding the production of diverse patient and expert knowledge about reproductive technologies, medical ideologies, therapeutic markets, and health care settings. However, both of these subdisciplines have failed to center anti-Blackness in these debates and inquiries; this is particularly evident when Black and Brown bodies are subjects of analysis. I follow the earlier work of Leith Mullings (2002) in thinking about how Brazilian gynecology is complicit in producing forms of what she has termed "Sojourner Syndrome." Mullings reminds us that race, gender, and sexuality are interlocking forms of oppression that too often are ignored in reproductive health. When Black women, like Sojourner, speak, they are neither heard nor taken seriously. Brazilian Black scholars Jurema Werneck (2016) and Emanuelle Goes and Elisa Santos (2014) have pushed the boundaries of structural racism in a central intervention for holding accountable private spaces that produce gynecologic racism, which drives other forms of gynecological violence such as sexism, classism, homophobia, lesbophobia, and transphobia.

The notion of a social clinic unveils these interlocking forms of oppression in gynecology. I observe how it maintains normative reproductive strategies regardless of what Black lesbians perceive as the core of their reproductive lives and encounters. This tension between normative gynecology and nonnormative lesbian patients' desires holds heteronormativity firmly as part of that center; significantly, this tension is underexplored anthropologically (see Lewin 1993; Mammo 2007; Craven 2019). The heteronormative center of reproduction in gynecology elicits the complicity of this "woman's" medical specialty to favor some (white) patients over (Black) others. Michel Foucault's work on *scientia sexualis* helps to rethink the social clinic as a gynecological space that produces "truths of sex" and "knowledge-power"; as Foucault phrases it, "the masterful secret: I have in mind the confession" (1978, 58). The gynecologist in the film and statements by physician interviewees expose these enactments of truth-power and confession-making about women's homosexuality. It is also essential to remain aware that gynecological discourses deploy societal silences of sexuality via iterative, hidden confessional acts in the public realm. In this sense, gynecology is the invention of heterosexuality and heteronormativity (see Katz 1996).

The subsequent sections connect key dimensions that intersect in the contact zone of the social clinic. I map a series of normative, oppressive, insidious logics (gendered, sexual, racial, heteronormative) that sit at the heart of this contact zone alongside a vexation of logics and practices redefining the "gynecological gaze" with its invisible social terms (Mulla 2014; Kapsalis 1997). Language and symbolism are also critical elements for "experimenting with care" (Garcia 2010) to rethink entrenched preconceito as a vital mechanism of interlocking oppressions, much as it does in the outside world, challenging how Black lesbians pursue *viver suas sexualidades*.

Gynecology medically heals and saves many women's lives. For example, gynecologists intervene in the early detection of breast and reproductive cancer. Breast and cervical cancer are among the top causes of women's mortality in Brazil. Breast cancer continues to be the most common cancer for women, with 66,280 cases and 17,572 deaths per year as of 2018, according to the Instituto Nacional de Câncer. However, Black women's health is disproportionally impacted compared to white women's. In Bahia, seven women per day are diagnosed with breast cancer; two women per day die from it. I met three Black women (two heterosexual and one lesbian) diagnosed with breast cancer.[3] One of the women was only in her forties; she has since died, leaving a young son behind in the care of his grandmother. Gynecologists and mastologists (a field of medicine in Brazil specializing in breast disorders) are at the forefront of treating breast cancers. The stakes are high. Yet women reported that gynecologists too often do not touch their breasts for exams—even when there is a complaint. My intent here is to dispel the notion that gynecology in Brazil is by any means a paradise for care, as it ought to be—medically or socioculturally, it is not at all. Christen Smith helps us to think about different forms of culturally constructed paradises that illustrate how "Brazil's approach to the black body is to invisibilize it" (2016, 20). Smith takes up Achille Mbembe's formulation of necropolitics as "contemporary forms of subjugation of life to the power of death" to interrogate the central role that Black death plays in the epidemic of police and state violence" (Mbembe 2003, 39; C. Smith 2016, 20). What does it mean to examine gynecological spaces as a microcosm of this violent social world? To interrogate gynecology as a contact zone for inter-locking oppressive logics and practices, I follow C. Smith's urging: "The focus on asserting humanity has to be seen within the anti-colonial analysis of impe-rialism and what were seen as imperialism's dehumanizing imperatives, which were structured into language, the economy, social relations, and cultural life of colonial societies" (2016a, 26). This is my anticolonial analysis of Brazilian medicine. Brazilian gynecology is a colonial space. At the root of the social clinic lie the same complex ways colonial subjects assert themselves in a multi-scaled imperialist infrastructure of power.

Ciência da Mulher, da Diferença

The Brazilian colonial imperialist enterprise established gynecology not just to study women's reproductive organs or to examine women's bodies medically, but also to "make female bodies": to establish gender norms and differences for social order (Kapsalis 1997, 6). In Brazil, gender ideologies are the sociohistori-cal patriarchal specters of gynecology behind the violent ways female bodies are continually made and constituted in power relations. In this section, I discuss how gynecology, as a social clinic, is contingent on violently making gender and sexuality into intertwined "social categories" for social order (Valentine 2007). One central mechanism is the volatile sexism reproduced in gynecol-ogy; another is the general practice of medicine as it has been denounced to me by women physicians and patients. Sexism, a violent, systematized set of patriarchal gendered and sexual logics and practices, was repeatedly reported to me by women physician participants to reinforce its chronic manifestation in power relations between heterosexual physicians (women and men) and pa-tients. For example, I recall sitting across from a white gynecologist working at a public clinic for STDs in a tiny office and asking myself, "Is she about to cry?" as she stoically expressed her utter exasperation with the sexism in the field. She said, "These male doctors are going to finish us women with their sexist, de-grading ways of treating us. Many women also act like them. Of course, patients experience sexism too." Indeed, sexism exists in medicine, with female physi-cians competing for recognition and authority from their male colleagues. As I see it, these reports from female physicians (and patients) about a culture of sexism and sexual preconceito in Brazil point to issues of both society and the history of the practice of medicine.

In October 2012, I had my first conversation with a gynecologist about Black lesbians' experiences. This conversation proved so disturbing that it com-pelled me to interrogate how gynecology inherited this depth of gender violence and culture of obliterating Black queer women. Her observations were that much more troubling given that she was a very respected and experienced white female professional. She told me, "Sexuality, in general, is not significant. Most doctors treat women mechanically in Salvador and sometimes don't even look into their eyes while speaking. Their first question is usually, 'What contraceptives do you use?'" Her insight not only confirmed what most women I interviewed reported; it also revealed how women's gendered and sexual lives are devalued, diminished, and even erased. When I asked her why discussing issues of lesbian sexuality was such a challenge, she said, "They [doctors] act in their masculinist superiority. They think it [lesbian sexuality] is not important, not attractive, and that it is not necessary to discuss any issues related to it." I was stunned by the matter-of-fact manner used to convey this insight in my first interview with a gynecologist—an insight, moreover, uttered by someone who was a prominent leader in her field. I was not naïve about gender violence in Brazilian society. But her severe frustration with her colleagues was palpable and unsettling. She provided a stark insider's perspective on how gynecological practices in Salvador-Bahia mirrored micro and macro modes of societal domination. After that interview, I began to pay attention to what medical control should not look like for my participants.

Dra. Sandra

Getting to Dra. Sandra's office required a long bus ride to the business district located in the north-central area of Salvador. Still, I was excited to speak with this white female gynecologist, because she was known for advocating for reproductive justice and humanizing obstetrics with her own birthing center. Her office was upscale, with warm, fuzzy colors and dramatic art like a meditation suite. I was her last appointment of the evening. Despite the late hour, when I greeted her, she was eager to speak to me. She was a huge critic of gynecologists' preconceito toward homosexuality. As I unexpectedly learned, her young adult daughter was a lesbian who had had adverse experiences with gynecologists.

Unsurprisingly, Dra. Sandra also first situated herself as not having the background, as a gynecologist, to "lidar com questões da sexualidade" (to handle or deal with issues of sexuality), being instead primarily trained to deal with "physical" issues. She insisted on the necessity of training for gynecologists to lead in matters of sexuality. She was also referring to being trained in sexology, which I discuss below. However, I understood her self-critique through her insecurities toward her daughter. I was grateful for the forty-eight minutes of audio-recorded conversation, since my time in doctors' offices was otherwise often curtailed by their need to carry out medical business as usual. We talked about a range of issues such as gender, sexuality, and racism in gynecology. When I asked about preconceito, Dra. Sandra unleashed her disdainful insights without much probing. She said,

> My daughter shared with me the shocked and frightened face of a gynecologist when she disclosed her sexuality. Gynecologists should deal with their preconceito and worldview even to try to understand. We can say that we have no prejudice, but they will show it if they clearly have [preconceito] and do not know how to handle it. They are too embarrassed to think about how to examine a woman [lesbian], you know. It is a matter of how to face the world and work through your biases. Doctors, as professionals, have a duty to deal with these things in a free and natural way and improve as human beings. It is not about training. It is about being a human being. All these years, I had to work on it and question my prejudices. I had so many gay and lesbian friends. I really thought I had no prejudice, and then I saw that I did have preconceitos. I spent a lot of time working on it inside of me when my daughter told me about her homosexuality.

Dra. Sandra's perspectives about physicians' inability to restrain and confront their abhorrent sexist and homophobic views and belief systems helped me think about physicians' embodiment of larger systems of gender ideologies. Their entrenchment in how sexism and sexual preconceito operate together becomes expressed in interactions and power relations. Since the effects of sexism in all its forms (microaggressions, insults, harassment, and gender inequity) are as rampant as that of sexual preconceito (prejudice against gender expression and homosexuality) in gynecology, what does it mean to think about how sexual preconceito and sexism function together to shape the attitudes of gynecologists? Dra. Sandra's strong opinions about preconceito derive from her concern for her lesbian daughter, which helped her recognize her preconceito as it emerged in her practice. Her sociality heightens what she knows about her colleagues and the field: the imminent, unchecked threat of preconceito toward lesbians such as her daughter. Her self-reflection challenges us to imagine how gynecologists' socialities play a role in shaping their patient encounters and relations. This glossed-over existential "discomfort" destabilizes gynecology's ingrained gender norms and ideologies, further sanctioning entrenched sexism and misogyny.

For Dra. Sandra, gender and sexual differentiation emerge in the "knowing" how to, or how not to, examine a lesbian. She referred to the heteronormative ways of asking questions and proposing to conduct speculum exams and to discomfort with the patient as a lesbian. I applaud her for deciding to become a practitioner for her daughter's lesbian friends because of their fear of other gynecologists. How Dra. Sandra visualizes and positions lesbian patients within the power relations of the social clinic is encapsulated by this remark:

> Most times, a lesbian will submit to that preconceito that is so harmful and bad that women become closed, do not return, and do not take care of themselves. They avoid the doctor. Masculine women are received with more profound prejudice, shaming them, marginalizing them. Sexuality is delicate because it is tied to issues of preconceito.

For Dra. Sandra, preconceito permeates gender and sexuality issues in gynecology. Her idea of "submit[ting] to that preconceito" resonates with the idea of a contact zone in a cultural phenomenon that reproduces submissive spatial relations and oppressive gendered, sexual consciousness and control. Leaving aside how women may respond today to the gendered and sexual subordination in Brazilian medicine, Sandra's interpretations point to the deeply ideological seeding of gender norms, codes, and "symbols of modernity" (Peard 1999, 110). These societal gender norms and codes are linked to the emergence of Brazilian gynecology and obstetrics during the nineteenth century as a *ciência da mulher* (the science of women), *da medicina da mulher* (area of medicine for women), or *ciência da diferença* (the science of difference). Fabíola Rohden (2001, 52) argues that Brazilian gynecology played a crucial role during the nineteenth century in marking the social distinction between male and female. Sex-distinction processes were an ideological move to reinforce biological evidence as a means to establish societal norms for differentiating genders and establishing gender difference through articulating what ought to constitute femininity and masculinity. Obstetrics focused on the discoveries and interventions of pregnancy, delivery, and neonatal care; in contrast, gynecology became society's pathway to construct womanliness and to measure women for cleanliness, healthy reproductive capacity, and sexual vitality for marriage and the ability to satisfy a man's sexual pleasures and desires for procreation (Rohden 2001; Peard 1999). Brazilian gynecology was central to designing how to name and reinforce sex difference in society. Between 1833 and 1940, medical schools published 7,152 dissertations on disease and social issues related to water, schools, and prisons. Of these dissertations, 22.3 percent (1,593) focused on sexuality and reproduction; the most significant spike occurred between 1850 and 1859, when 32.2 percent had this focus. These dissertations served as reporting and public documents to define and institutionalize social norms and codes of sexual and gender difference between men and women. The majority were produced at the medical schools in Bahia (the first medical school in Brazil, founded in 1808), Rio de Janeiro (founded in 1912), and Salvador. Fabíola Rohden further documents the gamut of gendered and sexual social constructions across these dissertations about puberty, menstruation, menopause, and the hysteria associated with curiosity about these biological processes.

Gender difference in medical discourses is ingrained in society. It normalizes various kinds of sexual preconceito through characterizations of women as perturbed, sensitive, erotomaniac, nymphomaniac and by designating them as morally responsible for caring for children and sexual pleasure in marriage. These social characteristics modeled European culture and the views of European doctors traveling to Brazil. Brazilian doctors invested in a scientific approach that placed the social study of women alongside medical advances to compete with and demarcate medical progress and promote civilized society on par with with European and North American medicine.

The term *scientific* suggests the ferocious institutionalization of gender and sexual difference in medicine and society. Extreme positions were accepted as truths to normalize the inferiority of women's socialities and women's subordinate place in the home as well as to establish a "natural femininity" by way of the medicalization of women's bodies in contrast to men's (Velasquez de Souza 2018, 1130). This sociomedical agenda further underscores gynecology's crucial role in defining women's sexuality and reproduction (menstruation, ovulation, sexual dysfunction, and reproductive diseases) as a way to regulate and sanction social mores. The science of gender difference was rooted in both moralist and misogynist ideologies that included forging representations of smaller brains, thinner bones, wider pelvises for reproduction, and correlations between "menstruation and hygienic preconceitos" (Rohden 2001, 150).[4] The gender principles to achieve national "bem-estar fisico e moral" were grounded in economic and political change for Brazil (70); these principles materialized during the nineteenth century as part of sociopolitical and scientific interventions directed at the social and biological hygiene of the population.

To define marriage and legitimize patriarchal relations, medical practices intertwined with the establishment of social norms in the form of public hygiene (see Neto 2001), sexual health, and reproductive control (see Rohden 2001). These nationalist efforts also grounded the history of gynecology in mobilizing moral and social codes about sexual hygiene and sanitary practices in urban spaces—especially to construct healthy, moral families (see Jacobina, Ribeiro, and Gelman 2008). Thus, gynecology, along with other rising medical specialties in Brazil such as bacteriology founded by Dr. Carlos Chagas (1879–1934) and Dr. Oswaldo Cruz (1872–1917), legitimated a *higienismo* (hygienist) doctrine that would ultimately construct a new "social body" of Brazil's urban life for the modern world.[5] The entanglement of medical and social ideologies—also referred to in the Brazilian literature as *medico-higienista*—is best understood in the context of the hygienist and sanitary movement called Junta de Higiene Pública, created by the government in 1851. The reformulation of sanitary legislation between 1882 and 1889 increased the formation of alliances among various national medical congresses and medical societies. It exerted public control of public hygiene for a new social order. Their scope escalated to the extent that the idea of "medical police" was circulated in medical texts during the late nineteenth century (Machado 2011).[6] This hygienist movement continued in full force into the twentieth century as part of nationalist initiatives such as Liga Pró-Saneamento do Brasil.

The *medico-higienistas'* public interventions were considered social experiments. They mobilized ideas of degeneration and regeneration that functioned as technologies to cleanse the nation of conditions that degenerated the human race, and masculinity in particular, such as syphilis (Rohden 2001). We imagine the control of women's sexuality and bodies in the hygienist responsibility placed on them as *formadora de homens* (trainers of men) (3858). These ideologies mobilized medical "knowledge into a new discursive field, into a specialty focused on female difference" (3880). Brazilian historian Ana Paula Vosne Martins (2004, 3072) reminds us how medicine invented women's image socially. She quotes a study from the medico-hygienist period by Brazilian physician Jurandir Freire Costa:

> Traditionally trapped in her husband's service, home, and family property, the woman will suddenly find herself elevated to the category of mediator between her children and the state. These charges redefine a Brazilian women's physical, emotional, sexual, and social characteristics. Hygiene started insistently asking the woman to reproduce the national wealth as a breeder of her husband's goods. (as quoted in Vosne Martins 2004, 3895; my translation.)

Despite the feminist movement's progress with the medical community in the twenty-first century to overcome these institutionalized, sociohistorically gendered ideologies, Dra. Sandra's work in creating her humanizing obstetrical facility and examining her daughters' friends point to the omnipresent specters of Brazil's sexism—especially in SUS public health care (see Caldwell 2017). Another white female doctor interviewed also shared her horror stories of pregnant women in SUS waiting days for admission into a hospital for a *vaga* (available bed). She reported ending her affiliation with SUS and working only in private care before "one of her patients' died because of SUS neglect." The sexism described by my participants evidences a continuing systematic production of power to maintain gender and sexual hierarchies. In Brazil, the early role of gynecology and medicine in systematizing these power dynamics in society continues to exist within contemporary power relations in the gynecological space. A social clinic is a contact zone for these colonial and modern tendencies to assert gender difference by constantly redefining women's and female bodies' as subordinate places in power relations. Feminists and gender studies scholars have long diagnosed such systemic medical violence as ideologically central to understanding gender and sexual constructions of the body (see Sanabria 2016; Kline 2010; J. Gregg 2003; Martin 1987; Roberts 1997). The fact that gynecology is a gendered medical specialty is not new; the conversation that is needed now concerns how it is constantly shaping its authority and expertise to maintain insidious violent and normative hierarchies of gender, sexuality, and race in gynecological spaces.

An Insidious Zone of Anti-Blackness

The *ciência da mulher* with all of its violence of gender subordination had, nonetheless, a vision of a new kind of social citizenship for white bourgeois women as mothers and wives. The hygienist and sanitary movements emerged during slavery and grew well past slavery's abolishment in 1889. Black feminist activist epidemiologist Emanuelle Goes (2016) reminds us that Black women were regarded as "grossly degenerative" reproductive beings during the nineteenth century, as evidenced in racist ideologies guiding patriarchal nationalist movements. The widely read journal *A Mãi da Familia*, founded by hygienist physician Carlos Antonio de Paula Costa in 1879, published new discourses about the modern woman that represented reconstitutions of religious, moral, and social views. These included the sexualization of white women and the denigration of women with "utero ardente" as "special hybrids," "vampires" (associated with menstruation), and "assassins" (associated with abortion)"—notions based on biological ideas such as menstruation or birth mortality. In addition, the Black female body was simultaneously desexualized and hypersexualized as unfit to be mother or wife and definitely not worthy of full citizenship. For example, the Law of the Free Womb, passed on September 28, 1871, was the first legislation to free children born to enslaved Black women in Brazil. Children remained in their mother's care until they were eight years old, at which time the slave owner could integrate them into child-adolescent labor until adulthood. This sociohistorical injunction is also critical for thinking about how enslaved Black women were punished by being forced to breastfeed white women's babies and through the widespread selling of their enslaved bodies for breast milk. The sociomedical discourses about Black female bodies mark Black women as a racial underclass worthy of consideration only for domestic labor and breastfeeding. The hygienist regeneration agenda urged white women to breastfeed their babies and not rely on the breast milk of enslaved women, who were likely to be Black (Rohden 2001, 81). This agenda purportedly guaranteed the physical, moral, and intellectual development of white babies.

Enslaved and free Brazilian Black women were "dangerous wet nurses" (Carula 2011), threatening the purity and morality of a new modern social order. In this period physicians of the hygienist movement demonized breastfeeding by Brazilian Black women. Costa called them *onianimistas*—women who masturbated or became sexually aroused during breastfeeding. While physicians castigated these immoral sensations and imagined the participation of all women in such acts, the accusation especially applied to Brazilian Black women's bodies. Thus, Brazilian Black women's breasts were exploited for capital gain yet also seen as dangerous to the moral health of society. These sorts of deviant and barbaric reproductive corporeal images and medical and moral discourses were central to creating Brazil's scientific racism and racial ideologies.

Physicians spearheaded Brazil's eugenics movement during the early twentieth century with racial ideologies linked to the social mores and codes of the hygienist movement and a nationalist turn to present a new social order on the world's stage. The eugenics movement focused on preventing degeneration of the human race and a breakdown of patriarchy. It is deeply seated in the aftermath of slavery to obliterate, in the name of creating one human race, the social and moral impurities of both Blacks and the history of slavery (Hartman 2007; Davis 2019). In yet another iteration of Saidiya Hartman's notion of the afterlife of slavery and the hauntings of slavery in the United States, the Brazilian eugenics movement further institutionalized the "racial calculus and political arithmetic that were entrenched centuries ago to devalue Black life" (Hartman 2007, 6). Brazilian physicians were key actors for institutionalizing such racial apparatus and what Katherine McKittrick (2013) calls "plantation futures." Hartman and McKittrick remind us that institutional colonial histories are intricately interwoven with the present. Plantation futures represent the ways the colonial history of Brazilian medicine and society shapes contemporary medical institutional practices and physicians' logics about Black female queer bodies as medical subjects. Physicians from the Bahia School of Medicine, such as Raimundo Nina Rodrigues (1862–1906) and Julio Afrânio Peixoto (1876–1947), interfaced racial superiority with new forms of urban population control for reconstructing the ideal marriage and family, institutionalizing criminality, and controlling reproduction through sterilization—mainly of Black and *mestizaje* women.[7] Nina Rodrigues was the most influential among the physician intellectuals. Also regarded as an anthropologist and sexologist, his work emerged amid new interest in urban "fieldwork" and examining African religions and other aspects of Black urban life. The goal of such research was to offer deterministic racial models of criminology. In one publication, "The Human Race," he argues that the Negro savage (in the city or forest) is without moral, mental, or intellectual capacity to integrate into the new civilization without contributing to miscegenation (see Rodrigues 2019, 271–72). Despite the presence of Black male physicians in Bahia during his time, white racial superiority was considered foundational to establishing modern national identity. Eugenicist Julio Afrânio Peixoto is often regarded as a "sensitive" physician because he abandoned medical practice after his first attempt to examine a woman with European vaginal forceps that had been given to him by his mother. He was the only physician in Bahia with forceps at that time. Instead, after writing his dissertation in 1897, "Epilepsy Is Crime," he became a leading eugenicist and pioneer of legal medicine sponsoring eugenic laws to commit the mentally ill, carry out criminal surveillance, and assess workers' health and suitability for particular occupations. All this work contributed to efforts to reorganize the population in light of the social concerns of the eugenics movement (Stepan 1991, 51; Vosne Martins 2004).

Well into the early twentieth century, the need to "improve the race" was discussed in terms of "eugenic and dysgenic factors" for the purification of society (Stepan 1991, 50). Brazilian obstetricians and gynecologists, such as Fernando Magalhães, who were leaders in gynecological and obstetric surgeries, were at the center of these efforts, focusing on a gamut of reproduction-related issues such as abortion, prostitution, infanticide, and madness. Issues surrounding abortion and its complications heavily affected the poor and Black populations at the time and continue to be significant sites of mortality and institutional racism in Brazil. Dr. Magalhães was invested in the idea of an *aborto criminoso* (criminal abortion) to counter women's attempts to control their reproduction. While abortion was eventually banned, the country legalized surgical techniques of reproductive control in the twentieth century.

These included hormones for birth control and forms of sterilization (such as tubal ligation for those twenty-five and older with two children) that mainly impacted poor urban dwellers and Blacks. Brazilian Black feminist scholars of public health consider the country's eugenic history as culpable for the ongoing degeneration ideologies concerning the Black population and reproduction today (Goes and Santos 2014).

Brazil is still a "racial laboratory" (Schwarcz 2001, 22) in its past and present ways of violently fusing race with the history of eugenics (Stepan 1991). Also, its racializing constructions and categories of body phenotypes have contributed to a long-standing national resistance to accounting for racial disparities in health outcomes and to considering government legal constructions of racial preconceito as a crime (Caldwell 2017). I was once struck by how even a Black male physician believed race is not an issue in SUS because most patients are Black. I eventually understood some physicians' negation of racist treatment toward Blacks to protect their professional conduct in light of a criminal law passed in 1997, Lei 9.459, which criminalized "discrimination or preconceito" against race, color, ethnicity, religion, and national providence.[8] Racial democracy continues to be an ideological and institutional upholding of white supremacy in Brazil (Stepan 1991). The history of racial preconceito as a criminal act is relevant for thinking about insidious forms of anti-Blackness through the erasure and negation of Brazilian Black existence (A. Guimarães 2008). Colorblindness, an ideological apparatus for racial erasure, was deeply ingrained in most of the physicians' narratives. With the country's turn toward democracy with the 1988 constitution that offered public health care for all citizens, racially discriminatory laws that center on "prejudice" are suggestive of its racial hauntings. For these reasons, many gynecologists, especially white ones, will not identify racist relations in gynecology, not even to assess their behavior. Regardless, as Black women in private care whose experiences should have been far better than those in SUS, Brazilian Black lesbians felt targeted.

The embodied racial democratic views of physicians were evident in their complex and distorted perceptions of race, racism, and racial inequalities and of the impact of all these on Black queer women's lives. I first approached Dr. Manuel, a gynecologic surgeon, at an OB/GYN medical conference in Salvador after watching his presentation about women's social and corporal perceptions of their uterine fibroids. Like many gynecologists I spoke with, he did not recognize that structural racism and racial preconceito contribute to health care access and socioeconomic inequity. These distorted beliefs obscure how race and racism function in institutional spaces and social interactions. Dr. Manuel further said on this topic,

The issue in health care is not racism but lack of access. Black women earn less than white women. If you see that 80 percent of Black women have no higher education level and 80 percent of white women have, it's not because you earn less to be Black. There is no Black bank manager who makes less than a white bank manager. You don't have Black doctors who have the same job and earn less; no, the question is not about being Black or white here. It is about why you have more incredible difficulty accessing education and those jobs, right, that comes with a better level of education, etc. It is not always the issue of race as a social issue. They go to the identical SUS, have the same jobs with low salaries. I do not think race is much of a problem—at least not here in Bahia in Salvador, where the Black population is enormous. In the south of the country, there is a different reality than here.

Dr. Manuel's observations signal how racial democratic views seep into the gynecological space. His perspective exemplifies the entrenched societal colorblindness and class wars that negatively impact racial relations in Salvador. He also argued that Black lesbians experienced discrimination based primarily on class and minimally on their skin color or putative race. He later depicted physicians treating white Brazilian patients more favorably than Black female patients due to their sartorial choices because of their skin color. Even though he believes the impact of social class overrides racial discrimination, he shows that Black women fall within racially coded subject formations in these spaces. Dr. Manuel recognizes that many Black women are disadvantaged in many ways, but he looks only to class to explain it. His lack of recognition of systemic racism and his support of unfair and colorblind practices and beliefs further systemic violence, particularly medical racism.[9] Racial democratic views such as those of Dr. Manuel invalidate concerns about racism and illegitimate racial preconceito across interactions. In the afterlife of slavery, this is institutional anti-Blackness. Brazilian Black lesbians argue that they are in an unsafe social space if there is racial preconceito—whether gynecologists admit it or not. Black lesbians understand preconceito to be an entrenched mechanism for all interlocking oppressions, not just individual experiences. Many physicians deny the existence of race issues; for example, they do not perceive racism in health care because the population of Salvador is predominantly Black and Brown. Still, Brazilian medical practices rely on the sociohistorical threads of racial democracy to negate anti-Blackness. These practices justify racialization, invisibilize medical racism, and legitimize ongoing medical and scientific production.

Gynecology is a contact zone for insidious and blatant institutional racism and racist behaviors, or what I see as gynecological racism grounded by mechanisms of anti-Blackness or "anti-Negritude" (Vargas 2016). The "logic of anti-Black exclusion" is insidious violence negating the body, affect, and knowledge in the gynecological space leading to gyno-traumas (Ferreira da Silva 2016, 185). It is similar to what Dána-Ain Davis discusses in her work on what she has called *obstetric racism* (2018, 2019); her term redirects our attention from obstetric violence to take seriously Black women's narratives about racism during pregnancy, delivery, and premature birth experiences. Davis argues that obstetric racism "lies at the intersection of obstetric violence and medical racism" (2018, 2). The social clinic is grounded in this long history of violence against Black women's reproduction, bodies, and sexualities as nonnormative (Morgan 2004, 2021; Cooper Owens 2017; Davis 2018, 2019; Roberts 1997; and Washington 2008). Gynecology's long history of making race by privileging medical authority is a continuum of present-day racial dominance. The subjective violence of racial *preconceito* in gynecology illuminates what Christen A. Smith argues for: "Blackness as presence, not absence" (2016a, 13), up against the *branquitude* (whiteness) of both elite physicians and the most favored ideal woman—a white woman or even a white lesbian. Smith argues for avoiding the deployment and erasure of "Blackness" in ways that mean we lose sight of the value of recognizing its presence. These critical stakes point to Sueli Carneiro's (2005) interpretations of racial *epistemicídio*. For Carneiro, *epistemicídio* "disqualifies the subjugated knowledge of Black people through mechanisms that delegitimize them as bearers and producers of knowledge" (97). Gynecological racism and its historical ties are *epistemicídio* through the insidious erasure and negation of Black women's bodies and, even more so, of Black lesbians' ways of existing in power relations.

The Invention of Heteronormativity in Gynecology

Suppose the social categories of *heterosexuality* (Katz 1996), *woman* (de Beauvoir 2011), and especially *Yoruba woman* (Oyěwùmí 1997) are inventions. What are the normative codes and limits by which gynecology constructs female homosexuality in Brazil? After Dra. Sandra's interview ended, she asked me, off the record, "How are women *masculinizadas* made? How does that work?" She was provoked by my gift of a brooklyn boihood calendar featuring Black masculine women as central bodies. According to my field notes, I offered a simple explanation about gender expression and representations of dress codes and the subjective orientation to masculinity.

I often found myself explaining these social issues to Brazilian gynecologists. I found that it took a lot of humility to restrain myself from exploding in frustration with them. Holding a critical distance as a clinician, anthropologist, and Black queer woman, I witness how race is made within a heteronormative system. We understand the Brazilian historical entanglement of anti-Blackness and heteronormativity by how "lesbianism within the white supremacist ideology of slavery becomes attributed to black and poor women who seduce white women" (Aidoo 2018, 95). Lamonte Aidoo documents this ideology by how the historical sexual exploitation and coercion by white women slave owners led to pathologizing and criminalizing the bodies and desires of enslaved Black women. The enmeshed logics of anti-Blackness and heteronormativity (also class) reinforces Evelyn Higginbotham's argument that race is made through sexuality and gender. According to Higginbotham, we must interrogate systems of gender and sexuality through the historical and material power of race as metalanguage (1992, 252). Like Higginbotham, I interpret the ways race through unseen language and power is made through heteronormative approaches to Brazilian Black lesbians' examination. When a medical interaction is violent in the ways women described it to me, race opposes power relations of whiteness and heterosexuality to demoralize and maintain inferiority. The history of eugenics also records investments in casting homosexuality and lesbianism as abnormal, degenerated, deviant, and animalistic (Moreira 2012; Aidoo 2018). As explained by Brazilian scholar Adilson Moreira, homosexuality and lesbianism were omnipresent in Brazil and subjected to medical and eugenic sanitation surveillance and control as well as to marginalization from society during the nineteenth century. Brazilian scholars consistently point to the institutionalization of heterosexuality as normative through appeals to its naturalness, or the "natureza, naturalidade, e naturalização" of the family and a moral society (Moreira 2012, 270). These are all terms used for naturalizing gender and sexuality, and they came up frequently in discussions with physicians; for example, Dra. Sandra stated "the feminine body is naturalized." These gendered and sexual processes also make race by unnaturalizing bodies nonnormative in relation to the heteronormative *padrão* (model). As Lamonte Aidoo argues, "homosexuality and homosexuals, like blacks and blackness, came to be seen as a threat, a transmittable disease that could potentially destroy white male supremacy and the white family" (2018, 161). Through the horrors of the history of Black homosexuals during and after slavery as told by Aidoo, I understand the particular systemic violence of heteronormativity that is most notable in the notion of a *cura gay* (gay cure) during fieldwork. Brazil's social sphere and medical history evidence a complex sexual and gender landscape for diagnosing and controlling homosexuality as "abnormal, deviant, and shameful" (Mott 2011, 18; Aidoo 2018). Notions of a "gay cure" in medical infrastructures and government policies provoke social resistance and political strivings in reforms such as Brasil Sem Homofobia. Despite these and other broad strokes, Brazilian gynecologists justified to me their limited understanding of homosexuality in how they related to their patients. Doctors were not "trained," yet they had language and strong opinions for framing and positioning the homosexual in their spaces.

This section examines the term *natural* and other coded language that surfaced during my interviews with physicians. I analyze the term through my clinical and anthropological lenses as I scrutinize the history-taking examination and its deployment of the heteronormative. Heteronormativity is evident in the pattern of questions reported by Black queer women and confirmed by physicians, such as beginning with "What contraception do you use?" Suppose a gynecologist wants to determine whether a patient is multipartum (multiple births) or nullipartum (no births) for their medical chart. In that case, they will ask, "Do you have children?" These translations enforce heteronormative power relations. The predictable first question, "Do you use contraceptives?" triggers lesbians, indicating that gynecologists may not be receptive to their queerness. While this leading question points to the ideologies of the hygienic movement, control of sexuality, and a heteronormative process, I am interested in the ambiguity of eliciting the "natural" aspect of sexuality and other heteronormative techniques of disclosure that are worthy of exploration.

The term *natural* points to heteronormativity in the history-taking process. The Brazilian naturalist movement inherited the term and adapted it during the eugenics movement. As Lamonte Aidoo notes, "Brazilian naturalism is distinguished by its pronounced focus on the physical body and sexuality. For the naturalist, physical desire was the result of environment, social conditions, and biology" (2018, 172). Dr. Manuel is aware of how the use and order of language in the clinic allow or disallow women to reveal their sexuality. It seems that asking patients about their sexual relations leaves room for heterosexual, bisexual, and homosexual patients to feel invited to answer freely.

In contrast, a question about sexual practices implying far less heteronormative intent might be, "Do you have sexual relations with men, women, or both?" Yet heteronormativity is foundational in both questions. The purpose is to elicit information to frame gendered practices or sexual identity as associated with a social determinant or medical condition such as sexually risky behavior and STDs. These forms of surveillance establish the social categories that naturalize gynecology (Martin 1987; Kapsalis 1997; Bordo 1993; J. Gregg

2003; Davis 2007; Kline 2010). These shifting techniques are undoubtedly heteronormative, yet they position the lesbian or gay patient as a medical subject.

Physicians also mobilize coded language such as *vontade* (will/willpower) to naturalize (or normalize) relations by naturalizing sexuality and gender. These naturalizing tactics are not necessarily equitable or without gender or sexual prejudice. Some doctors, such as Dr. Manuel, have nuanced techniques for inviting their patients to feel *com vontade* to be who they are and help guide their examination. I was intrigued by his insight and his concern for creating an environment that invites women to be who they are—in this case, to be recognized as lesbians. When I asked him how he did this, he replied,

> More recently, the number of women who report having [sexual] relations with women increases, coming forward more naturally. The posture of the gynecologist toward it is becoming more natural, too. I learned about their sexual orientation while doing the *anamnese* [history-taking questionnaire, also referred to as a gynecological semiology instrument]. I would ask, "Have you already had sexual intercourse? How old were you when you first had sex? How was your first sexual relationship? How many partners have you had? Do you have a steady partner now?" I always questioned these patients as though it was apparent [assumed] that their relationship was with a man. But it cannot be like this anymore. So, nowadays, I ask, "Are you sexually active?" Then, the person responds, "I am." Then, I'll ask, "How is your relationship now?" or "What kind of relationship do you have?" Finally, I ask a more open question. Many patients will then say, "I have a relationship with a woman." Yesterday I attended to a very young girl who told me about her [sexual orientation] in a very natural way. Before, people spoke in constrained ways or did not speak [about their homosexual orientation]. At times, only after several consultations would they come forward with this information, you know. Or, they would say they had not had [homosexual] relations when they had.

Vontade through a gynecological gaze presumes feeling natural and stepping out of a state of feeling unnatural; once accomplished, both parties can become comfortable relationally. This relation is a compulsorily heterosexual (Rich 1993) strategy to establish the dominant normativity of gender and sexuality. The gynecologist uses such reframed and repositioned questions as active social cues, codes, and normative systems to elicit the other's sexual positionality. During this discussion, I position the term *natural* to acknowledge preexisting social entanglements of language, body, and environment. Dr. Manuel attributes a gynecologist's "posture" to the capacity to become more "natural" and for more lesbians to feel comfortable revealing their sexuality and discussing their sexual practices; in his view, the *anamnese* facilitates this relational naturalness or comfort. A restructuring of normative questions for a routine gynecological *anamnese* would trigger possibilities for social fluidity in the interaction. Gynecology requires and involves questions about sexual practices, sexual health, sexual concerns, and reproductive and sexual conditions; thus, sexual orientation is always an eminent trace of gender relations in a gynecological inquiry.

Medical documentation is more than a medical archive. As Sameena Mulla notes, the history-taking process "presents material realities as well as the reference worlds of stakeholders" in which they circulate (2014, 174). Mulla also notes that "overcoming the perseverance of these problematic imaginaries requires us to think seriously about the institutional protocols practitioners inherit and embody over time, and the traces of imagined relations that inhere within these protocols" (175). Mulla helps me think about the heteronormative scripted inheritances as ideological and colonial. A history-taking process does not capture "truths" about patients' existential being or formulations of identity.

Sexology: Sex or Sexuality Disclosures

The role of sexology raises the question of whether it (and gynecology) is a science of desire or technology of control (Weeks 1985, 61). In Brazil, the fact that a gynecologist can specialize as a sexologist suggests a historical, medical, and institutional location of women's sexuality primarily as a tool that can inform their clinical practice (see de Oliveira 2019).[10] When I discovered that Dr. Manuel also trained in sexology, I better understood his interest in shedding light on issues of sexuality. Soon after, he squeezed my appointment into his busy patient-care schedule. Luckily for me, rain prevented many patients from turning up for their appointments on the interview day. He conveyed to me that as a sexologist and a gynecologist, he chooses words carefully to elicit a discussion of same-sex sexual relations. Gynecologists' rethinking of what to anticipate from patients and how to ask questions about nonheteronormative matters flags how gynecologists shape encounters with their orientations to the world. At the same time, gynecologists such as Dr. Manuel are reshaping gynecological inquiry through a social domain tied to their own cisgender, heteronormative socialities. In response to my asking how he approaches unidentified lesbians in his clinical practice, he said, "I do not assume that patients who present masculinized, who have a shaved head, wear masculine clothes, a male chain, a cap, are lesbian just because she is a masculine woman. I ask, 'How is your sexual activity currently; are you having sex?'" I had not asked about queer women who present with masculine features (clothing or otherwise), but they were the patients he imagined might be women who have sex with women. I kept in mind the reported experiences of Black lesbians, such as Luciana, who identified as a masculine lesbian under such a gyneco-logical gaze. His gendered and sexual interpretations of what he thinks he sees suggest that his sociality of gender expression shapes his social gaze of women's bodies and sexual practices. His social gaze constructs how he questions such patients to elicit sexual history for medical charting. The notion of revelation or confessing your truth is pronounced in this medico-social strategy.

Physicians' presumptions that more privacy or a more secure environment is needed for patients to reveal their sexuality or discuss issues related to their sexuality is based on regarding sexuality as a private issue. Indeed, it may well be for many women. In general, there is less privacy throughout SUS, not to mention that what SUS constitutes as privacy is itself questionable. It does not offer a suitable environment for revealing homosexuality precisely because of gynecologists' perceptions of homosexuality as somehow "more private" than heterosexuality. While sexuality is regarded as private, heterosexuality always enacts its privileged public advantage, including in medical spaces.

Sexuality is situated in medical discussion as least private for heterosexual women. For example, suppose a heterosexual woman describes pelvic pain with sexual intercourse and chooses to disclose that she has a male partner or husband and has negative emotions linked to this discomfort. In this case, her sexuality becomes far less private and more welcomed than it would be for a lesbian sharing similar symptoms that concern her relations with a woman. In gynecologists' efforts to give patients autonomy to disclose their sexuality, or not, they rely on ambiguous elicitation praxis to avoid engaging in discussion about sexuality, but such indirect or ambiguous tactics only legitimize physi-cians' heteronormative logics and behaviors.

Most gynecologists hold lesbians responsible for disclosing their homo-sexuality or same-sex practices if they are to be treated with full recognition. Ambiguity is a heteronormative strategy tied to questions such as "How is your relationship?" It is not just an implicit question about patients' sexual relations; it is a truth game that entails waiting for Black queer women to assert their sexual orientation and requires experimental strategies to invoke trans-parency about sexuality. Many Black lesbians believe that gynecologists should be more direct. But this is not a common strategy. This is because it presumes that any patient may be homosexual. It points out and disrupts the prioritization of caring for patient bodies that matter more socially and symbolically: white, feminine, cisgender, heterosexual bodies.

Give Care, Not Subjection or Subjugation

Brazilian gynecologists orient themselves in a gynecological encounter with Black lesbians in a "colonial matrix of power and intricate web of social interactions" (Reyes-Foster 2019, 114), bringing in their socialities. Gynecological encounters are ideologically driven not only by the medical privilege of physicians as medicine knowers but also by their ethics and belief systems. Gynecologists' socialities are central to imagining gynecology as a uniquely positioned encounter compared to other medical specialties that do not navigate intimate issues of gender and sexuality. These hierarchies of domination in medicine normalize Black lesbians' presence as unbelonging or simply not present in flesh and spirit.

In this section, I rethink the obstruction by hegemonic power to caring for patients' well-being through the medical term *iatrogenia*. *Iatrogenia* means "of or relating to illness caused by medical examination or treatment." The medical terminology encapsulates what doctors should want to prevent in general: causing mental anguish and harm with either direct bodily insult or inappropriate language. For example, K. Eliza Williamson (2021) documents the harmful causality between obstetric racism and its iatrogenic effects on Brazilian Black mothers and infants. However, these iatrogenic effects in reproductive medicine are neglectfully overlooked in Brazilian Black patients. Dr. Manuel suggested to me by use of this term, *iatrogenia*, that there are known medical approaches to avoid harmful affective experiences for lesbian patients. Dr. Manuel's sense of carefulness to avoid iatrogenic impact upon his patients from a negative experience during medical care indicates that gynecology is a social clinic for producing and ignoring the negative affective experiences of Black lesbian patients. The term also signals that a doctor's inquiry into patients' lives and medical histories can deviate from humanizing practices that ensure patients' well-being. Medical "care" should not be presumed to be limited to the actual "care" or tending only to the corporeal existence of Black women.

Care is a relational social act. Such relationality in care in medical spaces can also constitute violence (Mulla 2014). Bruno Latour posits that the social as an adjective is "a type of connection between things that are not themselves social (2005, 5)." In following Latour, if we designate the social in social entanglements as a function of "tracing associations," we can also designate such webs in the social clinic (5). Suppose social medicine tends to provide a humanistic approach to the social realities of patients. In that case, we must rethink what medicine means by *social medicine* when there is extensive abuse of power in medical spaces. Gynecologists create (or at least attempt to create) effective and respectful translations across gynecological interactions, viewing them as necessary mechanisms or technologies to prevent harm. However, a gynecologist's neutral or vague inquiry into with whom a patient has sex does not guarantee that lesbian patients will not experience preconceito. When gynecologists readjust their heteronormative strategies, they still too often negatively impact Black lesbians' experiences. Medical strategies are what Angela Garcia refers to as "experiments of care" to explore forms of responsibility for the care of others (2010, 203). Doctors reframing medical strategies fall short of caring for patients' humanity. Dr. Manuel referred to the medical term *iatrogenia* to name the stakes for lesbian patients experiencing preconceito due to their homosexuality. He described it as a harmful psychological effect on the patient if a doctor "behaves heteronormatively and excludes the patient and neglects performing the exam. Then, the patient omits information, may not come back and resolve any health issues."

How do terms such as *iatrogenia* frame gynecological subjects? Are they intended to guide physicians with care and awareness? I draw a critical distinction for this discussion between *subjection* and *subjugation*. Judith Butler argues that "subjection is, literally, the making of a subject, the principle of regulation according to which a subject is formulated or produced" (1997, 84). Medical subjection in gynecology reproduces broader forms of cultural or discursive domination reinforced by gynecologists through functional or conversational linkage. Most women almost always find the gynecological examination uncomfortable—both discussing various subjects and the physical exam itself. This discomfort is more than being subjected to medical technology and body precarity. As Butler points out, the struggle of being regulated and controlled subjectively and socially signals the making of gynecological subjects.

Medical subjection in gynecology is inevitable; however, there are degrees of medical subjection. All women are subject to the presumptions of heterosexual relations that socially gender women as feminine (*feminina*) in varying degrees.[11] Rohden documents this sociohistorical information in analyses of the 1882–84 legislatures, the 1887 *Brazil Medico* periodical affiliated with Faculdade de Medicina do Rio de Janeiro, and the 1866 *Gazeta Medica da Bahia*.[12] For example, most heterosexual women reinforce heteronormative systems of sex and gender, demanding that medical providers not mistake them for gay women (see Rubin 1984). Heteronormativity and whiteness remain as power modalities and then as forms of subjection to otherness. As Judith Butler argues, power modalities restrict, shape, and allow for the production of subjects (1997, 84). While female patients are subjected to the gender-normative codes of gynecology, lesbians are further subjected to heteronormative language and expectations. Heteronormativity is the restrictive mode of sexual subject production in gynecology.[13]

Subjugation is a demoralizing process that runs parallel to medical subjection, or control and power. Black lesbians' complaints of being belittled, disrespected, or mocked for their sexual identities and lesbian practices (sexual lifestyle and desires) by gynecologists point to experiences of subjugating processes that differentially target them. Social subjugation penetrates subjective experiences with aggressions, insults, and violence, undermining personhood and humanity. Through these processes, the social clinic produces gyno-trauma. The distinctions between subjection and subjugation in women's experiences in the gynecological setting help us understand the gynecological encounter as an inherent extension of structural violence and power and as a site of reproduction of compulsory heterosexuality. Let's also keep in mind that, as Veena Das notes, not all of the "experience of becoming a subject is exhausted by subjugation" (2007, 59).

A casual trip to a restaurant with friends exemplified how society is gynecology's social laboratory. During fieldwork, I took a trip to a restaurant on the northern beach coast of Salvador with a participant and a few lesbian friends. I had interviewed her in 2011. Subsequently, I did not follow her closely but enjoyed spending time with her on occasion. While sipping our drinks and waiting for the food, one of her *parda*, straight-hair friends, turned to me and said, "You research lésbicas Negras?" She then turned to the darkest lesbian at the table—someone I did not know—and said, "You should talk to her. You are a Black lesbian." The woman and I looked at each other in disbelief. The immediate racialization as Black thrust her roughly into my research and implied that no one else at the table may identify as Black except this one designated representative. The targeted woman may have felt a form of racial preconceito inflicted on her by her drunk friend. The shy woman did not express any interest in talking to me, which was fine by me.

Then, I went to the bathroom and saw entrances marked by binary gendered signs depicting underwear: blue briefs and pink thongs (see figure 3.1). I rolled my eyes, then laughed and took a photo. Racial and sexual heteronormative crossings, or a traversing across, from the past to the present are omnipresent

FIG. 3.1: Entrance to a bathroom at a restaurant. Photo by the author.

in the fabric of society. Emily Martin's (1991) work on how science constructed societal gender norms remains critical for interrogating how gender norms are scientifically sanctioned and naturalized in both medicine and society. Martin's perspective on gender stereotypes hidden in scientific language such as that of reproduction (egg and sperm) is also subtly framed by these bathroom signs. Symbols of masculinity and femininity attached to bathrooms reproduce the insidious social differences taken up in this book. Physicians often said to me, "preconceito belongs to society." Despite this common belief, Black lesbians hold gynecologists responsible for their racial preconceito when clinicians target them through insulting behavior and speech. This commonly used phrase suggests that preconceito is a problem for all people, including those residing within the perpetuating systems. The notion that preconceito belongs to society might in a sense be true—it is a social problem. However, people use it to dismiss the need for accountability for how it is embodied by those who reproduce it violently. As such, it is also a problem for all people.

The sociohistorical connections in this chapter thread the intersectional ideologies and forms of oppression that coexist in gynecological spaces. The social violence of gynecology is structural. As Donna J. Haraway has observed, "A speculum does not have to be a literal physical tool for prying open tight orifices; it can be any instrument for rendering a part accessible to observation" (1997, 197). Haraway's work is useful for thinking through how the sociopolitical scene in Salvador considers homosexuality a political topic concerning the racialization of bodies and social interactions. My interlocutors often referred to their sexual health as an instrument (see chapter 5) to shape sexuality, for better or worse. The idea of instruments takes many forms, such as physical, policy, or even educational tools, to render the humanity of others (patients) accessible and available for respect. Following Haraway, we can rethink how Black female homosexuality in Brazil functions as another speculum, symbolically speaking. We might recognize the dynamics of ethical citizenship that emerge between Black lesbians and their gynecologists.

"Brazil is one big hospital!" In the early twentieth century, this widely circulated statement by a Brazilian eugenicist physician, Miguel Pereira, became public discourse (Aidoo 2018, 149; Britto 1995, 26). Scholars have interrogated this statement to show how Brazilian society is deeply ideologically driven and influenced by sociomedical norms. Black lesbians' demands for respect and recognition of sexual, racial, class, religious, and other subjectivities challenge gynecologists' socialities emerging from society at large. Understanding gynecological encounters, then, provides a map to navigate the social world. For gynecologists to recognize Brazilian Black lesbians as agents of their lives, they must acknowledge their medical domain as a social domain that bridges their space and the world. The gynecological encounter is fraught with the colonial gaze, which is shaped by gynecologists' socialities and orientation. This chapter has shown that, in gynecology, many practitioners are aware of their limitations with queer patients. However, they lack awareness of their anti-Blackness. So reproductive freedom and justice also belong to society.

The next chapter opens Brazilian Black queer women's public world to link the ways they counter the erasures and destruction of their knowledge production about structural violence and self- and communal care, or *epistemicídio* (Carneiro 2005). Another way to visualize and embrace unseen flesh.

It Doesn't Matter

For the Santo Antonio (Saint Anthony) festival week, from June 1 to June 13, 2013, many people in Salvador practiced a thirteen-day ritual of praying to the Saint. The Santo Antonio festival led to the prelude celebrations for the São João (Saint John) festivities of the June 23–24 weekend. Downtown Salvador, especially the Pelourinho neighborhood, was quite festive, with elaborate decorations in the streets. Specially prepared liquors and desserts were everywhere in the city: stores, homes, and streets. Many people stopped into Bairro Dois de Julho to buy these. One of the most popular traditions is to cook *amendoins* (peanuts) in a pressure cooker with salt. The most common ritual for Santo Antonio is to place a miniature bread roll or miniature croissant inside of a bag of rice for a year. These rituals promise an abundance of food, never going hungry, and always having the means to care for yourself and your family, according to Marcia.

Nanda and I met for coffee at the Bola Verde bakery in Bairro Dois de Julho one evening during the Santo Antonio festival. We walked from Bairro Dois de Julho to Santo Antonio square, located in a neighborhood just above Pelourinho, which took us about thirty minutes. The streets were crowded. When we arrived, there were numerous food and alcohol vendors. The Santo Antonio Catholic church had a mass service, which ended soon after we arrived. There were hundreds of people in front of the church listening to the service. Then suddenly, many people ran toward the side of the church, where something was being handed out. Marcia charged in that direction. As usual, she was thoughtful: she got me two bags with mini rolls to put into rice. I asked where her roll was, and she told me that she already had one at home.

Then we searched among the vendors for the best *caipirinhas*. With our *caipirinhas*, we sat at a table. Nanda and I decided to share a table with a random man drinking a few beers because it was the only table even partially available. The white man in his early forties was friendly. We shared a few laughs about the public event. He inquired into what I was doing in Salvador. When I told him about my research in gynecology, he replied that his mom worked as a gynecologist, and he worked for her. Nanda and I raised our eyebrows in astonishment and chuckled, especially after he said that his mother's practice was in Bairro Dois de Julho, where I lived. Nanda got up to greet someone she spotted nearby—she is a popular person. I continued to chat with the gynecologist's son. He was very curious about my research findings. He asked, "Why does it matter that a lesbian comes out to the gynecologist?" He went on to answer his own question: "I don't think it matters."

In this public moment, amid secular music and lots of alcohol, sitting opposite a large and open Catholic church, I was being probed in casual conversation about whether lesbian sexuality should matter to the gynecologist (Falu 2021). I asked him whether any of his mother's patients were openly gay women. While he replied that he believed there had been a few, he did not know of his mother's strategies and relationships with them. As a manager of her practice, he also couldn't tell me if those women were content or disgruntled about how they had been treated. He reported that his mother was in her seventies and would soon retire. Nonetheless, his questioning of whether coming out "matters" points to an issue central issue to both lésbicas Negras and (some) gynecologists.

But Brazilian Black lesbian lives do matter.

4

ARE *WE* ETHICAL SUBJECTS?

Seeing Ourselves in Shapeshifting Ethics

This chapter contemplates Black lesbians' worth and worth-making through a different form of subject formation that emerges in the gynecology clinic: the ethical subject. My first impulse is still to identify the wrongfulness of uneven relations, such as devaluing Black lesbians' sense of self or the harm caused by racially coded subject formations in spaces of power. Being a subject or occupying a subject position usually points to having an uneven relation to something or someone. Yet, in this study, I continue to contemplate whether Brazilian Black lesbians are ethical subjects at any given moment. Subject formations can reflect the processes of power relations. The circumstances of a subject position can also invoke necessary pathways to responding to violence or limited freedom. However, being a particular subject does not always point to enslavement or subjugation. Instead, as I have shown, subject positions express our orientations in situations and spaces; these expressed orientations toward ourselves matter—even if they are invisible.

Over the long course of this research, I pursued—to the point of obsession—an understanding of whether Brazilian Black lesbians can be ethical subjects concerning their gynecologists. Beginning this chapter with the question "Can Black lesbians be ethical subjects?" would have left room for discussing the limits and boundaries of self-formation in power relations. But this question shifted when I was challenged at my postdoctoral symposium to rethink the point at which Black lesbians become ethical subjects when they have yet to move from being medical subjects, let alone medical objects? This led me to reengage with how Black lesbians see themselves as medical subjects, medical objects, or both. Through their own lens, they do not become ethical subjects within gynecological spaces. Rather, their agential orientation to themselves in these private medical spaces is a preexisting ethical turn shaped by belief systems and formations through resistance and abolitionist trajectories exerted within the public collectively. This chapter is an opportunity to discuss agency (of both the self and the collective) through a different lens: that of unseen flesh.

There are many recurring public messages circulating among Brazilian Black women (and Black lesbians in this study)—such as "*Não Me Violenta*!" (Don't Violate Me)—that denounce racist, sexist, homophobic, and classist behavior and systems everywhere. These messages drive my interpretations of how ethics operate in public spaces and are charted into private spaces. This protest chant is more than a demand. It is a collective push to eradicate, break down, and abolish all forms of violence against their existence, such as gyno-trauma and death. As Savannah Shange (2019) reminds us, we should not conflate or confuse acts of abolition and resistance. I am analytically interested in both pathways in this chapter. Abolition and resistance share ethical features when tracked into medical spaces. This chapter is concerned with the ways such ethical realms exist beyond medical spaces. Public messages such as "Não Me Violenta!" are communicative portals between private and public spaces. They import a collective consciousness that supports self-consciousness and belief systems to enact their ethical turns within power relations. The private and public always communicate through the permeable threshold of dominant social norms—hence the metaphor of Brazil's past society as a vast hospital. Since sociohistorical elite norms continue to infiltrate private spaces for social control, Brazilian Black communities also continually reinforce antiviolence responses to the rigidity and persistence of present social norms in the broader social world.[1]

The role of the public looms large in the discussion in this chapter concerning the ethical turns that gave rise to the thorough understanding of antiracism and other forms of antiviolence consciousness. Public terrain is an ethnographically vital tool in any conversation about private interactions in medical spaces to honor the work Black women have done to revitalize places of engagement and resist acts of violence, particularly in the context of Brazil still being "one big hospital." For these purposes, different forms of publics (from occupying the street or participating in closed meetings such as *encontros* and various other discussion platforms) provide avenues to address their invisibility. Public forums and spaces in Brazil are spatial interventions where Black lesbians shape and fortify themselves to overthrow intimate social violence and assert their human worth. I follow Black lesbians through social spaces, networks, collaborative demands, and collective praxes of visibility to demonstrate how ethical strivings work toward liberatory practices. For example, Xirê da Pretas events and the organization Amuleto engage in the ethics of social justice and transformations of wellbeing. My exploration is similar to Naisargi Dave's approach to "radical ethics," where lesbians in India push the boundaries of possibilities through activism and forge their own systems of norms and values (Dave 2012, 3). I follow Dave's work to emphasize my research on the relevance of exchanges to queer life; I also highlight the self-formation for social change carried out by Black lesbians in various public spheres to define the norms that drive their struggle for freedom. Like Dave (2012, 29), I am interested in the imperatives asserted by Black lesbians for the public visibility of transformation.

I deviate from Dave's work by not framing the sense of being political as an act of activism or being an activist. Most of my interlocutors do not identify as activists. Instead, they participate in *movimiento* (movement) work such as community organizing, collective work, or protest. As such, they have different understandings of perceived outcomes for Black bodies and of which bodies are least visible to the broader public and in public discourses within movement work. I focus on using different publics to emphasize an ethical self-formation and its challenges to anti-Blackness and antiqueer consciousness formation. In other words, activism is not the only generative response to the violence against Black bodies anywhere in Brazil. Instead, seeing and feeling social change can strengthen intersubjective relations among Black lesbians and Black heterosexual women. As I see it, the public realm is the critical extension of private institutional spaces. It is a site of struggle and transformation where well-being—and life itself—is defended. Through this lens, the reader should interpret the narratives in this chapter and how they tie into the entire book.

I explore the concepts of ethics and ethical subjects in the context of liberatory practices to argue that Black lesbians are not newly shaped in their own ethical dimensions of self-worth-making orientations in gynecological spaces. Some dimensions of ethics are already a daily part of everyone's life. For Black lesbians, their daily methodologies center on interconnected ways that ethical subjects would ordinarily be engaged, situated, or transformed by ethical practices, systems, and norms (see Lambek 2010, 2015; Faubion 2001, 2011). By following my participants into the spaces where they work for social change and justice, I reinterpret how ethics, for Black lives, enact resistance, justice, and freedom on behalf of the self and others. Responding to injustice is not just the right thing to do; it is the only thing to do, As such, ethical practices animate self-worth and worth-making tactics to defend Black life. This application of ethics does not presume that any given individual (Black lesbian or gynecologist) is operating within normative or universal truths. Because ethics, as a system of beliefs, norms, or values, are embodied and ritualized differently between individuals and groups, I center ethics' production of action (behavior, ritual, or strategy) to reveal the "conditions of value" of any given subject (see Miller 2017; Dave 2012; Keane 2016; Mattingly 2013, 2014). Black lesbians' value conditions illuminate the distinctions between resistance and abolitionist thinking and praxes in a social world that intimately reconfigures some Black lesbians as "shapeshifters" (see Cox 2015). Aimee Meredith Cox's notion of "shapeshifting" is instrumental in rethinking the choreographing of citizenship in various intentional ways. I take up Cox's work to map what I call *shapeshifting ethics* that serve to both shift and retain the intersubjective reconstitutions of being an ethical subject.

This chapter begins with Estelle, a community organizer who is deeply committed to confronting preconceito and transforming bem-estar for all Black women. Her community leadership and collaborative story express the intersubjective logics and optics of justice that anchor a shape-retained ethics formation in institutional spaces such as gynecology. The goal of the chapter is to narrate Black lesbians' intersubjective strategies to push the limits and boundaries—the enactment of ethics—interfering with bem-estar. An enactment of ethics reveals processes of becoming social agents charting abolitionist epistemologies rooted in Brazilian and transnational Black feminist legacies. The risks and sacrifices are shapeshifting courses to ground the self for justice work. I also stress the importance of photographs in eliciting the powerful messages of enactments. When Black lesbians ask, "Are we ethical subjects?" they are not seeking to confirm moral codes or satisfy conformity. Instead, posing this question is a provocation to see how relying on created social worlds is a necessary condition of value for enacting agency and justice anywhere, anytime.

How Estelle Shapes Her Groove Back

Urban living was my ethnographic terrain. Brazilian Black lesbians were scattered everywhere and without downtown central social spaces to gather and mingle. To meet new Black lesbians, I attended social spaces for Black women. Luckily, I crossed paths during my first month of fieldwork with Lalia, a Black lesbian community organizer I had known in 2007–8. She had moved to a rural city in Bahia for work but traveled into Salvador to promote a new monthly Black women's performance event, Xirê das Pretas, of which she was a founder. She said I would meet Black lesbians at the event, but I was thrilled mainly by the thought of a central social space led by Black lesbians where I could recruit participants and immerse myself in participant observation with enjoyment.

The last Tuesday in August 2012, I could not walk fast enough down the steepest hill in Pelourinho (the cultural center and tourist neighborhood of Salvador) to Casa de Benin, where the event was held at a small museum with a beautiful large private room featuring large brick walls, cobblestone paths, live trees, and a partial roof. Hanging on the foyer wall and stacked on a small table were pamphlets and small fliers promoting organizations advocating against gender violence, racism, and supporting domestic workers. I learned that Xirê das Pretas was put on by Amuleto, an organization addressing issues of violence against Black women. Xirê das Pretas was an extension of the community and institutional justice work being done by those affiliated with Amuleto.

Lalia, who is tall, with locked hair and a soft, friendly face, was standing at the entrance when I arrived. She greeted me and escorted me to meet the event organizers. I later learned that they were all Black lesbians and that their presence attracted other Black lesbians. The event featured open mike spoken-word performances, dancing, singing, an independent film screening, music, and short plays. The samba vocalist host and popular local entertainer Liliana, a Black lesbian, performed with her band each month. It was the new spot for Black lesbians! There was always beer for sale and often an *acarajé* vendor was there. I rejoiced whenever this vendor had codfish for the acarajé. Street vendors and local bars sold food and alcohol nearby, right in the lower valley of Pelourinho. I confess that I basked in my own Black lesbian subjectivities, absorbing the performances by beautiful women and the energy circulating in the intimate space with an audience that at any given event ranged from ten to twenty women.

By the third event, I noticed a consistent pattern in the programming that reflected a profound social change agenda beyond ordinary cultural and artistic entertainment. Each performer and artist exuded a justice-driven sense of self that collectively formulated a deeper anti-racist, antihomophobic, antisexist public message. For example, in November 2012, a Black lesbian community organizer (Nilda, from chapter 1) stood out as she performed a solo oration interpreting Frantz Fanon's text *Black Skin, White Masks*. Dressed in white clothing, with her face and head covered by a loose gold sparkly covering, she moved around the space, on and off the front stage area, dramatizing parts of the book. It did not matter whether the audience was familiar with Fanon's work. From what I remember, the lyrics that Nilda's lyrics permeated the air, sending a clear poetic message about anti-Negritude (anti-Blackness).

At the time, Xirê das Pretas provided the only space for these openly sociopolitical and transformative expressions (see figure 4.1). Word was still getting out about the event. Most of my interlocutors did not frequent Xirê das Pretas, except for Marcia, Sandra, and Estelle. Many Black lesbians made social spaces in their homes or in local bars in their neighborhoods. For me, Xirê das Pretas was my foremost opportunity to witness how issues of sexuality, race, and gender were celebrated in a space where fluid social boundaries allowed for a pronounced Black lesbian outness and for any of my participants in attendance to platform their concerns about those social categories. The space took up various social problems to disentangle complex issues and denounce toxic political agendas on the local and national levels. Xirê das Pretas was more than an artistic space of resistance and freedom. People overtly denounced racism, sexism, and homophobia to the audience and announced their protests and community activities and agendas. Often, invited community leaders and politicians stopped in and publicly denounced injustices against Black women and Black lesbians. The expressive combination of creativity and political resistance was a window into the strivings of organizers and communal allies specifically and Black lesbians in general.

Through such dynamics, I reflected on my quest to reinterpret how Black lesbians' ethics of social well-being allow them to shapeshift to promote self- and communal care. It was both a social space and a space of *axé* (good energy) where women collectively and unapologetically identified as lésbicas Negras (Black lesbians). I witnessed how they engaged in *assumir-se* (come out) with both Black and lesbian identities, as Black women participants discussed social issues that affect them. At all Xirê das Pretas events, the social interactions between Black lesbians were intimate and sacred. Their interactions pointed to their values and visions about their sense of belonging in the world.

Estelle was the main force behind the Xirê. I met Estelle at my first event. She had locks and dark skin and was a Candomblé member. Older than most other women working with Amuleto, she carried a shy, reserved aura yet commanded attention in the room. Over time, I learned about her high regard for her community and her sociopolitical work on behalf of Black women's issues in many circles. At Xirê das Pretas and other events, I listened to and observed her leadership. She was also playful. I remember her teasing me at one of the Xirê events about my girlfriend coming from the United States to visit me in

FIG. 4.1: Poster in an Amuleto tent during Parada Gay festivities. Photo by the author.

Brazil. I was notorious for playing hard to get when Black queer women flirted with me at the Xirê (or anywhere). Estelle said, "You are going to marry her in Brazil." What she meant was that when my girlfriend arrived, we would not be leaving my apartment. She was charming, with her easygoing and charismatic introverted personality, and subtly flirty with everyone, including me. She drew me close to her by these personal attributes and through her leadership. I also sensed that it would be essential to interview her about the sociopolitical landscapes in Salvador impacting Black lesbian life.

In May 2013, I walked down narrow stairs between houses into a small, quaint house in Barrio Garcia to finally meet up with Estelle for a more extended conversation about gynecology. My eyes landed on house walls covered with posters, memorabilia, and other ephemera of Amuleto. It felt like a material archive of the Black women's movement and Black women's empowerment. I was overjoyed to engage in conversation in that space, though it was a lot to navigate. The interview became part of an event, a *feijoada* (feast centering a dish of beans and assorted meats with side dishes) for a gathering of several organizers, whom I knew, at Amuleto headquarters.

After we ate and drank and laughed, I sat on a chair across from Estelle while she sat on a couch with others surrounding her. That is how we rolled with the interview. In front of several Black lesbian friends and Amuleto organizers, she adamantly told me that their work to empower Black women to navigate all spaces included visits to gynecologists. She strongly asserted that gynecologists must learn to interact with Black lesbians respectfully and appropriately. Estelle shared the following opinion about interacting with a gynecologist:

First, we must break barriers. We [women] must see that independent of being professional, gynecologists are human beings, not gods! And we must not hold on to the belief, "Oh, it is a gynecologist!" There must be a dialogue exchange if I seek a professional to receive guidance from him about taking better care of myself. We both must break barriers. The gynecologist is there to attend to the entire patient, not just our body parts. They may not know the patient's background, and too often, he or she may not know what to say and be lost for words when they see you are a lesbian and only follow their questionnaire. So I think that silence about sexuality should be a barrier that both parties break. The silence can be broken with a questionnaire that people fill out before talking with the doctor. The nurse should ask questions that include our sexual orientation. There should be a video in the waiting room that includes all kinds of sexuality and signals inclusion.

Estelle's call for a transformed clinic visit pushes to break down uneven power relations. The idea of "breaking the barrier" may appear as a reformative vision, but it is an invitation to coexist in the space and allow an experience of human dignity without violence or erasure in social relations toward her sexuality and Blackness. As Estelle talked, the other Black lesbians nodded and listened intently. Estelle had the floor during this audio-recorded session. She said, "And when talking about Black women, lesbians, and Candomblé, you are increasingly pointing out inequality, intolerance, and lack of respect for human dignity." Although other women did not use the word *dignity* during my interviews, they alluded to it in other ways, such as recognizing the lack of respect toward them. Neither respect nor dignity is negotiable. In medical spaces, Black lesbians such as Estelle shift into an ethical relation of pushing or breaking down the boundaries; this is especially true when the topic impinges on dignity. Dignity was tied to the notion of racial inferiority in Brazil. She said, "We may not be slaves anymore. However, white superiority continues as if we are still enslaved, and we are treated as racially inferior." The barrier to abolishing this injustice is a white consciousness that construes Blackness as inferior. Estelle offered more perspectives to address dignity in medical interaction:

For improved interactions, gynecologists must spend time with patients and find ways of relating to us. It is not enough to just have the doctor sit there and fill in a questionnaire. The doctor himself should ask the usual questions with more ease and not prejudice; instead, the doctor should move with a flowing dialogue. I think this is necessary to establish a humanitarian dialogue.

Dignity, or the state or quality of worth, when dishonored or disrespected is a sign of medical intolerance of such patients' self-value. Black women recognize when a lack of respect toward them is rooted in anti-Blackness. Yet Black lesbians must maintain and draw on their dignity as a source of self-esteem, confidence, and strength to navigate these interactions that are part of daily life. Black lesbians' expectations for dignity and respect hold the gynecologist responsible for initiating and guiding the conversation; gynecologists should know how to become partners in dialogue about their patients' sexual health, sexuality, and gynecological health care. Here, the concept of dignity expresses what Webb Keane (2016) calls a core component of ethical life. Keane argues that "dignity is an ethical quality that cannot be understood just in reference to the individual to whom it pertains: there must be someone else who respects it. It must also be perceptible to another; it cannot remain an inner quality alone" (113).[2] Keane's aim (to problematize interaction in his analysis of the semiotics of interaction about dignity and respect) urges us to consider how medical spaces can be potential spaces for ethical life. If anti-Blackness, alongside antilesbian views, is the main barrier to be broken or abolished, then the expression of dignity provides evidence that such ethical dimensions in medical interactions are predicated on just racial relations. Black lesbians such as Estelle may shift into an ethical subject mode in such relations in recognizing and communicating the absence of such ethical life. Such a sense of self and associated strategies are rooted in social formations of resistance and abolitionist thinking beyond medical spaces.

Are *We* Ethical Subjects?

Ethics in this chapter are best interpreted as processes of becoming in what Karan Barad (2007) refers to as "ethico-onto-epistem-ology." Barad argues that "the separation of epistemology from ontology is a reverberation of the metaphysics that assumes an inherent difference between human and non-human, subject and object, mind and body, and matter and discourse" (185). However, dignity is a reminder that all these relations are fused and dependent on conditions of value. Like Barad and many anthropologists of ethics, I regard the ethical as always intertwined with being and knowing (see Das 2015; Dave 2012; Davis 2012). Barad's notion of intra-action helps illuminate how

Black lesbians in their processes of becoming demanders of justice lift themselves up in moments of conflict to signal physicians to take responsibility for the outcome of their ethical orientations. Dignity, then, reveals the entanglements of intra-action. Barad says, "Ethics is therefore not about right response to a radically exterior/ized other, but about responsibility and accountability for the lively relationalities of becoming of which we are part" (393). In other words, Black lesbians do not need to be legible to physicians for intra-activity to transmit their agential nature to separate them from lack of respect and engage in antiviolence (whether the violence is prejudice or physical) relationality. This is one way to understand an ethics that produces ethical subjects with declarative voices about their value in the world and in their own worlds. Their articulations about injustices and how to address them, and how to learn to defend themselves and their communities, are a consequence of legitimizing their intersubjectivities in social spaces.

A conversation about ethical subjects frames just one of many dynamics of self-formation. Despite its complexities, the ethical subject is a valuable concept for understanding how Black lesbians adjust their ethical realm to illuminate the value systems that sustain their quality of life and sexually liberatory experiences.[3] An ethical realm is socially, culturally, and historically specific. Freedom alone is, then, insufficient grounds for ethics (Foucault 1985). Marcia and Estelle, for example, are ethical subjects who forge the "truth, culture, and freedom that stand both as instruments and as sites of responsibility" (Davis 2012, 17); they expose how public discourses travel into microsocial spaces and interactions, serving to further and more intimately reinforce their subjective sense of social well-being. Some dimension of action and praxis must be possible for an ethical subject to emerge in institutional spaces and engage their self-formation activity beyond those medical spaces.[4]

An ethical subject is a subject engaging in evaluative interpretations within social interactions (see Miller 2017; Keane 2016; Mattingly 2013, 2014; Faubion 2011). I am interested in how ethical subject formation questions how certain domains—such as a gynecology visit—become topics of ethical scrutiny. Ethical scrutiny is feasible when Black lesbians pay close attention to their fragility as well as to their strength. While constrained circumstances are often understood as social conditions that impede liberatory praxis or being, Black lesbians' ethics are never disengaged from social resistance in institutional spaces or elsewhere. Being an ethical subject as a Black lesbian means that self-advocacy is contingent on the evaluation and reflection of both constricting and liberatory conditions. Being an ethical subject is just one dimension of their strivings toward justice.[5] It is not always a radical sense of self. More importantly, the attempt to govern themselves in moments of conflict is rooted in antiviolence consciousness. An ethical mode of existence is grounded in a place of self-love and living in the self through space. It is the exertion of power, and in my view, that power is valuable, despite being subject to a power differentiation in a medical space.

Ethical subjects are not subjugated in their awareness about their various intersectional subject positions but are active strivers for liberatory praxis. These human complexities are critical tensions for understanding Black lesbians' relationalities to Black human value or the value other humans place on them as Black bodies. I qualify Black human value in relation to Blackness and ethics—not one inside the other. As race scholar and philosopher J. Reid Miller argues, "Value, it would appear, is not what the subject brings upon itself through social interaction, like a scarlet letter sewn to the soul; rather, value brings the subject itself into being. If the subject is always an 'ethical subject,' it is not because it is always 'good' but because it always resonates evaluatively" (2017, 16). Miller's perspective on ethical subjects and value centers on Black life as a human condition that signals inner value emerging in social interactions. The evaluative being brings us closer to defining *well-being* as a value for a subject, particularly in the face of prejudice. Black lesbians do not become ethical subjects within gynecological encounters and similar spaces of power but rather engage their ethics of resistance every day through their politics and praxis of social change. Their sense of individuality does not merely produce ethical subjects in the becoming, or emergence, of their humanity in the face of normative systems. The collective shaping of self-reflective beings is what they bring into the gynecological clinic; they embody ways of knowing the self with justice. Are Black lesbians ("we") ethical subjects? We can contemplate that Black women have always been ethical subjects in particular ways. They have been continually working to remove the stain on race left by normative ethics of whiteness and heteronormativity in their efforts to define or enforce their norms and value systems to exist and stay alive.

Shapeshifting Ethics

The public visibility of Black lesbians' social action to address violence has been a significant feature shaping their ethics for justice work. Creating this visibility usually requires infiltrating and aligning with government organizations at the local and national levels to disseminate public messages denouncing injustice. Black lesbians are often not as visible or present on these platforms as white lesbians. Because of entrenched divisive racial politics, white LGBTQ+ leaders and activists are usually the public faces of these efforts. Black lesbians push these racial boundaries even within LGBTQ+ platforms in response to the need to intervene on behalf of Black communities and raise awareness about the issues faced by Black lesbians. These embodied forms of collaborative care are vital in Brazil—particularly in Bahia—given its large population of Black and Brown folks and long histories of racial and gender resistance work. Sueli Carneiro (2019) reminds us of the importance of *enegrecer* (blackening) feminist or activist spaces to fight for the issues impacting Black women. Many Brazilian Black women heed Carneiro's charge to *enegrecer* the feminist movement by demanding that an anti-racist agenda is center to the social justice movements. Still, Black women have had less access to opportunities for gaining recognition for their contributions to these platforms and behind-the-scenes justice work. The notion of *enegrecer* should also be considered praxis and a philosophy or a system of values fueling agential relations. Public visibility for Black lesbians is no small act, given the prevalence of social violence in Brazil (see C. Smith 2016).

In this section, I consider how listening and following the involvement of participants in large-scale justice work gives insight into the formation of their shapeshifting ethics. I draw from Aimee Meredith Cox's reformulation of the term *shapeshifting* to expand our view of the production of ethics; like Cox, I regard these as shapeshifting practices. I reflect on the unseen value production attached to public materials, discourses, and networking for this analysis. Marcia talked ceaselessly to me about May as LGBT Diversity Month (Maio da Diversidade LGBT) for several months leading up to it. Being part of the planning committee animated her: the gossip, conflicts, joys, and rigors of working with LGBTQ+ leaders. When May finally arrived, I met Marcia at the opening plenary ceremony; she was very excited about and proud of the agenda she had helped organize. Then, I noticed that Marcia and Estelle were on the cover of a large pamphlet with a programming list (see figure 4.2).

I had not recalled her alerting me to this, but then again, she always shared many details. One thing was for sure: I dared not miss the event. It had been the center of her life, and she was rightfully proud of it. When I saw her face on the materials (pamphlets, posters, and large banners), I understood on a deeper level what she had been working toward: a grand "coming out" that would traverse Bahia and beyond. This act of visibility would not be the first time photos of faces were used as public representations contesting homophobia and anti-LGBTQ+ violence. When I arrived in 2012, I saw the faces of three lesbians plastered on a single billboard overlooking a major highway to make a public statement denouncing lesbophobia. I saw the billboard a few times, recognizing one of the women as an activist and academic white lesbian; in total, two were *brancas* and one *parda*. To my knowledge, Black lesbians were still not too open to "outing" themselves on materials for public circulation. This widely circulated pamphlet was the first in my findings to feature Black lesbians visually for an antihomophobia cause.[6] Things are a bit different now. Back then, the pamphlet was a massive deal for Marcia and Estelle.

I was also struck by the intensity of the May 2013 programming. There were approximately fifty-nine public discussion events in various locales on health, religious intolerance against Candomblé, LGBTQ+ youth, and education on homophobia. Employees of the state spearheaded this public intervention and involved many volunteers, including community leaders and social movement organizers. The programming spread across seventeen municipalities across the state of Bahia. In Salvador itself, there were seventeen events scheduled in different locations, including the plenary and opening celebration for Maio da Diversidade LGBTQ+, which was held at the building that housed the Secretaria da Justiça, Cidadania, e Direitos Humanos (Secretariat of Justice, Citizenship, and Human Rights). In addition, Estelle's group, Amuleto, had several *xirês* and *rodas da conversa* (conversation circle) events scheduled in various urban and rural cities. As Bahia's first effort to institutionalize and mobilize such social justice recognition, the Maio da Diversidade LGBT agenda centered on homophobia, racism, and religious intolerance to rethink education, antiviolence policy, and community healing.

Publicly circulating Black lesbian faces on printed materials was risky yet courageous. Being visible as lovers, partners, and even protesters is no small task in Brazil.[7] Nonetheless, it symbolized a call to action for social change. The LGBTQ+ social movement had long centered on the needs of gay men and the trans population (transsexual and travesti; this now includes transgender), mainly related to HIV issues and violence. Lesbians, including Marcia, who was active in the 1990s in the LGBTQ+ movement, were always present, yet they were not given full recognition. Public visibility for Black lesbians' labor—the integration of Black lesbian faces into LGBTQ+ social and policy work and public discourses—has gained momentum significantly. The public presence of Black lesbians such as Estelle and Marcia (and the month-long programming) inevitably push the discussion of LGBTQ+ issues further to center on racism, classism, sexism, and religious intolerance.

Marcia's intertwined politics of public visibility were more evident to me after witnessing her sense of self at Maio da Diversidade LGBT events. On May 4, my plans to take a bus trip to a rural city and participate in one of the events organized by Estelle's group were canceled. Disappointed, I instead at-

FIG. 4.2: Poster from a May LGBT Diversity event reading. We are all the same. Denounce homophobia. Understand. Comprehend. Respect. Photo by author.

tended Marcia's facilitation of a discussion circle in downtown Salvador at the Sindicato dos Comerciários on lesbian issues and lesbians in the workforce. Sindicato was a familiar place where I organized meetings of a lesbian collective, Lesbibahia, which Marcia also was part of. After arriving, I was relieved to be at Marcia's organized event. All twelve of us sat in a circle while Marcia explained how the discussion focused on fitting to a *padrão* (normative pattern) of gender expression. For two hours, long testimonies poured out about crises with nonnormative gender expression, stigma, and prejudice.

I took notes but my attention was on sharing space with everyone. First, a Black trans woman talked about self-identifying as a lesbian in her desire to sleep with women and men, yet not being accepted by the lesbian community. She also shared her difficulties with securing employment as a trans woman and convincing her coworkers to accept her name change. Others shared challenges in their relationships or families or with coworkers related to their masculinities. Listening felt therapeutic for everyone. Above all, the exchange of small personal strategies to overcome those challenges was affirmed. Then, Marcia shared her story about her experience in her first few jobs as a young feminine lesbian. The interviewers back then voiced strong disapproval of her not wearing earrings. Other employers would ask her to wear earrings; she would get fired each time for refusing. She lamented, still feeling discriminated against today for not wearing earrings though she considers herself feminine. It was not until then that I realized she never wore earrings. Jewelry is a substantial cultural production for women in Brazil. Her sentiment about those past experiences signaled her struggles in forging values about whom she needs to be—despite coercive norms and needing work. Everyone nodded, sighed, and chimed in with solidarity.

On May 10, I finally took a bus trip to a rural city for a Maio da Diversidade LGBT event. This time, I attended with Marcia. We visited a high school and a Candomblé terreiro in the city of Mata de São João, one hour outside of Salvador. I had impromptu opportunities to facilitate discussions at both events and engaged the audience on issues of anti-LGBTQ+ preconceito from my point of view. The event in the well-established small terreiro stood out for me given that it was my first time in a Candomblé space having a formal group discussion about homophobia. Candomblé is the most welcoming religion for the LGBTQ+ population, but it is not without gender normativity and homophobia (A. Allen 2012). Nearly everyone in attendance at the terreiro was Black or Brown; they were all very attentive to the three facilitators, including me. One Black woman had many questions about homophobia and how to educate the religious community on the topic. She also asked questions about pending legislation to prohibit animal sacrifice for religious purposes. She said, "What will our orixás eat! They are not vegetarians!" Everyone laughed.

Marcia's address to the group was testimonial and personal and instructive in sharing her own experiences as a lesbian in the social movement. The audience was very receptive to hearing about her early days in the movement when lesbians were far less visible. Marcia drew on her history to engage this religious community on issues of preconceito. To fight preconceito meant unifying Black communities to feel and imagine what keeps them interconnected in communal suffering. A Black woman in the audience said, "I think the orixás wanted us to know about you and all your work. It is very helpful for us." As it turned out, this Black woman was also a lesbian and invested in the discussion positively impacting their Candomblé community. For Black lesbians like Marcia, sharing parts of the self was part of caring about the different parts of themselves and others for the sake of justice.[8]

Shapeshifting ethics is an analytic drawing on what Aimee Meredith Cox refers to as what "Black women use to read and respond to the evaluations of their social value—evaluations having implications that unsettle the notion of unified and knowable identities and the presumed stability of geographic space" (2015, 27). Cox explores how low-income young Black women participate in the "dynamics of place making" in Detroit and establish their politics of the body through institutional displacement (27). Cox's framing of "shapeshifting" helps to rethink Black lesbians' bodily and subjective orientations to their community and political agendas for shapeshifting their evaluations of social value tracked from external interactions into and about medical spaces—such as in the experiences of Marcia and Estelle. *Shapeshifting* is a term used to talk about the nature of molecules, spirit transformation, and even computer coding. In her work, Cox redefines *shapeshifting* as a method by which Black women turn to memory, recall ideas, and mobilize their history to "give new meaning in social contexts that engender cartographic capacities beyond particular physical or ideological sites" (28). For me, shapeshifting ethics is the illuminating force of evaluating both social value and self-worth in designated places and times and tracking that force into spaces of constraint such as medical spaces. Black lesbians' praxes to denounce injustices are their visual politics reinforcing visibility. Through their visual politics, from being the face of a pamphlet to communal *rodas*, their acts of social change are their shapeshifting ethics to disrupt dominant institutional visual cultures of seeing only whiteness as social value, compelling us to reimagine intersubjective agential formations.

Shapeshifting ethics is a methodology of the oppressed (see Sandoval 2000) that does not situate Black bodies as destitute. Such methodological praxis is worth-making and embraces Black bodies as frontiers—to identify microcosms of a world in which oppressive mechanisms are omnipresent both systemically and intimately—with awareness and reflective evaluation. Chela Sandoval's work evidences how any "specific technology of the methodology of the oppressed that produces the differential movement of consciousness through meaning" is critical for social change (2000, 5).[9] Like Sandoval, I value knowledge that does not simply appear but is acquired through exercises of judgment and strategizing for praxes that travel into various spaces. In becoming ethical subjects that reclaim their minds and bodies, Black lesbians would rather "stay in their bodies," as Cox argues, to shift embodied trauma of their memories of violence into social action (29). Ethics charted through multiple intersecting identities unravel how resistance praxes are a critical product of a schema of feedback, perceptions, experiences, social systems, and interactions; how communal intersubjective connections—often tightly woven together—are the shapeshifting tools of assessment for social well-being.

These unseen shapeshifting ethics, or praxis and action, highlight the contested and invisible processes of human valuation that are antithetical to justice and freedom. Here, I understand ethics via J. Reid Miller's interpretation of stain [on/by race] removal: "to encounter and contemplate a being or phenomenon as it originally accedes to conscious awareness—as unmarked and uncolored—one becomes thereby obliged to strip from that existent all ethical and racial associations: to perform an interpretive exercise of stain removal" (2017, 7). In other words, both ethics and race are stained processes of the judgment of value. According to Miller, the ethics of race is not possible since race is not external to ethics; ethics stains race and race stains ethics with judgment about what constitutes value. I refer to a human value in any dimension from the selling and trading of Black bodies (see Berry 2017) to human worth in interactions from intimate to state violence. Normatively speaking, ethics through whiteness highly favors whiteness. Miller reminds us that a pitfall in interpreting ethics and race is the presumption that it immediately means to speak of racism. What is at stake is not whether a conversation about ethics and race is synonymous with addressing racism but instead treating the interrelational forces shaping the value and valuation of bodies, social worlds, and power, for example. Value is the substance of moral systems foundational to knowledge, existence, and action.

Miller's perspective on stain removal is helpful for rethinking how ethics, anchored by anti-racist values, is the only possible way to evaluate and recognize any shared value between ethics and race. Miller's reading of Frantz Fanon's racial difference as "color, hue, dye" suggests that social markers are more useful for getting clarity about other markers of representation and being, such as whiteness and anti-Blackness (Miller 2017, 48). If race is stained by skin color and ethics is also stained by skin color (judgment), then visibility—or the process of seeing race—does not guarantee that racial difference will not cause harm, socially, bodily, or systemically (9). Rather, it allows at least an entry point for seeing stained bodies sociopolitically in the face of a "disparate evaluative resonance" toward race (10).[10] Any possibility of removing the stain of ethics on race—in this case on Blackness as devalued—is then the ethical driver to racial liberation. This point of view helps us recognize and affirm, above all, that my participants are more than inactive, passive, silenced Black bodies; instead, they are ethical subjects constantly working toward stain removal, even if merely scratching them off slowly. Stain removal work is more than resistance. Abolitionist thinking leads to words, action, habits, character, and destiny (present value in reality and an envisioned future).

Therefore, oppressive preconceito (racial, sexual, classed, gendered) is external to ethics. Like Miller, I do not propose an ethics of race. As anthropologists, we study how people value things, events, and bodies, including themselves.[11] However, Black lesbians' processes of valuation—or rather how they place value—run against the grain of universal notions of the evaluation of value. Since Black lesbians see themselves as Black first, their evaluative praxis of value of life is what Miller calls "stain removal," or the removal of devaluation. As Miller states, "The productive features of race as an evaluative force become clear only through a structural reading of it—that is, as signifying a modern configuration that constitutes embodied subjectivities through differential relations of value" (2017, 35). What can appropriately remove the stain that whiteness has placed on ethics but whiteness itself?

I do not ignore that ethics, generally, is a normative realm and can be toxic. However, we can think about ethics that counter normative shapeshifting ethics to be necessary conditions in power relations. In shaping ethics by moral codes ingrained in belief systems and embodied social rituals and behavior, ethics is at best the framework by which society contributes to defining thresholds of "good" or "bad" conduct. People are driven to do what they do, and it is important not to presume either the transparency of their motivations or the stakes to be gained or lost by their actions. Otherwise, we take for granted the meaning-making aspects of life or social value, and we forget the weight of the labor needed to undo the devaluing of their lives. Black lesbians often told me, "As Black folks, we are always called upon to teach whites about our issues." For me, this is a problem but nonetheless the burden many of us carry.

Shape-Retaining Agential Relations: *Encontros*

Shapeshifting ethics are also necessary forms of "ethico-onto-epistem-ology" (Barad 2007); that is, they link ethics, knowledge, and being to shape-retain necessary parts of the self to be ethical subjects. *Shape-retaining* is a term I appropriate to think about political representation, character, and systems and how any of these may be as ad hoc or opportunistic as shapeshifting representations (Saward 2014).[12] I find the term *shape-retaining* helpful in reflecting on what shapeshifting makes available in terms of both retaining and seeding value concerning self-consciousness and collective consciousness. Wherever shapeshifting ethics appear, there must also be shape-retaining forces to ensure a reservoir of the self. But what does this reservoir of the self consist of? Here, I explore such a shape-retaining force of shapeshifting ethics poignantly evident in private gatherings called *encontros* (intimate, often invitation-only gatherings). Shape-retaining facilitates the strengthening of agential relations to others and the self predicated on the intersubjective exchange of epistemic production. This episteme represents the "speaking truth to power, speaking the truth to the people" that contributes to shaping a sense of "politics of location" at any given time (Rich 1986).

For example, Black women frequently employ informal *rodas de conversas*, such as encontros, to educate and empower each other as movement organizers and community educators. They prepare collectively to act against preconceitos and other forms of violence. From 2007 to 2013, I attended numerous *encontros* organized by Black lesbians. At these gatherings, participants educated themselves about theory and feminist politics and shaped themselves to move into social action. These think-tank gatherings often formed selective focus groups of Black lesbians and heterosexual Black women and held strategy sessions for community or public social action. Other times, such gatherings were community engagements focused on raising awareness on various topics such as Black women's health, domestic violence, and labor laws for domestic work. I witnessed rituals to inform and care for each other through these circles of communal engagement. Their rituals were about making space and time to listen to each other's pain and celebrate joys, even if the meetings also served a lot of beer and food. In all these spaces and encontros, everyone engaged in dialogue to understand, denounce, debate, and share their observations and personal experiences of preconceitos, social violence, and inequities.

One encontro in Bairro Nazare, in downtown Salvador, started at 9 p.m., which was relatively late. When I arrived, there were many snacks and coffee. People had sleeping bags and were camping out in this indoor space—it was, in fact, a sleepover. It was also a discussion of a short Marxist feminist text, titled "Divisão Sexual do Trabalho e Relações Sociais de Sexo," that addressed women, oppression, and labor. Young lesbians (a combination of *Negras, pardas*, and *brancas*) were reading it on the spot and discussing it page by page. In talking about the text, they interrogated sexism in domestic work and the workforce. Marcia was about fifteen years older than most women in the room; the invitation to join surprised me, but her insight proved valuable to the other women and me. Lesbians of all ages and socioeconomic and educational backgrounds drew close to Marcia for her capacity to stimulate anyone interested in becoming a conduit of social change.

As the night went on, the encontro truly felt like a robust underground network. They showed and discussed a film on gender inequity and the workforce. One young woman shared a personal story about her mother's domestic work; she said her mother often cried because of the racism and inferior treatment she experienced. Despite the group's theoretical content being inaccessible to ordinary Black women, this night demonstrated that discussions about class mechanisms related to racism were far more accessible. These encontros did not solely consist of women pursuing higher education; rather, they most often included community organizers and Black women seeking ways to empower themselves to empower their barrios.

These intimate, profound reflection opportunities also embrace shapeshifting ethics that shape-retain value for the self and value in knowledge production.[13] They constitute intellectual activism that, as noted by Patricia Hill Collins, can be defined simply as "the myriad ways that people place the power of their ideas in service to social justice" (2013, ix). Collins acknowledges the wide-ranging mechanisms that people use to engage in intellectual activism. Face-to-face and all other forms of communication before technology offered a plethora of virtual platforms—which are often not accessible to many in Brazil—are critical channels for shaping ethics in knowledge production. Such *rodas de conversas* or encontros are often critiqued for not bringing about concrete action or visible social change. However, I understood them as spaces and places where Black women practiced radical and intellectual self-care, becoming empowered with knowledge; managing and healing negative affective experiences; and deeply reflecting on who and what they are up against in resisting oppression.

Ethics is socially relational and, therefore, also agential. Suppose ethics is about the "kind of relationship you ought to have with yourself, *rapport a soi*, and which determines how the individual is supposed to constitute himself as a moral subject of his own actions" (Foucault 1994, 263). In that case, we must view Black lesbians' ethics (or at least one of many possible dimensions of ethics) as their agential orientation to themselves. Encontros are pathways to and the personal cultivation of ethical formation and forms of responsibility as a domain of relationships that my interlocutors (and other women) rely on—for themselves and collectively—to respond to racial oppression (see Laidlaw 2014, 2010; Dave 2010, 2012; Lefebvre 2018). Race is then the primary object of ethical scrutiny in structural hierarchy. To counter differential racial optics, "self-forming activities" (see Foucault 1994, 265) such as encontros are binding sites of assessment formation to interrogate their presence in the world and to counter negative judgments in power relations (see Miller 2017). This is the ethical life of shape-retaining inner power engaged within or by shapeshifting ethics in all necessary domains.[14]

Inheriting Networked Worth

Black feminist thought and labor is inherited worth and continually mobilizes network coalition and solidarity among Brazilian Black women (Pacheco 2013; Perry 2013; Caldwell 2017). Network alliances have always been shapeshifting ethical work that deserves attention for its production of collective worth. My observations during my travels to Brazil in 2007 clarified to me that Black lesbians' justice work is rooted in abolitionist intent.[15] The state of Bahia, and Salvador in particular, has a long-standing history of rebellion, revolt, and abolitionist activism. Black women's anti-racist strategies in solidarity work are grounded in what Carneiro (2003) has called "enegrecendo o feminismo" (blackening feminism). Carneiro argues for the urgency of hastening Black women's trajectory toward a solidarity that combats racism across all genders (198–99). Carneiro also draws on the work of Lélia Gonzalez to remind us that Brazilian Black women are responsible for the introduction of feminism to Brazil through their sociopolitical work; this happened before Brazilian Eurocentric feminism took center stage with its disregard for the need to address racism (200). I interpret Carneiro as pitching an overturning of whiteness as Black feminist praxis and as urging us to remain diligent about the sociopolitical landscapes in feminism that exclude the issues of all Black people. Black women in Salvador have always been at the forefront of social movements (see Carneiro 2019). In this section, I show the value of my Black queer feminism to public protests as a critical pathway for Black lesbians to cancel their invisibility and call attention to Black life. Public protests are also the shapeshifting ethics centering solidarity and networks. Public protest was my "homework" (Perry 2013) for an "anthropology in reverse" (Visweswaran 1994, 104) about the Black and queer diasporic community and our transnational solidarity (Gonzalez 1988, 1984; Thomas and Campt 2006; Campt 2011). I learned about Black lesbians' fullness not just through their medical narratives but by understanding how their core values shape all their narratives—including medical ones. I hit the streets with them and tuned into their worth-making and worth-retaining processes.

Brazilian Black women's social movements and sociopolitical circles are also profoundly informed by Black feminist thought in the United States, including the work of the Combahee River Collective, Patricia Hill Collins, Audre Lorde, bell hooks, Angela Davis, and many others. The exchange is mutual, with US Black feminists learning from Lélia Gonzalez, Beatriz Nascimento, Luiza Barrios, and Sueli Carneiro. For example, Collins is influenced by the thinking of Carneiro and others. This Black feminist transnational history is long-standing and well established.[16] My presence in Salvador truly felt like homework, not fieldwork.

What is networked when standing in solidarity? Brazilian Black queer women know that they cannot rely upon the homonormative white queer politics for social change. Cathy Cohen (1997) reminds us that the "radical potential of queer politics, or any liberatory movement, rests on its ability to advance strategically oriented political identities arising from a more nuanced understanding of power" (458). What I witnessed being networked yet unseen was an exchange of abolitionist ideas, goals, and strategies anchored by political subjectivities in pursuit of well-being that pointed to such radical potential of queer politics and solidarity. There are times when Black women and lesbians resist and engage in reform praxes. I observed that that my participants pursued elimination, eradication, and abolition of injustice that included and often centered on preconceito. Their political subjectivities informed how they engaged themselves as ethical subjects in constrained spaces like gynecology. Barbara Smith examines Black lesbians' organizing and reminds us that "the only activity that has ever altered oppression and transformed disenfranchised people's powerlessness is collective grassroots organizing" (2000, 168). I emphasize liberation through collective solidarity. Black lesbians' visibility, even among heterosexual Black women, is crucial for effective political solidarity and worth-making. Solidarity with all Black women is necessary not just because racism is central to the struggle; rather, as Smith cautions us, the "closet" is a deterrent to community organizing. How does community organizing free them all? In Brazil, Black heterosexual women in social movements stand in solidarity with Black lesbians. It

FIGS. 4.3–4.4: Two protests in Lapa, Salvador, 2007. Photos by the author.

is easier to learn to be a community organizer with heterosexual Black women than with white lesbians in Brazil. Ultimately, racial solidarity is networked.

We are not free until all Black people are free. Belief systems are central to the principles of the Combahee River Collective, as is evident in their statement, "What we believe: above all else, our politics initially sprang up from the shared belief that Black women are inherently valuable, that our liberation is a necessity not as an adjunct to somebody else's but because of our need as human personal for autonomy" (2000, 263). Again, in a world that devalues all Black women—particularly Black lesbians—understanding the common goals of networking and not taking them for granted gives visibility to ethical life and bem-estar itself. During my visits to Salvador in 2007, I witnessed these networked political subjectivities expressed in public resistance and protest by Black lesbians (see figures 4.3 and 4.4); it was clear that they were enactments of visibility. These enactments continually shape themselves as ethical subjects and signal to the world that Black women will stand collectively in opposition to patriarchal, colonial, and other forms of domination. In what follows, I share two public platforms (among many others) for networking Black lesbian political subjectivity.

Dia da Lésbica Visibilidade

August 29 is Brazil's Dia da Lésbica Visibilidade (National Lesbian Visibility Day). Lesbian groups organize many activities on that day throughout the country. In Salvador, this day showed me how such activities of recognition place homosexuality as a signifier for a universal lesbian solidarity. Still, only a few Black lesbians in my study participated in this public action for national recognition. I was eager to join queer women from the lesbian organization that I followed in Bahia, Lesbibahia. This group, composed of white, *parda*, and Black lesbians, made banners that denounced all forms of oppression. I sat with the participants in attendance, made posters, and participated in a public chant held indoors. Lesbibahia circulated an open letter denouncing the recent murders of two young Black lesbians by an ex-boyfriend in the city of Câmara in the metropolitan area of Salvador. Every Black lesbian I knew talked about this tragedy. The media reported that the couple was walking through a parking lot when confronted by the assailant who shot them to death. The buzz around these murders among Black lesbians that I knew reinforced, with anguish, why they engaged in resistance and abolitionist strategies. It was also a reminder why continually addressing the roots of social violence is a matter of life and death. During the following few weeks, my main interlocutors told me that Black lesbians were protesting against the violence in Câmara. One Black lesbian said to me, "They were killed not just because of lesbophobia and masculinist rage, but because they are Black lesbians, women, and nobody will care. The police will not care. The government will not care." Many women at the protest chanted, "Pelo fim da violência contra as mulheres" (For the end of violence against women), and "Mexeu com uma—mexeu com todas" (Mess with one—mess with all).

The visibility of Black lesbians who protest is an ethical matter. Nanda was a Black lesbian participant whom I had met in 2007. At the time, she worked for the now-closed lesbian advocacy organization Palavra da Mulher. Nanda was a catalyst for integrating me into these public resistance praxes. With Nanda, I attended both protests shown in figures 4.3 and 4.4 in 2007. In November 2012, Nanda and I also attended a public vigil in the Lapa area of downtown Salvador. Women of all racial identities, ages, and sexualities gathered to mourn and chant against gender violence for an evening. One young Black woman held a sign announcing that Salvador placed fifth in the country for assassinations of women and Bahia placed third for violence against women. I understood these moments as evidence that Black lesbian presence itself is a moral action. Ethical subjects work through their moral grounds in justice and integrate visionary solidarity in their presence. They are collective knowers of how to push for the eradication of intimate and systemic violence. I witnessed how action and demands reinforce ethical life in solidarity among Black lesbians and Black women driven by shared shapeshifting ethics.

(Un)seeing Dead Bodies

The day before I left my fieldwork in early August 2013, Sandra, one of my participants, insisted that I witness her protest. Amid the chaos of exiting fieldwork, saying goodbyes, and tying up loose ends such as donating my apartment furniture, I managed to witness some of the protest. In figures 4.5 and 4.6, we see acts of resistance against the deaths of young Black men at the hands of police. The protest took place at the same public plaza in downtown Salvador where Dia da Lésbica Visibilidade took place; however, the protest was in daylight. I started at the staging of a dead Black body, recalling an actual dead Black body I had seen a month earlier. This had been when I was walking back to my apartment around noon, and I walked into Avenida Sete (the main shopping and business area) just minutes after a Black man had been shot. The police had not killed him, but his body was mostly covered with a white sheet saturated in blood—just like the staged body. As a physician assistant, I was used to seeing dead bodies, and many times I had pronounced people dead and had to deliver the news to their families. However, seeing a freshly killed Black man in the streets of Salvador raised the stakes of life and death to a different register for me. Sandra's staged protest signaled what whiteness does not care to see: the disposability of Black life. Such staged proclamations are demands to be seen with human value and dignity; they call for an end of being seen as disposable targets of racial preconceito and anti-Black violence.

Seeing living bodies politically means to acknowledge and respond affirmatively to their political subjectivities in protests, vigils, marches, chants, posters, and more. Black lesbians' collaborations with other Black community members are central for achieving justice for the deaths of all Black lives, including those of Black lesbians. As Savannah Shange argues, "abolition is not synonymous with resistance" (2019, 10). Like Shange, I understand abolition to deviate from resistance by its means, and I appreciate the attention to everyday life to illuminate these differences in the calls to action. I have written a lot about preconceito and the violence it produces to emphasize that the labor for justice matters at the deepest levels in ways that are not always immediately evident in interactions and everyday life. Shange's provocation to "care more than we know" is a direct message about work addressing state violence and anti-Blackness to eradicate preconceito at all levels, from the individual to the state. Black lesbians' unseen social movement labor is the sacrificial work to compel the public in their responsibility to not reproduce violence. Visual engagement with the public charts the ethical terrain for pronouncing calls for Black well-being. After all, when Black lesbians say to me, "We are invisible," they refer to the negation of their humanity when others see only their Blackness.

Bem-Estar Matters

Julho das Pretas (July for Black Women) in July 2013 celebrated the first anniversary of Odara, Instituto da Mulher Negra, an organization founded by Black lesbians and heterosexual Black women to focus on the social and physical well-being of Black women in Salvador. I had known one of the cofounders of Odara since 2007. As during Maio da Diversidade LGBT, the full calendar of events included local discussions on Black women's issues such as health, religious intolerance of Candomblé, and social violence.

I lived in Barrio Dois de Julho in Odara's neighborhood. I quickly walked to interview one of the Odara organizers, Emanuelle Goes. She shared their plans for Brazil's first-ever million-women march in 2015. Goes, then a doctoral student in epidemiology and feminist studies and an organizer of Black

FIGS. 4.5–4.6: Protest against Black genocide in Salvador, 2013. Photos by the author.

women's reproductive rights and antiracism, said that the goal was to promote the bem-estar of all Black women. I was excited to hear that bem-estar was the thematic emphasis for this large-scale national march. I attended their next organizing meeting in June 2013. During this meeting, Odara members planned the launch of Bahia's first month dedicated to recognition of Black women, Julho das Pretas in 2013. She handed to me a flier titled, "Julho das Pretas anuncia a March Nacional das Mulheres Negras Contra o Racismo e Pelo Bem

Viver na Bahia" [July for Black Women announces a national march of Black women against racism and for living well in Bahia]). Julho das Pretas signaled a profound, concerted effort to address the failures of government and society toward Black women's bem-estar. As a primary demand for social justice, Black women must become empowered to chart their bem-estar. Emanuelle's emphasis on demanding Black women's bem-estar also pointed to the impulse that drives particular ethical subjects to pursue recognition for all parts of their well-being or bem viver (living well), as noted on the flier. Resistance is not enough to ensure well-being. An abolitionist demand is a chant, "Pare de ser racista!" (Stop being racist!), repeated by Black women in downtown Salvador at the seventh anniversary march during Julho das Pretas in 2019. Bem-estar matters if reproductive freedom entails a life without gyno-trauma, reproductive racism, and any related violence that targets Black female bodies. Reproductive freedom is living in bem-estar.

I began this chapter with a question: Are *we* ethical subjects? The answer for Black lesbians lies in whom they become in seeking the abolition of intimate violence in gynecological spaces and, indeed, anywhere. They understand that in a gynecologist's office, "racialization is the product of embodied experiences, occurring over time and through space" (McCallum 2005, 100). Black lesbians in this project ride out multiple intersectional parts of themselves in ways that at times make shapeshifting ethics a necessary condition to survive. They do not just survive. As Dána-Ain Davis asserts, "If you're looking to address inequity, then you may fail. If we seek justice, then abolition is necessary for healing. Justice will not accept inequity" (Davis and Scott 2020).[17] Equality and human rights may be among the demands of Brazilian Black queer women. In this book, bem-estar is a justice issue that does not allow room for racism, homophobia, heterosexism, sexism, or classism (Werneck 2016).

5

BEM-ESTAR NEGRA

Lésbicas Negras' Beautiful Experiments of Worth

Somos preta, mulher, sapatão, pobre, e de Candomblé.
—Luciana

We remember and honor deceased loved ones who have sustained the lives of a few of the Black queer women in this book. I concur with Savannah Shange when she says "writing is ancestral work" (2019, ix). Our ancestors look to us to fight and make sense of the world to ensure a better present and future. I had the humbling honor to attend three funerals for relatives of Black lesbians I followed: Marcia's maternal grandmother, Nanda's maternal grandmother, and Luciana's mother. I had met all these Black queer women and these opportunities allowed me to learn how Black queer women shape their sense of legitimacy through their relationships with loved ones. Knowing these women meant knowing the families that sustained their bem-estar through hardships, burdens, anger, sadness, joy, and love. In June 2018, I was traveling back from a respite in the mountains of Bahia with Nanda and her new partner, Luciana. While on a bus, we got a call that Luciana's mother had passed that day. Her burial would be the next day, as is customary in Brazil. Though Luciana was the "rock" of her family, her mother was her rock in many ways.

During my primary fieldwork, from 2012 to 2013, I found it valuable to spend time with Luciana in various situations—hanging out and drinking beer with her partner or friends, spending one-on-one time together, or visiting her terreiro. Perhaps the most important event for me was seeing her among her family on Good Friday. On March 29, 2013, I rode the bus to her sister's home, north of Salvador, where her family members were gathering. I had received invitations to join other friends and their families, but I chose to visit Luciana's family. I wanted to rekindle a relationship with two of her sisters I had known since 2007 (one of whom had recently suffered a debilitating cerebral stroke). Also, I had not yet met her mother, and I was curious. Luciana, like Marcia, Estelle, Nanda, and nearly all the Black lesbians I followed, plays a significant role in caring for family members. For Luciana, this included caring for her mother, siblings, and youngest niece. Her family values and principles are strong; though Luciana does not have any children, she is very close to her two-year-old niece. Luciana has four sisters and a deceased brother. She is the second-youngest.

One of her sisters is also an initiated member of her terreiro. Thus, they are both blood sisters and initiated members in the same Candomblé terreiro. One of her blood sisters had been diagnosed with breast cancer and received treatment in 2011. She was now cancer-free, and, of course, all the sisters must get yearly mammograms. Luciana is a *guerreira* (warrior) for her family, intervening in their health and social challenges. Luciana shared with me how she aggressively confronted her father during her younger days when he was abusive toward her mother. These family dynamics allow us to see the fullness of her bem-estar in all its multiplicities. This story recalls how much Luciana wanted her mother to affirm her sexuality and be in solidarity with related social justice issues; indeed, her mother evolved and eventually obliged.

Luciana met me at a bus stop in Itinga, a barrio in Laura de Freitas (a large municipality sharing a border with Salvador). When we arrived at her sister's house, everyone was sitting in front of the house drinking beer, listening to music, and chatting. Beer flowed all day and night. Good Friday was like a holiday in Bahia. Banks and most businesses were closed; the bus schedule was limited. Because it is a Catholic holiday, fish was the main protein for the day in most homes. At Luciana's family feast, fish was served in two ways: baked *bacalhau* (codfish) and *moqueca* (fish stew). The other dishes included rice, *vatapá*, *caruru*, and stewed black-eyed peas. The intimate familial conversations and negotiations regarding household work such as cooking and cleaning were in themselves a valuable source of ethnographic detail; they allowed me to hear and see a side of my interlocutors that I might not have otherwise.

An example is Luciana telling me, "I don't like doing domestic work like washing dishes but will do it anyway for [my] family." This domestic work is particularly poignant because, while many Black women detest it, Luciana's family has a history of doing domestic work for the elite as a way to make a living. In 2007, her youngest sister told me that she was sent at a young age to perform domestic work and experienced significant violence at the hands of her employers. Such wounds plague Black families in Brazil. The only cohesive way of healing as a family is to promote well-being, individually and collectively.

I felt welcomed and happy to be amid her family. Her mother, seventy-four years old, was a tall, dark-skinned woman who looked remarkably good and strong for her age. She was wearing a T-shirt that read, "Diga Não a Homofobia, Respeita as Diferenças!" (Say No to Homophobia, Respect Differences!). Luciana confided in me that she had "put it on" her mother. Her mother did not wear the shirt on her way home but had changed into a gray blouse. The shirt change was understandable, as she was taking the bus home alone very late at night. Since Luciana did not voluntarily tell me why she put that T-shirt on her mother, I assumed it was an affirmation of and welcoming gesture toward my visit and research. After all, it was Jesus's and Oxalá's day, not National Antihomophobia Day. This seemingly unexpected moment from my fieldwork stuck with me. As an ethnographer, I appreciate the interactive ways my interlocutors convey the significance of their lives, the details through which they construct their narratives, and the material ways they strive to facilitate their well-being. Luciana's story is significant for the deep values that affirm and promote well-being at all levels, even amid the health and social challenges of the self or family. The vulnerabilities and strengths within their lives, including their families, influence Black lesbians' pursuit of well-being.

Bem-Estar Negra

Bem-estar Negra is a reproductive justice framework that centers the humanness of Negritude (Blackness) as liberatory modes of being in their fullest expression (sexual, gendered, affective, religious) in gynecology and all spaces. This chapter takes up the notion of *Bem-estar Negra* more intimately to invite you into worlds of both joy and pain that "shapeshift and choreograph" life as Black women with nonnormative sexuality and gender expressions (Cox 2015, 28). Only within these racial lives is sexual health reconceived and lived as liberatory. Bem-estar Negra means breathing fresh air and drinking clean water; equally, it means not having to experience the social toxins of society. As Maya Angelou has said, "The plague of racism is insidious, entering into our minds as smoothly and quietly and invisibly as floating airborne microbes enter into our bodies to find lifelong purchase in our bloodstream" (1993, 121). Maya Angelou's words are important for reimagining Black lesbians as the protagonists of their lives precisely because their experiences of systemic oppression cannot be allowed to win against their simple everyday pleasures. The Black lesbians in this study need the world to understand that racism and other interlocking oppressions are symbolic (and literal) pollutants that they breathe into their bodies and that negatively affect their bem-estar. Bem-estar Negra encompasses the vital life substances for living our truths in power; this is because self-power in collective healing sets us free. Black lesbians existing in their bem-estar is what Zora Neale Hurston, our beloved anthropologist, novelist, and cultural critique, has expressed as, "I love myself when I am laughing and then again when I am looking mean and impressive" (as quoted in Walker 2011). Hurston's self-assurance amid fraught race relations, racism, and white supremacy—from being put in a closet to be examined by a gastroenterologist to critiquing white publishers for not valuing work about the life of Negros— was a defining feature of how she narrated her life and the lives of others (see Walker 2011, 162–63, 168–72). Bem-estar Negra, in all of its complexities, commands clarity about what matters. I understand these women's narratives much like Alice Walker describes Zora Neal Hurston's *Their Eyes Are Watching God*: "There is enough self-love in that one book—love of community, culture, traditions—to restore a world. Or create a new one" (Walker 2011, xiv). The narratives in this chapter reveal this self-love. Bem-estar Negra is itself nonnegotiable within these terms. Like Hurston's writings, these narratives should move us to create new worlds. Bem-estar Negra grounds the necessary nurturing and sustenance of the self, positive energy and health, improved social conditions, and strong relationships that Black queer women must do.

Bem-estar Negra considers how freeing ourselves from holding pain, insult, and trauma reveals various articulations of life in its fullness and the healing pathways created by Black lesbians. Black feminist activists Jurema Werneck, Nilza Iraci Silva, and Simone Cruz discuss how first-person narratives of Black women have value because "to be woman, Black, indigenous, lesbian, poor, migrant is to live the different ways within the asymmetries of gender and race that characterize a society organized by the rules of racism and patriarchy" (Werneck, Iraci, and Cruz 2012, 11; my translation).[1] When I visited Porto Alegre in 2013, Simone Cruz gave me a copy of this text. The text narrates lived experiences—Conceição Evaristo's "escrevivências." As Sueli Carneiro asserts, the protagonisms of Black women are critical to legitimize them, a sentiment echoed in Werneck, Iraci, and Cruz's description of "women who are references of affirmation of Negritude, of combating the stigmas and stereotypes of gender and race, that push change and broaden horizons for other women, their families and communities" (Carneiro's book-sleeve commentary about Werneck, Iraci, and Cruz 2012).

Evaristo's escrevivências also inspire my presentation of the stories below. Since the stories blend imagination and reality about Black women's lives that are not so separate from our own, I narrate these intimate lives to express how I witnessed the women's storytelling and the making of Black lesbian life as a journey to worth-making in their own contexts. This chapter is a full return to the power of Black lesbian living and storytelling as method for Black life.

I return to the Brazilian expression *viver minha sexualidade* to engage and position bem-estar Negra as a realm of erotic power and freedom that comes at a great sacrifice, as described by Black lesbians. I also return to it for a final reflection on the questions driving this book: Why do these Black queer women understand sexual health to be about liberty and well-being? Under what conditions is this kind of sexual health expressed and embodied? We benefit from paying attention to how this feeling plays out in the particular context of subjects who are engaging their homosexuality in heteronormative, gendered, and classed institutions. It might be possible for us to understand this engagement as a transcultural feature of the lives of all lesbians who move through medical establishments across the globe. However, as anthropologists, we must consider how unique contextual and historical meanings inform the value individuals and collectives place upon particular self-care modes beyond these institutional spaces. This is my approach in this book. Black lesbians' bem-estar is qualifiable as a valued state of being when we hear and believe their concerns and align ourselves with their humanity. This inquiry into intersectional Black/queer well-being captures the conditions that make self-formation in liberatory ways possible. Some ethnographic particularities of the coming-into-being of these enabling conditions are situated here.

Viver minha sexualidade is self-worth-making in flesh and spirit. Living your queer sexuality openly may be considered a privilege by some, but living openly as lesbians is a necessary condition of self-legitimacy for my interlocutors. Here, living openly is not about reinforcing normative disclosure practices in institutional spaces or to the public. Instead, it centers on the making of well-being in any given moment. We live openly to ourselves in many ways, including our affective selves and in the care of mind, body, and spirit. Bem-estar Negra is about making the quotidian matter, sustainably and pleasurably. I see my interlocutors as existing and forging their principles to reject social constraints for their bem-estar. To them, self-care in search of modes of freedom means expressing life as much as possible through their erotic subjectivities (see J. Allen 2011). When my interlocutors define *sexual health* as "cuidado de bem-estar" (care of well-being) and "uma forma de estar bem" (a form of being well), this is sexual health as liberation. Liliane, a participant discussed in the introduction of this book, described sexual health as well-being, "as not being enough to be one issue such as disease but about not having the sexual body invisible, to feel pleasure, desire. Sexual health is also an awareness about the invisibility of the body." Liliane's description calls attention to Black queer women's awareness that their bodies as desiring and sexually alive are invisible in the context of biomedical engagements with sexual health. Her definition of sexual health legitimizes Black lesbians' sexuality and sexual practices as deserving and not taboo. Discussing sexual health as well-being is a radical deviation from normative ways of understanding sexuality for Black lesbians. As we see above, my interlocutors are quick to point out that well-being ought to be achieved by knowing our desires, pleasures, bodies—even while being aware that it risks making those bodies invisible, *corpo invisibilizado*. We cannot miss when focusing on Black lesbians, for example, the intersectional weight of intersubjective labor to balance well-being in all aspects of their lives. Self-care is part of their lived experience of their sexual health as bem-estar Negra, and this includes their legitimizing ways of responding to the demands in their lives.

Blackness, or Negritude, is central to understanding these women's lives. Negritude is the site of oppression that relegates sexuality and gender to the unseen sphere of existence. Among the key participants I followed, Taina was not the only one who had a strained relationship with her mother or other family members at the start of her lesbian life. The precarity within such a racialized context when coming out with one's homosexuality is what Carneiro (2011) refers to as "a dor da cor" (pain of color) that reflects on the racial and sexual aspects of citizenship formation for Black communities in Brazil through the mechanism of *embraquecimento* (whitening). "It hurts us to be Black," said Taina, referring to the weight of racism on their lives. Taina conveyed to me the heaviness of that racial weight on her family, yet she upheld her sexuality as what Luciana describes as freedom. That is, not just because it symbolizes freedom to have sex and indulge sexual desire, but because it embraces the freedom to live openly and healthily as someone who loves others of the same sex. For some Black lesbians, this is bem-estar Negra. And its possibilities for joy are nonnegotiable—despite the pain it may bring.

My approach to rethinking Negritude is through Carneiro's notion of *a dor da cor*. I rethink a layered Negritude through queerness and sexuality as *a dor da cor, a cor da sexualidade* (pain of our color, the color of our sexuality). Brazilian race scholars such as Jurema Werneck (2016), Lélia Gonzalez (1984, 1988), and Abdias Nascimento (2016) compel us to ground Negritude in vivências and the quotidian experiences of Black culture and life. Blackness is an aliveness that exerts agency and power and that transcends a racial democratic society with a nationalist agenda centering on whiteness and class hierarchies. Negritude is the expression and embodiment of Black pride, Black love, Black hair, and Black freedom, which are all crucial elements of bem-estar Negra.

Black well-being is rarely valued or respected in society, and Black lesbian well-being even less so. Moving toward abolishing the mechanisms that cause gyno-trauma, bem-estar Negra must stand as the wakefulness of consciousness, as argued by Christina Sharpe (2016, 13). Like Sharpe, I contend that to be in the wake and to occupy such space in "the continuous and changing present of slavery's as yet unresolved unfolding" requires a form of consciousness to mediate survival and triumphs (14). The wake work that Black lesbians enact daily is the making of their bem-estar Negra. In this chapter, and throughout the book, we must read their narratives as that wakefulness and aliveness that "insists Black being into the wake" for existence (11). In the wake, gyno-traumas are survived and transcended.

Ethical-Willful Subjectivities: We Have Always Been Here

Black women and lesbians must transcend the gyno-traumas of the world, moment to moment. In rethinking subjectivity for the Black/queer mode of cultivating being and knowing, it is clear that Black lesbians are not docile bodies in the Foucauldian sense (Falu 2019; see also E. Williams 2013). They are prepared to resist forms of "secondary marginalization" (Cohen 1999, 9)—even when exerted by their own family and friends—since institutional marginalization forces them to live within their best bem-estar Negra. Ethical subjectivity is a valuable concept for considering a dimension of subjective formation and for seeing how it intersects with provocative subjectivities such as race, sexuality, and gender. Drawing from J. Reid Miller (2017, 3), I also question the nature of the "nonmaterial substance" to grasp subjectivity. What can such a subjectivity consist of if factors of race, gender, and sexuality that are based on appearance cannot be used to judge Black bodies? Ethical subjectivity must then be an inner landscape of self-expression endowed by a "discrete possessor, giver, and arbiter of value" (3); as such, it renders the nonmaterial substance for this discussion of human worth. In this way, I rethink how an ethical subjectivity that intersubjectively produces human value opposes judgments preventing the capacity to exist freely. Like Miller, I push back against the logic—as well as against the history—that suggests that marked Black bodies cannot assess or critique institutions with ethical qualities. As Brazilian scholar Adilson Moreira states, "They [Brazilian Blacks] are not blinded by how 'negritude represents that which cannot be moral and aesthetically appreciated'" (2019, 135).

Black lesbians do not forge pathways of resistance and well-being solely via ethical subjectivities. As Black lesbians, their self-understandings are shaped not just by interactions within power relations; instead, shaping occurs across communal interactions and in same-sex relations. Intentionality is a dimension that is most salient to my understanding of their ethical subjectivity. Because they are reflective beings about social conditions, the pursuit of freer possibilities, and making room for bem-estar Negra, intention carries the affective and physical labor of overcoming traumas, experiences with limited resources, and public images of inferiority. Intentionality, or a consciousness-raising modality of addressing the world, is "the method of inducing reflexivity through interaction" when rendering in explicit ways various verbal and praxis formulations for qualifying bem-estar in any given instance (Keane 2016, 98).[2]

A study of *auto-sabedoria* (self-understanding) is not a cognitive exercise; rather, it is an epistemic and ontological trajectory within the scope of social justice. In other words, it is what Tanya L. Saunders (2017) has termed "epistemologia negra sapatão." Saunders's epistemic analysis is sociopolitical. For Black lesbians, ethical subjectivity is a more profound ontological reformulation oriented to empowerment that is not reduced by social conditions or subjugating experiences. Saunders rethinks intersectionality for Brazilians by observing that to be a *lésbica Negra* in a "nonhuman" colonial construction must mean being a *bruxa Negra* (2017, 104). African diasporic associations and intersectional forms of power (race, gender, sexuality) in Brazil equate being a *lésbica Negra* with being a Black witch (*macubeira*), particularly in association with African religions. For Saunders, although being a lésbica Negra and *bruxas Negra* serves to construct a "nonhuman" existence that privileges white, male, heterosexual, Christian privilege and power, it serves for lésbicas Negras as an "organic rupture" of those racial hegemonic logics. I concur that it is the pathway to liberatory existence. Saunders's rethinking of the liberatory epistemologies of lésbicas Negras critically reminds us of the invisibility and erasures over the past, present, and future of being and knowing in the world. Saunders and Jafari S. Allen understand that Black queer folks care for their bodies and souls in ways that rupture undesirable notions of being human; indeed, they "work toward not only transgressing but transcending and finally transforming hegemonies of global capital, the state, of bourgeois, limited and limiting notions of gender, sexuality, or Blackness" (J. Allen 2011, 97). J. Allen reminds us that such reformulations are themselves entanglements, in transformative ways, of notions of love, desire, social death, and death in the context of social justice. It is not possible to keep the intention of achieving freedom to express love separate from the freedom to not die by structural violence. Human existence, then, does not blind them to liberating possibilities in how to live and love.[3]

Ethical subjectivity as it pertains to Black lesbians expresses the sense of "to be and to know" in intentionality produced across collective interactions.[4] Importantly, it should not be confused with eliciting a sense of ethical responsibility toward their total environments—their selves and the medical professionals, contexts, and objects with which they interact. Ethical subjectivities are always sociopolitically mediated by willfulness. Like Savannah Shange, I agree that to understand the "effects of willfulness," we should bring into question, "What is willfulness *doing*?" instead of "What is willfulness?" (2019, 16; Ahmed 2014). The narratives in this chapter get at what willfulness *does* through ethical subjective possibilities that push the boundaries of erotic desire, love and struggles, and devout commitments to African diasporic religiosities in a society with deep religious intolerance. In other words, Black lesbians may be unseen bodies to many, but their willfulness reveals how they counter these erasures. Like Shange and Ahmed, I ask: What is their willfulness doing through the ethical? The complexities of self-care as intention, intersubjectively, for example, in Marcia's case, and as a dimension of an ethical-willful subjectivity, became even more apparent during our filming. Though she had recently lost her grandmother, Marcia exuded a strong sense of lesbian pride during our filmmaking process. For the film, Marcia chose to depict her self-care in two ways: (1) having a conversation about her hysterectomy with her dear friend Carmen, and (2) showing her love for the ocean water and the deity Yemanjá.

Carmen's interview at her small apartment in Bairro de Tororo, a *periferia* (a poor neighborhood of Salvador), was profound. Carmen, a dark-skinned out lesbian, lived with her girlfriend. I occasionally spent time with Carmen at various social and political events. Her community admired her as a *guerreira* or *militante* (militant/activist). She had overcome many social obstacles and remained faithful to several Black movements. Like many Black lesbians, Carmen was always striving for a better life. Based on Marcia's friendship with her, I was not surprised that Marcia had selected Carmen as the person to create a conversation about her life in the film.

A great deal transpired during our thirty-five-minute conversation. The purpose of this filmed conversation was to discuss Marcia's struggle while waiting to see a gynecologist. We created a scenario in which Carmen listened and advised her friend on her remembered issues. As it turned out, Carmen had not had much opportunity to talk to Marcia about those past experiences. While it was evident that Carmen knew of the tormenting fibroids, it emerged on film that she had not been privy to the extent of the connection between the endurance of her fibroids and her commitment to not go to just any gynecologist. Through consideration of Marcia's past and present laments, their connection on film raised the common issue of the limited ways in which women generally share their disgruntlement with their gynecological experiences. Still, they understood each other and agreed that the praxis of demanding respect for their Black female lesbian bodies too often calls for intentionality in order to claim space. If they did not make these demands, nobody would do it for them. Marcia reminds us that, as a lesbian in Salvador, it is not easy to choose a gynecologist, even when there is a compelling reason for a visit. When Black queer women, such as Marcia, are willing to speak on a film about these matters or seek an ethical domain for recognition, it is vital to contemplate the social place in such medical interactions. Doing so illuminates complexities that ultimately are grounded in conceptualizations of bem-estar Negra.

Black/Queer Beautiful Experiments

How do Black lesbians breathe renewal into their bem-estar Negra? They breathe renewal as radical thinkers, communal lovers, artistic expressions, and through ancestral ties. They are Black queer futures making sense of social life in the present and reimagining desire and desirable, beautiful bodies in other times and places, always foregrounding agency and creativity. By attending to these lives, intimacy is radical existence and healing. I, like Saidiya Hartman (2019, xiv), offer of "beautiful experiments—to making living an art" in the lives of those surveilled, targeted and disposed by violence. Hartman helps us reimagine the transformations of Black intimate life consequent to "economic exclusion, material deprivation, racial enclosure, and social dispossession; yet it too was fueled by the vision of a future world and what might be" (xv). In response to Hartman, I object to the idea of bem-estar Negra as always concerning the present moment. I understand it also as a vision of different futures or transformative moments. For Black lesbian bodies, Afrofuturist vision is about the impossible turned possible at every moment. I recall participating in a one-time capoeira event led by a close Black lesbian friend of Marcia's. The purpose of the capoeira lesson was not necessarily to learn how to do capoeira; rather, it was the opportunity to experience an exercise that would release energy and promote embodiment as a group of Black women. This embodiment exercise reminds us that capoeira is an African movement (bodily and socially) to rebel and free ourselves of bondage. While walking to the bus stop after the event, our facilitator, whom I have known since 2008, told me, "Capoeira is about releasing negative energy that traps us. It is important to step away from situations and negative experiences because it causes too much mental anguish. Mental anguish must be given space to be released." Concerning what "giving space to release" negative affect might mean for Black women, I think of it as intervals that repeatedly reimagine different futures; making a claim for a different future in the now is essential for survival and nurturing well-being in the present. The release of mental anguish is central to how Black lesbians step away from gynecologists' microaggressions and often delay their medical visits. The importance of stepping away is not about being irresponsible but about preparing ourselves to more ably reenter the institutional space. Black women do not have to delay medical visits to engage in this strengthening, releasing self-engagements before the next microaggression occurs. I interpret these women's actions—such as walking out of or avoiding gynecological visits— as acts of resistance that do not immediately point to neglect of their bodies or health.

In 2019, Salvador's Julho das Pretas celebrated its seventh year. As I walked with Black women (many lesbians), adolescents, elders, and small children, the message remained consistent: *Fogo a racista! Vamos romper com o racismo!* (Burn the racist! Let us break down racism!). The chant that stood out the most to me was, "We are Black women; we are free." All Black women's individual and collective messages were about a better life and future, possible only without racism. *Romper,* as in breaking down racism, is the central goal to imaging a different present and future. This is not the end-all. These women are not waiting for racism to end. It is an impossibility in a world that not only denies its existence but depends on it. It is abolitionist thinking and demand. Black/ queer Afro-futures is about staying connected to the processes of becoming free. "Sou uma mulher livre" (I am a free woman) does not apply equally to all women. To be free is to already live through a reimagined reality and a world without racism. This reimagination is critical for survival with daily encounters, self-care, and revitalization for the struggle against racism. For Black lesbians, the disappearance of homophobia, lesbophobia, and transphobia would primarily benefit white LGBTQ+ people and leave racism to ravage the lives of all Black bodies.

The new directions of Afrofuturism bring light into and through my narratives, visuals, and the visionary contestations of lived realities that reimagine new possibilities against oppressions (see E. Jones 2016, 187).[5] Reynaldo Anderson and Charles Jones describe "Astro-Blackness" as an Afrofuturist concept of "Black consciousness releasing bodies from crippling slave, colonial mentalities" and as an "emergence of Black identity framework within emerging global technocultural assemblages, migration, human reproduction, algorithms, digital networks . . ." (2016, vii–viii). This shift in the discourses of Afro-futures is critical for anthropological inquiry at the intersections of body, technology, material culture, nonnormative sexualities and queerness, and racial consciousness. Afro-futures remind us that Black women "are the ones we have been waiting for," to rethink our intentions in the world through space, time, science and technology, and social change (Walker 2006, 3). The mere fact that Black women prepare to occupy space and be in relations with those who descend on them with violence suggests that Black women are always trying to grab hold of freedom. This is not a question of something not yet conceived that is waiting ahead. Afrofuturist imagination is hope turned into resistance. For Black lesbians, liberatory sexual practices depend on a world without racism. Their liberatory visions foresee new possibilities where there may, or may not, exist the potential for change.

What would Black lesbians' lives be without the power of radical imagination? This chapter is concerned with such musings on, fascinations with, strivings for, and realities of Brazilian Black queer futures. I agree with Kara Keeling that "imagination makes temporality possible" (2019, 33). As part of an ethical agenda, Black queer people deeply invest in their survival and transformations. Keeling deepens our thinking about Black flesh and culture through queer temporalities and a variety of logics about risks, creative engagements, and reimagining the self in the afterlife of slavery. Black lesbians who recognize their Negritude as beautiful and full of resistance ground their worth in affective experiences shaping how they navigate the world. Black women who come out as lesbian in institutional spaces risk feeling the fragility of racialized bodies. These risks valorize their self-image of being beautiful and as bodies that resist the negation of that valorization. Disrupting the flows that devalue their presence allows the possibility of an Afrofuturist self and collective. Blackness is disruptive in the gynecological setting because when women out themselves as lesbians, they risk stirring the racial boundaries of inferiority imposed by some white physicians. Sexuality is at the forefront of these women's narratives about interacting with gynecologists as lesbians in the humanity of their Blackness.

Rethinking bem-estar as Afro-futures by and for Black women is to acknowledge, as noted by Hortense Spillers, that "we do not want to know that the cost of our being here has been inestimable and that our current peace swims in blood and the truncated bodies of the violent dead" (1987, 5). Thinking through Spiller's notion of imaginative encounters, I consider what I refer to as bem-estar Negra not as a fantasy but as the continuation of an imagined future without racism that lends much room for creating space for different lived realities in the slow process of social change. Bem-estar for Black women and lesbians cannot ignore mental anguish. It entails releasing the experience to create physical, mental, spiritual, and relational space for *axé* (Harding 2000, 76).[6] *Axé* means positive energy and forces created by the cosmic and circulated through the people. All Black lesbians I followed walked and sought axé not just within religious spaces but beyond to protect their bem-estar "para ficar bem" (to be well). If there is an achievable balance of well-being, characterized by the legitimation of their sexuality as an intersubjective variable, Black lesbians who pursue and negotiate such recognition help us develop a more in-depth view of the social intricacies characterizing the relations structuring patient-physician interactions.

Afro-futures dismantle anti-Negritude (anti-Blackness) because it is the most painful systemic impediment grabbing hold of Black lives. When I asked Luciana's priestess what it means to be a Black woman in Salvador, she responded, "That is based on whether you first come out as Black (*assumir-se Negra*)." This statement was very provocative. As a Black woman herself, she suggested that many Black women negate the social and historical Blackness that the color of their skin represents in Salvador. She further suggests that Black women must recognize themselves as Black women proud of their skin color despite their place in colonial history as descendants of Africa.

Afro-futures is a beholding of our ancestors. It is a bank of windows into unseen interconnections, cast on the shadows from past to present and stepping into the future. As a frame through which to hold together multiple windows, we see partial connections of vivências and catch glimpses of Afro-futures and beautiful experiments. Below, I offer three stories to show how beautiful and ingrained resistance can coalesce to define bem-estar Negra—not simply bem-estar. Ultimately, I see these unseen Afro-futures as holding together what it means to be a Black lesbian and something far more important than being simply a patient.

Bem-estar Negra is the fabric of Black lesbians' Afro-futures. As an ethnographer, I acknowledge that seeing and understanding Brazilian Black lesbians' lives with each other, themselves, and even me as a Black lesbian, are best viewed as unique windows. They provide a means to narrativize intimately about *vivências Negras* and spotlight aspects of Black lesbians' lives. Here, windows are used metaphorically for the privilege of experiencing life as it happens with my participants. Their world and its moving flow of forces make a life for the better for the present, the next day, the following year, and subsequent life for generations to come.

To Paint My Sexuality

Emilia has been Luciana's partner for nine years. I tried my best to honor what they shared with me individually about themselves and each other. The time I spent with Emilia was among the most illuminating yet challenging experiences for those reasons. As a result, I tuned in closer to their well-being, how they honored themselves in love and conflict, and how they interacted with the world professionally and socially. I learned a tremendous amount about Emilia's perspectives on cultivating social well-being as a Black lesbian in Salvador. She was very outspoken in her opinions about injustices. She also was susceptible to various life difficulties, which I got to know firsthand. As an ethnographer and friend, I did my best to balance listening to and observing her. Following lesbian couples such as Luciana and Emilia allowed me to witness forms of gender transgressions (Blackwood and Wieringa 1999). Luciana was masculine gender presenting and identified as a woman. However, these Black queer women strove to foreground their racial identities as Black women; only after did they consider their identities as Black lesbians. I gained much more insight into their understanding of affirmation by sharing their spaces and reflecting on what was valuable to them as Black lesbians. Indeed, my discomfort in balancing the dynamics among the couples and circles of friends offered the most insight into their lives as Black lesbians.

I spent a vast amount of time with Emilia in various social activities before we sat down for an audio-recorded interview at my place in March 2013. We enjoyed ourselves together on the beach, dancing, drinking caipirinhas at the local bars in the Dois de Julho neighborhood, celebrating her birthday in November 2012 (when I met her mother and siblings), drinking lots of coffee at my place, and talking privately. I met her darling teenage son. I visited her terreiro and attended ceremonies she participated in that were open to the public. I witnessed her in a trance in her orixá Oxum clothing among her religious community.

Our reconnection in 2012 was timely. I rekindled our relationship in conversations about her doctoral studies in Salvador, her Candomblé participation, her partnership with Luciana, and her relationships with her family and friends. Emilia's reflection about what a gynecologist ought to have as tools for interacting with a lesbian indicates her ideas about institutionalizing a humanized practice.

One example of an illuminating interview moment was Emilia drawing (literally) how she perceived the relationship between sexuality and sexual health (see figure 5.1). She picked up a pencil and began drawing a square and some arrows on my field notebook during our conversation. For Emilia, sexuality was the square (walls and inner space) and sexual health was the pencil that drew the square. She pictured sexual health as a brush and sexuality as the framework. "I am the artist," she said, laughing, as she began to draw. She continued saying, "Sexuality is my vital energy. Sexual health is an instrument to paint information about sexuality, my vital energy. That is because it helps me to be able to take care of my sexuality and to understand it and access information about it; it makes me take care of my sexuality, my *energia vital*. Then, I will have to think about this brush there."

Her illustration was unique and creative. Sexuality is the energy driving the pencil or imaginative brush (or forces of sexual health) for painting sexuality. It was very intuitive, particularly Emilia's reference to the pencil as an instrument representing sexual health as liberatory. If sexual health were a pencil, it would draw sexuality in terms of malleable features. In this drawing, she represents her sexuality as needing care; sexual health helps to take care of her sexuality. Emilia is referring not just to the prevention of STDs or other medical problems but also to the social conditions that give meaning to sexuality through various social meanings driving sexual health. Hence, sexual health is an instrument that shapes sexuality. As she explained, "Information helps paint and guide our sexuality. Sexual health for me is always connected to the possibility of acquiring independence subjectively, emotionally, and financially, and that is what I call politics. When I talked about politics, this is something to think about." Emilia's statement about sexual health as more than biological health outcomes exemplifies sexual health as contributing to well-being. Her imagination to paint or draw her sexuality enacted an agential way to reimagine, feel, and capture what consumes negatively, such as stress; she pictures the body as a liberatory vehicle: an instrument.

Emilia had a hysterectomy in 2011 as a result of a rare uterine fibroid tumor. She always refers to her gynecological experiences of fear when discovering that tumor before she learned after surgery that it was benign. Still, Emilia interprets the importance of managing and understanding the sexual self as a woman, a Black gay woman in particular, through the social conditions that shape such identity markers. Emilia's statement about sexual health refers to the importance of understanding how, as a Black woman, the possibilities for affirmation and legitimation in her social setting depend upon realizing the sociopolitical effects on her well-being. Emilia recognizes how prejudice looks

terapia →

Saude sexual → acesso, participação.
  guardo.

contecimento.

cannot take care of

  Saude sexual artral de saude.

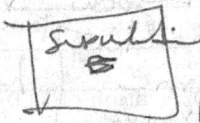

Saude sexual cuidar
de mista

yoga·
learn to swim.
massage

FIG. 5.1: My field notebook with drawing guided by Emilia.

and feels and understands its implications for her more global well-being. Afro-futures lie within the metaphors, visual imaginations, and instruments that guide our deepest selves into grounded worth.

Emilia shows that to paint is to be introspective about Black lesbian life and guided by the inner landscapes of worth in free imagination and with self-permission to be in awareness.

Love and Struggle

Love heals. We recover ourselves in the act and art of loving (hooks 2005, 97).[7] The coupled life of Nanda and Kamila offers an intimate ethnographic view into the social complexities structuring many Black lesbian relationships. Race, class, and sexuality collide and destabilize love. Black lesbian relationships reinforce bem-estar Negra by shaping personal visions of worthy ways to live. Nanda, my closest informant and a friend, is thirty-five years old and a native of Salvador. I met Nanda in Salvador in August 2007 at an advocacy organization addressing lesbians' social issues. Initially, her attractive, butch appearance struck me. Over subsequent years, I grew to appreciate her as a self-identified Black lesbian with strong political, racial, and social views and as someone with intense community involvement despite her middle-class background. In her efforts to frame enabling conditions from her same-sex relationship, Nanda experienced joys and struggles as a young Black lesbian in Salvador.

My friendship with Nanda provided insight into the density of the social world inhabited by Black lesbians. My key interlocutors spent much time reflecting on and critiquing the social systems that contributed to the *condições* of their lives and those of *Negros/as* in general, and their political practices often brought them into contact with one another. I enjoyed seeing Nanda during those moments, animated and opinionated. Nanda's and Kamila's negotiations with their gynecologists present somewhat different realities from those of my other interlocutors. Nanda is privileged to remain on her mother's health insurance even at the age of thirty-five. Her mother has excellent health insurance because of her government job, which in Salvador means relatively good pay, security, and benefits. This health insurance permits Nanda to see a white female gynecologist who is a friend of her parents. When I formally interviewed Nanda in November 2013, she told me that she had never experienced preconceito from a gynecologist because she always sees her mother's gynecologist. She believed that her gynecologist would never treat her poorly because she is a family friend. For Nanda, negotiations about her sexuality with her gynecologist involved different tactics given these familial ties. In our interview, Nanda expressed her fear of large speculums; she also talked about how she suffers from strong *cólica* (menstrual cramps) that often require birth control pills to minimize her menses flow and menstrual pain. While these discussions do not necessarily involve directly addressing her homosexuality, Nanda believes that her doctor treats her neutrally to avoid the awkwardness that would accompany greater awareness of her sexuality. Of course, her top-of-the-line health insurance pays for that respect—literally.

Kamila relies on SUS physicians (scouting out the "good ones") more than Nanda. When she worked for Globo television for eight months in 2012, she had excellent health insurance. Indeed, she commented, "I must take advantage of my health insurance!" She maximized the benefits of her coverage by consulting a variety of private specialists (orthopedic, neurological, and gynecologic). She even got dental braces. Once her Globo health insurance ended, she returned to SUS. Kamila, unlike Nanda, has a strong opinion about how gynecologists treat women, gay women in particular. One day I happened to meet Kamila on the bus. She was eager to tell me about her experience with a white female gynecologist from SUS. Wishing I had my recorder with me, I listened as Kamila animatedly recounted the poor quality of her experience, presenting details that ranged from the gynecologist not using gloves and barely touching her legs during a pelvic exam to giving dismissive and rude responses to her concerns. Though she did not think that the treatment she received was related to her sexuality, we both agreed that it is hard to identify whether inappropriate treatment of patients reflects preconceito or simply neglect. This quality of service is consistent with the general impression of care from SUS clinicians. Kamila told me she was not returning to the SUS doctor for her follow-up, and Nanda agreed with her decision. Making these decisions as a couple is instrumental for bem-estar Negra.

Even as a middle-class daughter of parents holding upper-level government jobs, Nanda could not escape the obstacles that the fractured employment and salary system presented to her self-care and social progress. When I met Nanda in 2007, she had just lost her job at which she had been earning R$500 per month. (At the time, the mean monthly salary was around R$350.) Nanda preferred to work for social movement organizations. Unable to find work for over a year, she decided to return to college instead. As of 2011, she was still struggling to find employment until she found a place in the administrative office of a public lower school. This work was sufficient until, in 2012, the *empresas* (the employment agencies contracted by the government) began to delay her pay for months at a time. Nanda and other workers were required to continue working without pay or risk losing their secured positions. Even once pay began again, it would not come at once. Instead, it would trickle in slowly, month to month. During my fieldwork, I saw Nanda struggle to pay for food, rent, and college expenses because her monthly pay had been "frozen." This problem was more common than I realized. With the help of her father, she finally transferred to another school where she received pay through a different *empresa*.

Kamila is an actress. Beginning at the age of seventeen, she worked for Bando de Teatro Olodum, a theater company located in the heart of downtown Salvador. The company prides itself on excellence in Afro-Brazilian performing arts. If your *carteira* (portfolio) reflects work experience in a profession for a significant length of time, even without a college degree in a related area, the government accepts it as your profession.

Coming from a working-class family, Kamila's strivings for a better life are somewhat different from Nanda's. Her work is essential to maintaining her self-esteem and self-love. When I returned to Brazil in 2012, Kamila had left the Bando for a role in the *novelas* at Globo television. She was proud and excited, not just for the opportunity to earn more money and travel to Rio de Janeiro, but for the possibility that she might transition into steady work as an actress on television. Kamila was cast as an extra; she played a domestic worker in scenes depicting elite white families and life in Brazil in the 1920s. She appeared on the *novelas* less frequently than she expected. She sat at home collecting her pay and benefiting from her health insurance while waiting for her role to appear, and she traveled to Rio for a few days at a time for production.

In contrast, she enacted and embodied her racial and sexual worth when she was working at the Bando. After not being recast by Globo after the *novela* ended, the anxiety caused by not returning to the Bando was painful; nevertheless, it proved transformative in allowing her to imagine greater possibilities. Nanda, as her partner, was a vital part of this transformation.

Nanda reminds me of a young Black intellectual radical. She debates and recounts politics, history, issues of oppression, and social violence in Brazil and Salvador over beer or coffee in ways that bring to mind a form of collective "Black resistance inspired by an enduring cultural complex of historical apprehension" (Robinson 1983, 5). However, Nanda is only interested in employment that engages with social change for Black communities. She was completing her college degree in history with a focus on Afro-Brazilian history and labor relations. This emphasis directly resulted from her raised consciousness regarding the political situation and structural violence in Salvador.

As a Black lesbian, she is out and proud, though she carries herself carefully; she is very aware of the extent of violence against LGBTQ+ folks in Salvador.

Nanda is a *buffie*, a femme-butch, according to Kamila. These intimate Black/ queer moments for me were amusing, daunting, and illuminating. Nanda, who never wears skirts, dresses, high heels, or makeup, would likely be considered both a *buffie* and *ledie* (lady) according to some views on lesbian gender roles. Nanda's long hair locks and serious face reads against Brazil's femininity and she often pays the price for it. Early in our relationship, she told me she was likely to be rejected for a job due simply to being a Negra with hair locks. Later, I learned about Brazil's *carteira de trabalho e previdencia* social system. It is a citizen's passport for applying for jobs, services, and much more; employers access your photograph on the *carteira* before offering jobs to prospective applicants. However, that employers might discriminate based on this photograph does not deter women such as Nanda from maintaining their preferred hair styles associated with their sense of Negritude. As a buffie, neither does she stay single for long, and she values live-in (*casadas*) relationships. Her flirty, romantic appetite gravitates toward a particular type of person, such as Kamila. Kamila, with her dark skin, full figure, big hair, big smile, and femme presentation, was Nanda's love, pride, and joy. Nanda described Kamila as complementing her intellectual appetite and commitment to issues of race and social justice. Kamila once told me in front of Nanda that she courted Nanda at an outdoor social event. She said, "Oooohhh, gostei dessa buffihna." Nanda's eyes just glittered back at her in front of me. Nanda is shy. Kamila is not. The extent to which couples can support each other in reaching new heights of bem-estar was evident in their relationship.

Kamila takes pride in how being part of the Bando taught her how to think critically about race and even sexuality. She is an intellectual artist and wanted to understand the world in ways that fostered self-love and love of the world. Kamila sought respect for her talent and artistry. After all, as an actress, singer, and theater performer in the Salvador Black arts community, she embodied her ideas and work, envisioning herself as a free agent forging change. She was acutely aware of the limitations that her Black body was subjected to, aware of the obstacles to her striving. Navigating their social *condições* required Nanda and Kamila to hold their passions tightly in their shared reality as Black queer citizens.

The term *casadas* was strikingly deployed in Salvador to rethink Afro-futures. Being casadas means being married in everyday Portuguese. If an unmarried couple lives together or is in a committed relationship, they are *casadas* (*casados* for male couples). However, I strove to find a distance that would allow me to entirely appreciate what it meant for them in their context. I knew better than to assume that all casada Black lesbian couples would live and move about in the same way. Black lesbians as partners play in each other's lives her personal freedom both within and beyond their casada space. By following couples, I bore witness to their worth-making through engagement with social conflict in a manner that allowed for personal freedom through desire and escape. This way of managing relationship conflicts enhanced their Black queer worth-making in quotidian ways as they navigated this world. Black lesbian casadas disrupt heteronormative understandings of familial and sexual health. If these Black lesbians' sexualities are not part of their liberatory mode of being in the world, social death may be imminent in the most intimate spheres of their socialities.

Nanda and Gabriela show that to love and struggle is to be guided out from the shadow realm of life by the realm of Black lesbian futures.

Collective Bem-Estar Negra

This window shows Black lesbians' Afro-religious formations of communal or collective belonging to ensure well-being at the individual level and create family ties (see M. Moore 2011; Weston 1991). Black lesbians organizing themselves as same-sex couples, mothers, biological sisters, Candomblé members, or simply as friends create enabling conditions for bem-estar. The racial formations linked to the African origins of the Candomblé religion and people produce for many initiated members (and for others who are not initiated but who frequent terreiros) an enormous sense of pride and worthiness as a Black community. Candomblé terreiros are spaces of resistance (see Harding 2000). For example, the deep pride in Blackness is a sociocultural marker in their religion, pronounced in protests, marches, and festive events held within and outside of the terreiros. The communal synergy in the protest of religious intolerance by Candomblé members and supporters shapes interventions to defend and protect their traditions. This is critical bem-estar Negra for Candomblé members.

Taina, Emilia, Cinthia, and Luciana honored each other as initiated Candomblé members and Black lesbians supporting each other's bem-estar. Taina, Emilia, and Cinthia belonged to the same terreiro; Luciana belonged to a different terreiro. Both of these terreiros were highly respected and historically recognized by the community. The possibility of creating bem-estar as religious women became more apparent when I spent time in their terreiro space and its social life. The social life within terreiros is starkly different from the dominant Christian communities of Catholics and Protestants. I witnessed a burial ceremony of an elder of one of their terreiros in 2008. With other terreiro members, I climbed aboard an empty city bus and rode down to one of the beaches in Bairro de Rio Vermelho, where the deity Yemanjá was honored for her dominion over the ocean.

When I returned to the same terreiro with Luciana in 2012, I remembered the sanctuary. It is common, if not customary, for the priestess or priest to live on the premises of their terreiros. In 2012 and 2013 I experienced many Candomblé *festas* (Candomblé ceremonies) and social events at the same terreiro I visited in 2008. Attending festas was important in appreciating the women's lives and their commitments. They spent much time in their terreiros throughout the year preparing for the festas or carrying out other duties for their terreiro. While the festas were open to the public, the women's invitations were also about recognizing them as Candomblé women. There were times when my absence generated some disappointment.

I sincerely appreciated joining their religious community at the terreiro, particularly the social events. At this terreiro, I saw a famous Black singer named Lazaro perform at a fundraising night. This fundraiser was extraordinary because one-third of my key interlocutors were present, including Taina, Emilia, Cinthia, and Luciana. I appreciated their relaxed demeanors in the terreiro space while the music, food, and beer flowed. Of all other activities, the party for São João (Saint John) connected me most to this collective. São João in Salvador, always the last weekend in June, is a festive holiday period with lots of unique flavored liquors, steamed peanuts, and holiday cakes and desserts sold and consumed everywhere. The city, especially Pelourinho, was decorated with street ornaments and pictures of São João and other saints such as São Pedro and Santo Antônio. The terreiro prepared elaborately for São João. For the evening, women wore tailored dresses in pink plaid; men's shirts were yellow plaid. I dressed the part as well. I arrived at the terreiro early and walked in just as the priestess and others prayed to Santo Antonio. Shortly after, seasonal cakes and liquors were arranged on a buffet for self-service. The night was long with lots of music, beer, liquor, and rodeo dancing.

The magic began at 5 a.m. First, my sleepy eyes noticed the priestess and others, including Luciana, gathering everyone to head outside. Then, a few more men arrived with different instruments. Indeed, a different party took place outside. Finally, everyone still there (about thirty people) walked the streets about a quarter of a mile away from the terreiro, singing, chanting, drinking some liquor, dancing, and giggling. Even an initiated member 86 years old hung with us, wide awake, until it all ended at 6:30 a.m. By the time I was driven home, it was fully daylight. I refer to this night as magic because of that communal social-cultural dimension of religious tradition for the terreiro that manifested late into the night. This event is one of many examples of how Candomblé contextualized for me collective bem-estar and showed me how religion acts as an enabling condition that affirms members of the community as proud and communally loving Black lesbians. Unfortunately, for many other same-sex-loving women or lesbians in Candomblé, feeling comfortable as openly gay women is not easy (see A. Allen 2012).

Spirituality and the body pose their Afrofuturistic demands. Luciana once said to me,

> If someone touches my body, it is like touching [connecting to] my spirituality. I am not alone [in the space with my body]. Within me is my spirituality. If you are violent to me, my spirituality is also violated. When I respect a person, I respect her spirituality, too, regardless of what she [or I] believes. I like doing it [respecting others' bodies]; I have practiced that a lot. I have learned so much. I cannot invade the body of another without their permission, without a dialogue on how I may access your body and your spirituality. That, to me, is sacred. When I talk about our humanity, any professional [gynecologist] needs to treat others as human in that way.

Luciana reminds us that there is minimal distinction between touching her body and connecting to her spirituality, as touching her body and spirituality is touching her humanity. Luciana and others have told me that there is very little connection, if any, between their spirituality and religion. Spirituality is constantly present in them outside the terreiro. The terreiro is merely a place in which their orixá is honored in various ways. Caring for their orixá, which principally governs the stability of their head, is an everyday task beyond the terreiro—caring for the orixá means caring for your body and mind. For them, this is bem-estar. Luciana's response is significant for imaging an Afrofuture that does not separate her bem-estar from social and physical wellness and justice. Racial formations that reinforce self-pride contribute to bem-estar. As described to me by another gynecologist, gynecologists' preconceito toward and often fear of touching Candomblé female patients is palpable to these Black queer women. As the protest chant goes, "Mess with one, mess with all." We are a perfect image of Black lesbians who have lovers and are looking for lovers who might be waiting for us out there (see McKinley and DeLaney 1995).[8]

To what extent might Black lesbians in Latin America understand themselves as agents of their sexual freedom through their symbolic presence and lived participation in an African diaspora?

How might we bring together ongoing conversations about the African diaspora, race relations, and same-sex sexuality? How do these relations change in an era of moving bodies, ideas, practices, and media that interconnect Black women across national and international borders? Brazilian Black feminist, physician, and community organizer Jurema Werneck (2005), in "De Ialodês y Feministas Reflexiones sobre la Acción Política de las Mujeres Negras en América Latina y el Caribe," cautions us to pay attention to how the collective lived experiences of Brazilian Black women in Candomblé shape their movement work, strategies for living, and resistance through their African diasporic and Afro-Latina struggles.[9] I also build on the work of Deborah A. Thomas and Tina M. Campt (2006). In their dialogue on diasporic transnationalism, they argue for foregrounding the diaspora as a lens to correct the disconnections in feminist transnationalism between gender, class, sexual and racial subjectivities. Jafari S. Allen's understanding of "erotic self-making as entailing individual and collective (re)articulation of race, gender, and sexuality, and the creation of new social and political subject(ivities)," is consonant with how my interlocutors express their sexuality in public as well as with the structural historical-political tensions encountered in self-images (2011, 14). Their *pelo duro*, or "kinky hair," for example, is marked as African inferiority. Despite these views, many Black women in Brazil continue to adopt natural hairstyles, creating a movement toward a sense of racial freedom in the domain of beauty. Many lésbicas Negras in Salvador occupy the center of these social and aesthetic movements, and there are ways to identify the "small practices of self-making through erotic subjectivity" as politically and even ethically transformative (14).

Bem-estar Negra is as Catherine E. McKinley and L. Joyce DeLaney (1995, xv) state "a perfect creation of the Black lesbian feminist imagination." Bem-estar Negra is a Black queer self-care praxis through the contradictions about ourselves that trouble identity politics.

A collective bem-estar Negra is the avoidance of being lost without light. A yellow moon is shining on their intersubjective landscape and beautiful experiments.

So, bem-estar Negra is . . . and bem-estar ain't.

We are AFREKETE.

A Gynx-Project: Hold Space for Us

What will our narratives be in gynecology's futures? Our Black queer reproductive futures?

In 2017, Dora excitedly reported to me that since I left fieldwork in 2013, she started feeling more confident about speaking out in the gynecologists' office about her pelvic exam needs. This is our Black queer reproductive future. I recognize that this project centered research for an academic book. But when people ask me who my target audience for this is, I say: Black lesbians. Why? My hope is that this book opens conversations and propels action for change inside and outside of all of us.

That change starts with the Brazilian medical community. This book challenges all gynecologists to reflect on how they can make room with intentionality in their practices and daily lives and ask themselves what it would mean to hold space for Black female bodies with different narratives, practices, and expressions. Written from the perspective of a physician assistant and medical anthropologist, it argues that an approach to patient care is caring only if undertaken with affirmation and legitimation of patients' truths. I follow the Black feminist health science studies (BFHSS) intellectual tradition and praxis of Moya Bailey and Whitney Peoples (2017) to "build on social justice science, which as at its focus the health and wellbeing of marginalized groups," specifically Black queer women (2). This book is BHFSS rooted in an "emergent lens and praxis" to eradicate medical injustice in gynecology through "narrative medicine and abolition medicine" (Bailey and Peoples 2017, 4; Iwai, Khan, and DasGupta 2020, 158). My goal has been to wrap Brazilian Black queer women's and nonbinary people's narratives around biomedical power, and not the other way around.

Black lesbian life matters. Giving patients room to breathe into the physician-patient interaction is critical for honoring their existence in every way possible. In Brazil, Black women have very little space, if any, with the gynecologist to breathe deeply in the moment and for their future. This is part of larger gender and race problems. Bem-estar Negra holds that breathing room for many Black lesbians. I expand our view of well-being as a unique aspect of Black life pursued and accumulated to transform pain, negate impactful insults, and ultimately return to a good quality of life. Black lesbian life reveals the colorfulness of strivings to protect it, resist injustice on varying scales, and reimagine a different world.

If a gynecologist must ask what race or sexuality has to do with their practice, then their privilege or racism, classism, sexism, or colorblindness is evident. They may not have Black friends, but only Black domestic house workers or nannies. They may not even have a Black front-desk worker in their private office. This book has framed a different vision of and gaze on Black lesbians (and all Black women) because Black lesbian lives matter. In the absence of a just and nonviolent medical establishment, Black lesbians hold themselves accountable for the care of their sexuality; this self-care permeates and shapes their inner selves, social practices, and personal routines concerning their sexuality. It is a highly developed relationship of the self to itself; it is an awareness of responsibility to the self and others in the quest for their Afro-futures.

This gynx-project is a Black queer feminist call for the present that reaches into a future that proliferates projects, or *projetos* as my informants would say, to deterritorialize gynecological spaces producing anti-Blackness. Black lesbians project change on the gynecological encounter. As a clinician, there is nothing more important than Black women's safety in all senses. While this change seems specific to suggesting, even demanding, that gynecologists restructure how they engage with the encounter, their imaginaries and critiques are a projection into ontological shifts of how to occupy space in relation to power dynamics. Thus, this book would not be complete without *um projeto*—a call to action for social change.[10]

I honor the instruments and instrumenting, like making music, ourselves as Black lesbians within institutional spaces to stand in worth. How do we write ourselves and histories today as part of all well-lived experiences, including healing from traumatic memories of microaggressions and violence? We cannot reduce Black women to a questionnaire as an instrument for social change. Black women already create the instruments by which they negotiate their humanity and well-being, even in gynecological clinics. The institutionalization of such instruments imagines sexual health as a sociopolitical instrument that reminds women, their gynecologists, and even the institutions that train doctors about the factors that lead to recognizing and engaging sexuality as part of a transparent and nonthreatening social interaction between patient and gynecologist.

Thinking of ways to revamp the clinical approach into a humanized practice requires the abilities to see the human first and to recognize how preconceito looks and feels and understand its implications for well-being. Gynecologists who do not affirm the humanity of all sexualities within the social and medical bounds of the consultation have overly narrow biomedical interpretations of sexual health that are experienced as traumatic in the gynecologist's office and beyond. This is not acceptable.

Along with Deborah Thomas and Tina Campt, I have turned to Black lesbians' lives to ask the following questions: "How (and where) are diasporas, and particularly the African diaspora, produced? How have African diasporas been politicized?" (2006, 164). This book opens avenues to explore other sociocultural structures in Brazil, specifically in Salvador, that shape the intersections of race, gender, class, and sexuality for Black gay women occupying other medical spaces such as cancer hospitals and even fertility clinics. I continue to be interested in how sexual categories cut across medical spaces, but I have become less interested in disease processes themselves. This book offers a next step toward critically and directly engaging the sociocultural negotiation of same-sex sexuality for Black women in Salvador and across the African diaspora when faced with acute medical dilemmas. In this book I have woven together various social justice discourses in Brazil; to date, they have had only a limited reach into the entrenched systems of structural racism.

Listen to Black lesbians and all Black women.

Notes

1. Throughout this book I refer to Black lesbians variously as *lésbicas Negras* (the Portuguese translation) or Black queer women. Some participants identify with being a *lésbicas Negras,* but many prefer to identify as *sapatonas*, a word that translates as *dykes*. The term *lésbica* is often associated with white lesbians. My participants identify as women and with cisgender even when they also identify as masculine presenting; they are not transgender or transitioning in gender. The pronouns used by my participants at the time are she/her/hers. I also use *heterosexual* and often *cisgender* because *heterosexuality* is a more common term in Brazil than *cisgender*. I use the acronym *LGBTQ*+ to include all identities beyond transgender, including transsexual, travesty, queer, and others.

2. During my hysterectomy, my cervix was removed because of the severity of my endometriosis. I left the field in mid-December 2012 and returned to the field in mid-February after five weeks of recovery. After surgery, I experienced sudden menopause because of the removal of my ovaries, which my fallopian tubes had wrapped around like curly fries, according to my surgeon.

3. I use the terms *homosexuality* or *homosexual* throughout the book to reflect the language that my participants and public discourses used and continue to commonly use today. At times, I will also use the term *queer* to ground my analysis and discussion to situate Black queer desire (J. Allen 2013, 553).

4. See Castro and Savage 2019; Chattopadhyay et al. 2017; Smith-Oka 2013.

5. Christen A. Smith's article, "Counting Frequency: Un/gendering Anti-Black Police Terror," helps me think about the entrenched injustice of Black women's gender being treated as "immaterial and unimportant" in all institutional spaces (2021, 27).

6. Ana-Maurine Lara (2020) in *Queer Freedom: Black Sovereignty* rearticulates the term "arrivant" to interrogate Christian coloniality past and present and future in Dominican Republic. It offers a way to conceptualize colonial power, national landscapes, and Indigenous presence (8). Brazilian gynecology can be viewed as a "project that emerged out of colonialism, and its policies continue to mobilize colonial power, especially in negotiating hierarchies of race, gender, sexuality," and class (9). Faye V.

Harrison (2008, 1994, 2010) has also been deeply instrumental in rethinking decolonizing anthropology for this work. I am cautious about not referring to the idea of freedom in ways that erase their social conditions and constraints as well as their racial consciousness about Brazilian slavery and its ties to racial injustices in Brazil in my analysis.

7. Anthropologist Linda-Anne Rebhun's work demonstrates the varied ways Northeastern Brazilian women manage, negotiate, and perform different emotions in the face of normative patriarchal control as well as class and racial difference in order to sustain everyday life with agency and even creativity (1993, 2004). Furthermore, anthropologist Jessica Gregg's (2003) work focuses on "the conflict between cultural ideals of Brazilian women's sexuality and the lived reality of sex for impoverished *Brasileiras* in the Brazilian Northeast" to examine the "interplay between sexual expectations, sexual reality, and disease in that same context" (3). Gregg's work is vital for reflecting on how Brazilian women's agencies that serve to strategize against medical institutional violence are entangled with how the medical establishment participates in an agenda centered on blame and risk, casting women's sexuality as "dangerously excessive for the spread of disease such as hpv which causes cervical cancer," and "dominant cultural constructions" of sexuality and gender that establish relationships to their sexuality (43, 4). Also, queer anthropology is foundational for rethinking nonconforming gender analysis in our discipline that takes seriously matters of social difference and intersectionality characteristic of female nonnormative sexualities and the ways categories generated understanding about gender and sexuality interconnected representations (Boellstorff 2007; Valentine 2004, 2007; Weston 1991; Lewin 1993; Lewin and Leap 2002). Richard Parker's (1991) work helped me during my formative years to rethink my approach to gynecology to be a complex window into Brazil's "sexual universe," offering us the opportunity to understand how homosexuality is permitted or prohibited within specific social hierarchies and imaginaries. My research also follows Don Kulick in studying how "gender is grounded not so much in sex as it is grounded in sexuality; and such grounding allows and even encourages the elaboration of cultural spaces" (1997, 575; also see 1998). My general undertaking grounds gender in sexuality to the extent that I point to gynecology as an entrenched space and practice of *desexualization*, of removing the person from their body parts and sexuality until the consultation ends (Kapsalis 1997). Also see Mammo 2007.

8. David Hellwig (1992) documents African Americans' experiences with entrenched racial prejudice after traveling to Brazil (1900–1970s) despite the absence of Jim Crow laws and prohibitions as in the United States.

9. See Telles 2004; Weinstein 2015; Farfán-Santos 2016.

10. See SOUBH, "Pesquisa: 33% das brasileiras não vão ao ginecologista regularmente, February 14, 2019, " https://soubh.com.br/noticias/viva-bem/33-das-brasileiras-nao-vao-ao-ginecologista-regularmente. There are many Brazilian journalistic sources documenting women's reservations of going to a gynecologist.

11. In analyzing intersectionality, I also think with Iris Marion Young, who identified five "faces of oppression": exploitation, marginalization, powerlessness, cultural imperialism, and systemic violence (1990, 63). This is not an exhaustive list, but for Young, these were critical elements for contemplating distributive injustice. We understand intimate violence through these faces of oppression inculcated in gynecological spaces. Also, this

intersectional preconceito is the steep power differentiation of intersectionality. See Crenshaw 1991; Akotirene 2019; and C. Moore 2012).

12. These emotions in particular raised questions about injustice, echoing Christina Sharpe's (2010) point that "if justice depends upon the point of view or is only recognized through a white gaze passed on from slavery (colonialism, segregation, incarceration, genocide, etc.) to Blackness (or being Black), then how is such injury addressed and redressed?" (13).

13. LGBT is a more commonly used acronym than LGBTT that would otherwise include transsexuals/*travesti* in Brazil, especially during my fieldwork period of 2011–13. The acronym may also include queer as of the publication year of this book, though it continues to not be a widely used term and is insulated in the Brazilian academy and public discourses. However, LGBTQI is now widely circulating in Brazil to include queer, questioning, and intersex people.

14. See the Ministry of Health's 2013 document for LGBT reform (Ministério da Saúde 2013b). During fieldwork, I accessed its original 2010 document online, which was a work in progress until its final version in 2013. Sistema Único da Saúde, or SUS, is Brazil's public healthcare system. It was created in 1990 following the 1988 Social Democratic constitution instituted after the fall of a militarized nation-state. See the *Lancet* for a history of SUS (Castro et al. 2019).

15. See Carneiro 2020.

16. This public health care policy agenda emerged on the heels of the country's 2004 initiation of another sociopolitical agenda, Brasil's em Homofobia: Programa de Combate a Violência e a Discriminação contra gltb e de Promoção da Cidadania Homosexual (Brazil without Homophobia: Program for Combating Violence and Discrimination against LGBTT and for the Promotion of Homosexual Citizenship), which sought to recognize the various areas in which discrimination impacts homosexual citizenship, such as "racism and homophobia, health, women's issues, etc." (https://bvsms.saude.gov.br /bvs/publicacoes/brasil_sem_homofobia.pdf). See also Knauth (2009) for a discussion of discrimination against lesbians in Porto Alegre. I had the opportunity to meet and converse with Dr. Danielle Knauth, an anthropologist, during my visit to Porto Alegre. I am grateful for her time and perspectives.

17. In Salvador, white lesbians promoted public discourses on lesbian health, but issues of medical racism impacting Black lesbians were not central to their movement and knowledge production. See also Prefeitura Municipal 2011.

18. From this document I also learned that homosexuality was legalized in Brazil in 1830, well before slavery was abolished in 1889. These changes clarified the ways I understood how the term is taken up in public discourses and everyday speech. Secretaria de Políticas de Promoção da Igualdade Racial 2011.

19. Document produced and distributed nationally by Articulação de Mulheres Negras Brasileiras 2012. The quotes in this paragraph are from page 11 of this document. See also Batista, Werneck, and Lopes (2012) for work on health, race, and racism in Brazil. See also Paim et al. 2011.

20. I also follow John Jackson Jr.'s notion of "flat ethnography, where you slice into a world from different perspectives, scales, registers, and angles—all distinctively useful,

valid, and worthy of consideration" (2013, 16–7). Otherness will never be transparent or fit neatly within a "thick description" as the object of power and hierarchy. My data collection and analysis fall within a "thin description or thin-slicing" approach not because details and patterns can be readily identified, but because of what I see in societal persistence to *unsee* Black lesbian existence in the moment and everywhere (Jackson 2013). See also Mullings 2005 for how we move toward an anti-racist anthropological inquiry.

21. Michel Foucault's understanding of ethical work is what he refers to as "moral": "for an action to be 'moral,' it must not be reducible to an act or a series of acts conforming to a rule, a law, or a value. Of course, all moral action involves a relationship with the reality in which it is carried out, and a relationship with the self" ([1985] 1990, 27–28). This study is not a focus on morality, but rather a study of interpretive processes grounded in justice by action and responsibility. Therefore, the works of some medical anthropology scholars are instrumental here for assessing the structural violence in medicine in order to challenge how the "meaning and structure" (see Dressler 2007) of the sexual subject might be unraveled from their power relations (Janes and Corbett 2009). Foucault defined ethics as "the kind of relationship you ought to have with yourself, *rapport a soi*, and which determines how the individual is supposed to constitute himself as a moral subject of his own actions" (1994, 263). I move beyond this widely taken perspective on ethics to interpret ethics as evaluative praxis within a social realm where Black lesbians hold multiple subject positions within a gynecology encounter; how they respond to preconceito as an entrenched and accepted social norm. While Foucault's ethics turns to morality as the defining feature of ethical action and patterns of conduct, I draw upon Naisargi Dave's understanding of radical ethics as primarily "a commitment to philosophical exercise, to think differently, to ask new questions of oneself in order to analyze and surpass limits upon what can be said and done" (2012, 8).

22. See Carneiro (2003, 123) where she takes up an anti-racist conversation to address Black women's health in Brazil.

23. An anti-racist Black/queer *olhar* forges empowerment "as having consciousness of the problems that afflict them and to create mechanisms to combat them" (Ribeiro 2018, 136).

24. I think about Brazilian Black lesbians' evaluative practices to reclaim "subjugated knowledge" for a politics of empowerment within spaces of power (Collins 2000, 13). Audre Lorde (1984) also charged us to think about how to not turn to the master's tools to dismantle oppressions and systems of power.

25. The scholarship on Afrofutures guides me to engage the value of Black futurity and narratives for ethnography (see Anderson and Jones 2016). Mark Dery coined the term *afrofuturism* in 1994 to describe "speculative fiction that treats African-American themes and addresses African-American concerns in the context of twentieth-century techno-culture" (Anderson and Jones 2016, viii). Kudwo Eshun asserts that "Afrofuturism may be characterized as a program for recovering the histories of counter-futures created in a century hostile to Afrodiasporic projection and as a space within which the critical work of manufacturing tools capable of intervention within the current political dispensation

may be undertaken" (Anderson and Jones 2016, viii). These perspectives signal potential for our ethnographic work of Black studies to assess Black futures through creating the present. I also draw upon the scholarship on well-being from Haworth and Hart (2007); Matthews and Izquierdo (2009); and Pickering (2007). My methodologies were also influenced by the work of Linda Tuhiwai Smith (1999).

CHAPTER 1. THE VIRGIN WHO LIVES WITHIN HER EROTIC WORTH

1. I bought this book of poetry at a book signing to which I was invited by my participant, Emilia, at Katuka, a store in Pelourinho. Katuka is a Black-owned store that also sells African cloth and jewelry. Contributing poets identify as Afro-Brazilian women or members of Candomblé. The book is written in Portuguese but also has its own English translation, which is used here.

2. The history of public health for sexual health is entwined with Brazil's history of eugenics and its hygienist movement. Nonetheless, it is a relatively recent public health concept emerging forcefully during the early HIV/AIDS era. It continues to be tied to family "health" construction and reproduction (see Ministério da Saúde 2013).

3. Lesbibahia is a small lesbian community organizing group that I followed in 2011 and 2012–13.

4. I am interested in O'Grady's work for rethinking how forms of self-expression are a stage of being *seen*, though inferiorly, yet experiencing being seen also resists the normative shaping subjectivity.

5. I'm influenced by how Samar Habib's (2009) accounts of Arabo-Islamic texts between 850 and 1780 A.D. period demonstrate women's contestations toward their prohibited erotic practices. The below poem by a ninth-century grinder and resident of Baghdad captures how nonpenetrative sex carries both erotic and resistance against patriarchal power. This poem speaks to the endurance of erotic sexual play (ninety pilgrimages) in resistance to patriarchy. The poem below, from Habib's findings, expresses the embeddedness of erotic political freedom.

> How much have we grinded sister, ninety
> Pilgrimages
> More delightful and invisible than the entries of the penis head and than
> A pregnancy that pleases the enemy and worse than
> That, the reproaches
> Of the censures
> And we are not limited in grinding,
> Like in fornication, even though it is more
> Delicious to the inclined.

6. I also think with Cymene Howe, who asserts in her work on Nicaraguan lesbians and activism that "sexuality is a vast category that has been used to give name and voice to desires and practices, to codify political solidarity, and to define subjectivity and identity" (2013, 16).

7. Terms like *virginity* or *sexual health* are routinely ascribed heteronormative meaning. My analytic intentions are to dig into these ascribed meanings to show how such terms are socioculturally taken up in varied ways for Brazilian Black queer women.

8. See also Foucault's (1973) analysis of the clinical gaze as an act of first seeing organs and body parts, then the human. See also Rohden (2001, 107), who documents how eighteenth- and early nineteenth-century gynecologists published on how to conduct the pelvic exam, which included careful identification of the hymen membrane.

9. My participants were attended to by white physicians only. They reported not knowing any Black female gynecologists. The two Black female gynecologists I interviewed stated that they represented a very small percentage of Black gynecologists in all of Brazil, including Salvador.

CHAPTER 2. UNSEEN FLESH: GYNECOLOGICAL TRAUMA,
EMOTIONAL POWER, AND INTIMATE SOCIOMEDICAL VIOLENCE

1. I prefer the use of *pelvic exam* over *speculum exam*." However, I use *speculum exam* intentionally to emphasize the fear of the use of the speculum. Pelvic exams for cervix swabbing can be done with a long Q-tip and without a speculum. However, manual vaginal/pelvic examinations for palpation can also be painful and performed with aggression.

2. Emily Martin describes how all women feel "alienated or separated from themselves during gynecological and obstetrical procedures such as cesarean sections and other medical procedures and technologies that elicit the feeling of a self and body separation" (1987, 82–85; see also Inhorn 2006, 2007). See also Rosaldo 1980 on the importance of emotions as an object of anthropological inquiry.

3. See Gunter 2019. See also Taylor, McDonagh, and Hansen 2017; Kline 2010.

4. Bianca Williams's interpretation of Sara Ahmed's work has also been helpful for my work on emotions through a transnational Afro-diasporic lens.

5. Kia Lilly Caldwell (2007) reminds us that Brazilian Black women's politics of identity are tied to the anti-Blackness body politics such as "bad hair" and other corporeal constructions inferior to whiteness, including natural hair and locks.

6. Zigon points out that an "unreflective mode of being-in-the-world" is not necessarily a passive or inactive state of being but an ethical mode of reflective evaluation for self-honing and embodying relationships to the self and others in relation to discourses.

INTERLUDE ONE: ANGELA

1. I recognize that the term *rape* is triggering and a sensitive topic for many readers. See my upcoming article "Erotic Senses: Powering Brazilian Black Queer Existence in Gynecological Spaces," forthcoming in *Medical Anthropology Quarterly* later in 2023. In this article, I explore the roles of senses, language, and knowledge tracked into gynecological spaces and situate Angela's story alongside those of others from my research.

1. The film, *O Fio das Masculinidades: Uma Reflexão das Masculinidades em Mulheres* (*The thread of masculinities: A reflection on masculinities in women*), made by Brazilian anthropologist Sueli Messeder, is a twenty-minute documentary produced by Grupo de Atuação Especial em Defesa da Mulher. Unfortunately, I could not attend its screening during my fieldwork and partake in the productive discussion about the film reported by Marcia.

2. Other medical anthropologists' works that have influenced this book include Bridges 2011; Brives et al. 2016; Csordas and Deomampo 2016; Hannig 2017; Kleinman 1990; Martin 1991; McCallum 1998; McCallum and dos Reis 2005; Mullings 1997; Mullings and Wali 2001; Nguyen 2010; Petryna 2002; Petryna, Lakoff, and Kleinman 2006; Street 2014.

3. See Gauthier 2018.

4. Rohden documents this sociohistorical information to analyze the 1882–84 legislatures and the 1887 Brazil Medico periodical affiliated with Faculdade de Medicina do Rio de Janeiro and Gazeta Medica da Bahia, 1866. Also see Rodhen's review of the long list of gynecology *revistas* (journals) from the nineteenth century (2009, 80).

5. Dr. Carlos Chagas (1879–1934), is known for discovering Chagas disease and pneumocystis. The Institute of Oswaldo Cruz was created in Rio de Janeiro. Dr. Oswaldo Cruz is known for discovering trypanosome.

6. Segundo Machado says, "The term and the concept of medical police date from the second half of the eighteenth century, being defined by some doctors as: defense art; the doctrine that teaches to protect man, and the animals that are useful to him from the harmful consequences of numerous cohabitation, and to promote his bodily well-being, so that, subject to the lesser evils, one may, as late as possible, suffer the fatal fate that awaits us" (my translation) (1978, 257).

7. Other leading physician eugenicists include Dr. Renalto Kelh.

8. Lei 7.716, instituted on January 5, 1989, is a law that designates as crime preconceito of race or color. Physicians often refer to this law to claim the absence of preconceito in health care. Also see Theodoro 2008; P. Pinho 2010; O. Pinho and Sansone 2008; Telles 2004; Sansone 2003; Twine 1998.

9. On the issue of *boa aparência*, see Figueiredo 2002. See also Hoberman 2012 on medical racism.

10. Gynecologists in Brazil can spend an additional year during their medical residency training as sexologists. See also Russo and Carrara 2013.

11. Butler says that a form of subjection of all women "is a kind of power that not only unilaterally acts on a given individual as a form of domination, but also activates or forms the subject. Hence, subjection is neither simply the domination of a subject nor its production, but designates a certain kind of restriction in production, a restriction without which the production of the subject cannot take place, a restriction through which that production takes place" (1997, 84). See also Eve Kosofsky Sedgwick's (1990) early theorizations of heteronormativity (1990).

12. See also Rodhen's review of the long list of gynecology *revistas* (journals) from the nineteenth century (2009, 80).

13. Tithi Bhattacharya argues for social reproduction theory as "displaying analytical irreverence to 'visible facts' and privileges 'process' instead" (2017, 2). Thinking of social reproduction as "the complex network of social processes and human relations that produces the conditions of existence for any visible, finished entity" as opposed to just naming the entity also helps me think about gynecology for its social reproduction of Black lesbian bodies and how they are treated as "nonreproductive" and only concerning labor power relations and capital.

CHAPTER 4. ARE *WE* ETHICAL SUBJECTS? SEEING OURSELVES IN SHAPESHIFTING ETHICS

1. Aimee Meredith Cox gets us to think about social citizenship as deviant, nonnormative, and consumed as labor by normative practices that represent the state—in this case, medical infrastructures that mirror state and social regulatory codes and mores (2015, 9).

2. I also agree with Keane that "ethical life is intersubjectivity, or people's capacity to share and exchange perspectives and intentions with one another" (2016, 81).

3. J. Reid Miller (2017, 60) refers to the ethical subject as "inheritable, bodily worth by addressing the ethical subject as both autonomously responsible for its performed deeds as well as determined through racial histories of responsibility" and draws on Martin Luther King Jr., as an example. Miller challenges us in his reading of Emmanuel Kant and Franz Fanon by asserting that "autonomy as 'self-discipline' has no meaning outside of determining forces such as those of evaluative bodily context. Autonomy in this respect operates as that through which heteronomous forces are themselves mediated and represented as such. This logic functions as a 'clip' in the sense of what executes at one stroke differentiated ethical subjectivity as well as the subject as irreducibly the effect of genealogies of value" (60).

4. See Foucault ([1985] 1990) on self-formation activity and ethics. For Foucault, the ethical has four aspects: ethical substance, mode of subjectivation, self-forming activity, and telos (263–65). While the book has explored some of these aspects, such as mode of subjectivation, here I am most interested in self-forming activity.

5. I rethink ethical life through the concept of ethical affordance as "any aspects of people's experiences and perceptions that they might draw on in the process of making ethical evaluations and decisions, whether consciously or not" (Keane 2016, 27).

6. This pamphlet cover also features Brazilian trans women and gay men native to Bahia.

7. The murder rate of the LGBTQ+ population is high in Brazil, according to a 2013 report by the Secretaria Especial de Direitos Humanos do Ministerio das Mulheres, da Igualdade Racial e dos Direitos Humanos. In 2018 I submitted a legal report documenting the extensive violence against the LGBTQ+ population to assist a Brazilian lesbian seeking asylum in the United States as a result of police violence and domestic violence from her partner's jealous ex-boyfriend.

8. During fieldwork, I attended a large protest held at the municipal legislative building in downtown Salvador. Initiated members of Candomblé, including priests and priestesses as well as nonmember supporters, chanted and gathered to protest proposed legislation to ban killing animals for religious reasons. Ultimately, the legislation did not pass.

9. I rethink Black lesbians' methods of life with Chela Sandoval's (2000) analytics of lived methods as "differential movement of consciousness through meaning" to conceptualize what she further argues as "a theory and method of oppositional consciousness, methodology of the oppressed, and hermeneutics of love" (5).

10. See Miller's (2017) interpretation of Linda Alcoff's work on race and ethics in his introduction to *Stain Removal*.

11. See Webb Keane (2016), "In other words, race as ethical always functions with value because it is (1) a historic and material coordination of signifiers or marks through which embodied ethical subjectivity becomes recognizable, and (2) the idiom that sustains simultaneously the causal logic of responsible subjectivity and the logic of transferable responsibility and thus inheritable worth" (8).

12. Saward states that "shape-shifting representative is a political actor who claims to represent by shaping strategically (or having shaped) his persona and policy position for certain constituencies and audiences" (2014, 727). Saward develops an analysis of shape-shifting representation in politics to demonstrate how such representatives can also adopt subject positions and such practices having close ties to concepts such as shape-retaining.

13. Alexandre Lefebvre (2018) in *Human Rights and Care of the Self* also helps us to think about ethics of resistance as "care of the self" in the Foucauldian sense. See also Foucault 1994; Dalton 2018.

14. James Laidlaw (2010) says, "Appreciating an ethical life agency as a concept that might be reformulated to accommodate proper recognition and facilitate perspicuous description of ethical life" (143). Also see Webb Keane 2016.

15. See Porta Geledés 2009. See also Catraca Livre 2018, a story about abolitionist enslaved Brazilian Black women.

16. I am deeply influenced by the Black feminist trajectories both in Brazil and the United States and use care to map on my own transnational Black feminist lens to write about my interlocutors' demands, strategies, sociopolitical positions, and ways of moving in their social worlds.

17. Dána-Ain Davis's statement here after her presentation at "Translating Obstetric Racism into Patient-Reported Experience Measure" on July 24, 2020, has been a guiding light in rethinking healthcare "inequity" and its difference to "injustice." I agree with Davis's and Scott's assertion that we must approach medical racism with an injustice approach first and foremost, not just as an inequitable matter.

1. In the original Portuguese, "Ser mulher, negra, indígena, lésbica, pobre, migrante, e viver de diferentes modos as assimetrias de gênero e raça que caracterizam a sociedade organizada sob as regras do racismo patriarcal."

2. If we consider that an ethical subject emerges intersubjectively through multiple positionalities, the ethical subject rotates and merges various modes of self-knowing and awareness of society as she negotiates several subject positions, ethical identities, and ideas of freedom inside of a sometimes seemingly futile and abstract ethical domain (Foucault 1985; Das 2007; Lambek 2010; Faubion 2011; Dave 2012).

3. I draw on Michel Foucault's (1994, 284) assertion that "freedom is the ontological condition of ethics. But ethics is the considered form that freedom takes when it is informed by reflection." My dissertation studies of Foucault's ethics was formative to interpret ethical subjectivity through his notion of practices of freedom (284).

4. Ethical telos of lésbicas Negras is an important consideration. James Faubion defines ethical telos as "the conditions that mark or define the consummation of any given subject position" (2011, 116). Ethical telos in my study is the conditions that inform some of the self-formation processes of my key interlocutors as ethical subjects: a set of enabling conditions that allow them to achieve what they describe as well-being. The connections among well-being, sexual health, and sexuality are used by my key interlocutors to interpret how these interconnected understandings shape the ethical telos or enabling conditions.

5. Esther Jones's (2016) essay "Africana Women's Science Fiction and Narrative Medicine" is critical for rethinking narrative medicine in constructing Black women's narratives. She draws on fiction for her analysis, but ethnographic narratives are central tools for this critique as well.

6. See Harding (2000) on healing and cultivating *axé* in Candomblé in Salvador.

7. See bell hooks to think about a beloved community as "understanding that love was the antithesis of the will to dominate and subjugate, we allowed that longing to know love, to love one another, to radicalize us politically" (2005, 265).

8. See McKinley and DeLaney (1995) in *Afrekete: An Anthology of Black Lesbian Writing*, xv.

9. See Jurema Werneck 2005.

10. I am inspired by a section on *viver bem* in a pamphlet from the SOGIBA conference (an OB/GYN conference I attended in 2012 in Salvador) discussing solidarity, affective experience, and subjectivities in lay terms and the contradiction therein of such personal narratives for an audience of gynecologists to read.

References

Abbott, Elizabeth. 1999. *A History of Celibacy*. Cambridge, MA: Da Capo.

Ahmed, Sara. 2010. *The Promise of Happiness*. Durham, NC: Duke University Press.

Ahmed, Sara. 2014. *Willful Subjects*. Durham, NC: Duke University Press.

Ahmed, Sara. 2015. *The Cultural Politics of Emotion*. New York: Routledge.

Aidoo, Lamonte. 2018. *Slavery Unseen: Sex, Power, and Violence in Brazilian History*. Durham, NC: Duke University Press.

Akotirene, Carla. 2019. *Interseccionalidade*. São Paulo: Polen Editora.

Alexander, M. Jacqui. 1994. "Not Just (Any) Body Can Be a Citizen: The Politics of Law, Sexuality, and Postcoloniality in Trinidad and Tobago and the Bahamas." *Feminist Review* 48: 5–23.

Alexander, M. Jacqui. 2005. *Pedagogies of Crossing: Meditations on Feminism, Sexual Politics, Memory, and the Sacred*. Durham, NC: Duke University Press.

Alexander, M. Jacqui. 2007. "Danger and Desire: Crossings Are Never Undertaken All at Once or Once and for All." *Small Axe* 24 (November 2007): 154–66.

Allen, Andrea Stevenson. 2012. "'Brides' without Husbands: Lesbians in the Afro-Brazilian Religion Candomblé." *Transforming Anthropology* 20, no. 1: 17–31.

Allen, Andrea Stevenson. 2015. *Violence and Desire in Brazilian Lesbian Relationships*. New York: Palgrave Macmillan.

Allen, Jafari S. 2011. *¡Venceremos? The Erotics of Black Self-making in Cuba*. Durham, NC: Duke University Press.

Allen, Jafari S. 2012a. "One Way or Another: Erotic Subjectivity in Cuba." *American Ethnologist* 39, no. 2: 325–38.

Allen, Jafari S. 2012b. "Black/Queer/Diaspora at the Current Conjuncture." *GLQ* 18, nos. 2–3: 211–48.

Allen, Jafari S. 2013. "Race/Sex Theory 'Toward a New and More Possible Meeting.'" *Cultural Anthropology* 28, no. 3: 552–55.

Allen, Jafari S. 2016. "One View from a Deterritorialized Realm: How Black/Queer Renarrativizes Anthropological Analysis." *Cultural Anthropology* 31, no. 4: 617–26.

Anderson, Reynaldo, and Charles E. Jones. 2016. *Afrofuturism 2.0: The Rise of Astro-Blackness*. Lanham, MA: Lexington Books.

Angelou, Maya. 1993. *Wouldn't Take Nothing for My Journey Now*. New York: Random House.

Articulação de Mulheres Negras Brasileiras. 2012. *Saúde Da Mulher Negra: Guia para a Defesa Dos Direitos das Mulheres Negras*. Porto Alegre, RS: Secretaria Executiva-ACMUN.

Avilez, Gershun. 2020. *Black Queer Freedom: Spaces of Injury and Paths of Desire*. Urbana: University of Illinois Press.

Bailey, Moya, and Whitney Peoples. 2017. "Toward a Black Feminist Health Science Studies." *Catalyst: Feminism, Theory, Technoscience* 3, no. 2: 1–27.

Barad, Karen. 2007. *Meeting the Universe Halfway: Quantum Physics and the Entanglement of Matter and Meaning*. Durham, NC: Duke University Press.

Barbosa, Cléa. 2012. "Vivência." In *Importuno Poético*, edited by Jocelia Fonseca, Cléa Barbosa, and Lutigarde Oliveira, 32–33 Salvador: Edições Revoluo.

Batista, Luis Eduardo, Jurema Werneck, and Fernanda Lopes. 2012. *Saúde da População Negra*. Petropolis: DP et Alii Editoria Ltda.

Bernau, Anke. 2008. *Virgins: A Cultural History*. London: Granta Books.

Berry, Diana Ramey 2017. *The Price for Their Pound of Flesh: The Value of the Enslaved, from Womb to Grave, in Building of a Nation*. Boston: Beacon Press.

Berth, Joice. 2019. *Empoderamento*. São Paulo: Polen Editora.

Bhattacharya, Tithi. 2017. *Social Reproduction Theory: Remapping Class, Recentering Oppression*. London: Pluto Press.

Biehl, João, Byron Good, and Arthur Kleinman, eds. 2007. *Subjectivity: Ethnographic Investigations*. Berkeley: University of California Press.

Blackwood, Evelyn, and Saskia E. Wieringa. 1999. *Female Desires: Same-Sex Relations and Transgender Practices across Cultures*. New York: Columbia University Press.

Boellstorff, Tom. 2007. "Queer Studies in the House of Anthropology." *Annual Review of Anthropology* 36: 17–35.

Bordo, Susan. 1993. *Unbearable Weight: Feminism, Western Culture, and the Body*. Berkeley: University of California Press.

Botelho, Denise. 2012. "Plenary Speech." 16 Dias de Ativismo na UNEB Pelo Fim de Violência Contra a Mulher. Universidade do Estado da Bahia, November 20–December 10, 2012.

Bridges, Khiara M. 2011. *Reproducing Race: An Ethnography of Pregnancy as a Site of Racialization*. Berkeley: University of California Press.

Britto, Nara. 1995. *Oswaldo Cruz: A Construção de um Mito na Ciência Brasileira*. Rio de Janeiro: Editora Fiocruz.

Brives, Charlotte, Frederic Le Marci, and Emilia Sanabria. 2016. "What Is in a Context? Tenses and Tensions in Evidence-Based Medicine." *Medical Anthropology* 35, no. 5: 369–76.

Brown, Elsa Barkley, Deborah King, and Barbara Ransby. 1991. "African American Women in Defense of Ourselves." In *The Black Feminist Reader*, edited by Joy James and T. Denean Sharpley-Whiting, 271–72. Malden, MA: Blackwell Publishers.

Browne, Simone. 2015. *Dark Matters: On the Surveillance of Blackness*. Durham, NC: Duke University Press.

Butler, Judith. 1997. *The Psychic Life of Power: Theories in Subjection*. Stanford, CA: Stanford University Press.

Caldwell, Kia Lilly. 2007. *Negras in Brazil: Re-envisioning Black Women, Citizenship, and the Politics of Identity*. New Brunswick, NJ: Rutgers University Press.

Caldwell, Kia Lilly. 2017. *Health Equity in Brazil: Intersections of Gender, Race, and Policy*. Urbana: University of Illinois of Press.

Campt, Tina. 2011. "What's the 'Trans' and Where's the 'National' in Transnational Feminist Practice?—a Response." *Feminist Review* 98, no. S1: e130–35.

Carneiro, Sueli. 1995. "Defining Black Feminism." In *Connecting across Cultures and Continents: Black Women Speak Out on Identity, Race, and Development*, edited by Achola O. Pala, 11–17. New York: United Nations Development Fund for Women.

Carneiro, Sueli. 2003. "Mulheres em Movimento." *Estudos Avançados* 17, no. 4, 117–32.

Carneiro, Sueli. 2005. "A Construção do Outro como Não-Ser Como Fundamento do Ser." PhD diss, Universidade de São Paulo.

Carneiro, Sueli. 2011. "Racismo, Sexismo e Desigualdade no Brasil." São Paulo: Selo Negro Edicoes.

Carneiro, Sueli. 2019. *Escritos de uma Vida*. São Paulo: Polen Livros.

Carneiro, Sueli. 2020. "Enegrecer o Feminismo: A o Situação das Mulheres Negras na América Latina a Partir de uma Perspectiva de Gênero." NEABI—Universidade Catolica de Pernambuco. https://www.patriciamagno.com.br/wp-content/uploads/2021/04/CARNEIRO-2013-Enegrecer-o-feminismo.pdf.

Carula, Karoline. 2011. "Carlos Costa e Mãi de Familia." *Anais do XXVI Simpósio Nacional de História*. São Paulo: Associação Nacional de História.

Castro, Arachu, and Virginia Savage. 2019. "Obstetric Violence as Reproductive Governance in the Dominican Republic." *Medical Anthropology: Cross Cultural Studies in Health and Illness*. 38, no. 2:123–236.

Castro, Marcia C., Adriano Massuda, Gisele Almeida, Naercio Aquino Menezes-Filho, Monica Viegas Andrade, Kenya Valeria Micaela de Souza Noronha, et al. 2019. "Brazil's Unified Health System: The First Thirty Years and Prospects for the Future." *Lancet* 394: 345–56.

Catraca Livre. 2018. "17 Mulheres Negras Brasileiras que Lutaram Contra Escravidão." August 20, 2018. https://catracalivre.com.br/cidadania/17-mulheres-negras-brasileiras-que-lutaram-contra-escravidao/.

Chattopadhyay, Sreeparna, Arima Mishra, and Jacob Suraj. 2017. "'Safe,' yet Violent? Women's Experiences with Obstetric Violence during Hospital Births in Rural Northeast India." *Culture, Health and Sexuality* 20, no. 7: 815–29.

Clarke, Cheryl. 1981. "Lesbianism: An Act of Resistance" In *Still Brave: The Evolution of Black Women's Studies*, edited by Frances Smith, Beverly Guy-Sheftall, and Stanlie M. James, 12–21. New York: Feminist Press.

Clough, Patricia T. 2010. "The Affective Turn: Political Economy, Biomedia, and Bodies." In *The Affect Theory Reader*, edited by Melissa Gregg and Gregory J. Seigworth, 206–25. Durham, NC: Duke University Press.

Cohen, Cathy J. 1997. "Punks, Bulldaggers, and Welfare Queers: The Radical Potential of Queer Politics?" *GLQ* 3: 437–65.

Cohen, Cathy J. 1999. *The Boundaries of Blackness: AIDS and the Breakdown of Black Politics*. Chicago: University of Chicago Press.

Cole, B. and Luna Han, editors. *Freeing Ourselves: A Guide to Health and Self-Love for Brown Bois*. Oakland, CA: Brown Boi Project.

Collins, Patricia Hill. 1989. "The Social Construction of Feminist Thought." *Signs: Journal of Women in Culture and Society* 14. no. (4): 745–73.

Collins, Patricia H. 2000. *Black Feminist Thought: Knowledge, Consciousness, and the Politics of Empowerment*. New York: Routledge.

Collins, Patricia H. 2013. *On Intellectual Activism*. Philadelphia, PA: Temple University Press.

Combahee River Collective. 2000. "A Black Feminist Statement." In *The Black Feminist Reader*, edited by Joy James and T. Denean Sharpley-Whiting, 261–70. Malden, MA: Blackwell Publishers.

Conrad, Robert Edgar. 1983. *Children of God's Fire: A Documentary History of Black Slavery in Brazil*. Princeton, NJ: Princeton University Press.

Cooper Owens, Deirdre. 2017. *Medical Bondage: Race, Gender, and the Origins of American Gynecology*. Athens: University of Georgia Press.

Cox, Aimee Meredith. 2015. *Shapeshifters: Black Girls and the Choreography of Citizenship*. Durham, NC: Duke University Press.

Craven, Christa. 2019. *Reproductive Losses: Challenges to LGBTQ Family-Making*. New York: Routledge.

Crenshaw, Kimberlé. 1991. "Mapping the Margins: Intersectionality, Identity Politics, and Violence against Women of Color." *Stanford Law Review* 43, no. 6: 1241–99.

Csordas, Thomas J., and Arthur Kleinman. 1990. "The Therapeutic Process." In *Medical Anthropology: A Handbook of Theory and Method*, edited by Thomas M. Johnson and Carolyn F. Sargent, 3–20. New York: Greenwood Press.

Dalton, Drew M. 2018. *The Ethics of Resistance: The Tyranny of the Absolute*. London: Bloomsbury Academic.

Das, Veena. 2007. *Life and Words: Violence and the Descent into the Ordinary*. Berkeley: University of California Press.

Dave, Naisargi N. 2010. "Between Queer Ethics and Sexual Morality." In *Ordinary Ethics: Anthropology, Language, and Action*, edited by Michael Lambek, 368–75. New York: Fordham University Press.

Dave, Naisargi N. 2012. *Queer Activism in India: A Story in the Anthropology of Ethics*. Durham, NC: Duke University Press.

Davis, Dána-Ain. 2018. "Obstetric Racism: The Racial Politics of Pregnancy, Labor, and Birthing." *Medical Anthropology* 38, no. 7: 560–73.

Davis, Dána-Ain. 2019. *Reproductive Injustice: Racism, Pregnancy, and Premature Birth*. New York: New York University Press.

Davis, Dána-Ain, and Christa Craven. 2016. *Feminist Ethnography: Thinking through Methodologies, Challenges, and Possibilities*. Lanham, MD: Rowman and Littlefield.

Davis, Dána-Ain, and Karen Scott. 2020. "Translating Obstetric Racism into Patient-Reported Experience Measure." University of California, San Francisco Department of Humanities and Social Sciences. Video, 1:08:25. https://vimeo.com/441631241.

Davis, Elizabeth Anne. 2012. *Bad Souls: Madness and Responsibility in Modern Greece.* Durham, NC: Duke University Press.

Davis, Kathy. 2007. *The Making of Our Bodies, Ourselves: How Feminism Travels across Borders.* Durham, NC: Duke University Press.

de Beauvoir, Simone. (1949) 2011. *The Second Sex.* New York: First Vintage Books.

de Oliveira, Vanilda M. 2019. "Precisam as Lésbicas de Identidade? "In *Lesbianidades Plurais: Outras Produções de Saberes e Afetos*, edited by Mayana Rocha Soares, Simone Brandão, and Thais Faria, 110–18. Simoes Filho: Editora Devires.

Deomampo, Daisy. 2016. *Transnational Reproduction: Race, Kinship, and Commercial Surrogacy in India.* New York: New York University Press.

dos Santos, Renato Emerson. 2012. *Questões Urbanas e Racismo: Coleção Negras e Negros: Pesquisas e Debates.* Petropolis: DP et Alii Editora.

Dressler, W. W. 2007. "Meaning and Structure in Research in Medical Anthropology." *Anthropology in Action* 14, no. 3: 30–43.

Edmonds, Alexander. 2010. *Pretty Modern: Beauty, Sex, and Plastic Surgery in Brazil.* Durham, NC: Duke University Press.

Edmonds, Alexander, and Emilia Sanabria. 2014. "Medical Borderlands: Engineering the Body with Plastic Surgery and Hormonal Therapies in Brazil." *Anthropology and Medicine* 21, no. 2: 202–16.

Edu, Ugo Felicia. 2018. "When Doctors Don't Tie: Hierarchical Medicalization, Reproduction, and Sterilization in Brazil." *Medical Anthropology Quarterly* 32, no. 4: 556–73.

Eribon, Didier. 2004. *Insult and the Making of the Gay Self.* Translated by Michael Lucey. Durham, NC: Duke University Press.

Evaristo, Conceição. 2017. *Becos da Memoria.* Rio de Janeiro: Pallas Editoria e Distribuidora.

Falu, Nessette. 2019. "Vivência Negra: Black Lesbians Affective Experiences in Brazilian Gynecology." *Medical Anthropology* 38, no. 8: 695–709.

Falu, Nessette. 2020. "Ain't I Too a Mulher? Implications of Black Lesbians' Well-Being, Self-Care, and Gynecology in Brazil." *Journal of Latin American and Caribbean Anthropology* 25, no. 1: 48–66.

Falu, Nessette. 2021. "Shadowboxing the Field: A Black Queer Feminist Praise Song." *Feminist Anthropology* 2, no. 2: 242–49.

Fanon, Frantz. 2008. *Black Skin, White Masks.* Translated by Richard Philcox. New York: Grove Press.

Farfán-Santos, Elizabeth. 2016. *Black Bodies, Black Rights: The Politics of Quilombolism in Contemporary Brazil.* Austin: University of Texas Press.

Faubion, James D. 2001. "Toward an Anthropology of Ethics: Foucault and the Pedagogies of Autopoiesis." *Representations* 74, no. 1: 83–104.

Faubion, James D. 2011. *An Anthropology of Ethics.* Cambridge: Cambridge University Press.

Ferreira da Silva, Denise. 2016. "The Racial Limits of Social Justice: The Ruse of Equality of Opportunity and the Global Affirmative Action Mandate." *Critical Ethnic Studies* 2, no. 2: 184–209.

Figueiredo, Angela. 2002. "Cabelo, Cabeleira, Cabeluda e Descabelada': Identidade, Consumo e Manipulação da Aparência entre os Negros Brasileiros." *Trabalho Apresentado no*

XXVI Encontro Anual da Associação Nacional de Pós-Graduação e Pesquisa em Ciências Socials. Caxambu (MG).

Foucault, Michel. 1973. *The Birth of the Clinic: An Archaeology of Medical Perception.* Translated by A. M. Sheridan Smith. New York: Vintage Books.

Foucault, Michel. 1978. *The History of Sexuality. Vol. 1: An Introduction.* Translated by Robert Hurley. New York: Random House.

Foucault, Michel. (1985) 1990. *The History of Sexuality. Vol. 2: The Uses of Pleasure.* Translated by Robert Hurley. New York: Vintage Books.

Foucault, Michel. 1994. *Ethics: Subjectivity and Truth.* Edited by Paul Rabinow. New York: New Press.

Franklin, Sarah. 2013. *Biological Relatives: IVF, Stem Cells, and the Future of Kinship.* Durham, NC: Duke University Press.

Garcia, Angela. 2010. *The Pastoral Clinic: Addiction and Dispossession along the Rio Grande.* Berkeley: University of California Press.

Gauthier, Jorge. 2018. "Sete Mulheres Descobrem Câncer de Mama por Dia na Bahia; Duas Morrem." Correio, accessed March 28, 2023. https://www.correio24horas.com.br/noticia /nid/sete-mulheres-descobrem-cancer-de-mama-por-dia-na-bahia-duas-morrem/.

Geronimus, Arline T. 1992. "The Weathering Hypothesis and the Health of African-American Women and Infants: Evidence and Speculations. *Ethnicity and Disease* 2, no. 3: 207–21.

Gill, Lyndon K. 2018. *Erotic Islands: Art and Activism in the Queer Caribbean.* Durham, NC: Duke University Press.

Ginsburg, Faye D., and Rayna Rapp. 1995. *Conceiving the New World Order: The Global Politics of Reproduction.* Berkeley: University of California Press.

Goes, Emanuelle. 2016. "Racismo Científico, Definindo Humanidade de Negras e Negros." *Combate Racismo Ambietal,* June 16, 2016. https://racismoambiental.net.br /2016/06/16/racismo-cientifico-definindo-humanidade-de-negras-e-negros/.

Goes, Emanuelle Freitas. 2021. "Um Giro Epistemológico, Contribuição da Teoria Interseccional nos Estudos sobre Direitos Reprodutivos." In *Saúde-Doença-Cuidado de Pessoas Negras: Expressões do Racismo e de Resistência,* edited by Leny A. Bomfim Trad, Hilton P. Silva, Edna Maria de Araujo, Joilda Silva Nery, and Alder M. De Sousa, 127–48. EDUFBA: Brasil.

Goes, Emanuelle Freitas, and Enilda R. do Nascimento. 2012. "Mulheres Negras e Brancas, as Desigualdades no Acesso e Utilização de Serviços s de Saúde no Estado da Bahia, PNAD-2008." In *Saúde da População Negra,* edited by Luis Eduardo Batista, Jurema Werneck, and Fernanda Lopes, 255–65. Petropolis: DP et Alii Editoria Ltda.

Goes, Emanuelle Freitas, and Elisa Maria Santos. 2014. "Racismo, Gênero e Saúde no Brasil." *Universidade Federal Rural de Pernambuco. 18 Redor,* 2532–39.

Gonzalez, Lélia. 1984. "Racismo na Cultura Brasileira." In *Revista Ciências Sociais Hoje, Anpocs,* edited by Bruno Bolognesi and Glauco Peres da Silva, 223–44. São Paulo: Associação Nacional de Pós Graduação e Pesquisa em Ciências Sociais.

Gonzalez, Lélia. 1988. "A Categoria Politico-Cultural de Amefricanidade." *Tempo Brasiliero,* nos. 92/93: 69–82.

Gregg, Jessica. 2003. *Virtually Virgins: Sexual Strategies and Cervical Cancer in Recife, Brazil.* Stanford, CA: Stanford University Press.

Gregg, Melissa, and Gregory J. Seigworth. 2010. "Introduction." In *The Affect Theory Reader*, edited by Melissa Gregg and Gregory J. Seigworth, 1–26. Durham, NC: Duke University Press.

Guimarães, Antonio Sergio. 2008. *Preconceito Racial: Modos, Temas e Tempos*. São Paulo: Cortez Editora.

Guimarães, Marco Antonio C., and Angela Baraf Podkameni. 2012. "Racismo: Um Mal-Estar Psiquico." In *Saúde da População Negra*, edited by Luis Eduardo Batista, Jurema Werneck, and Fernanda Lopes, 211–24. Petropolis: DP et Alii Editoria Ltda.

Gunter, Jen. 2019. "What to Do When a Doctor's Visit Is the Cause of Pain," *New York Times*, February 21, 2019, https://www.nytimes.com/2019/02/21/well/live/what-to -do-when-a-doctors-visit-is-the-cause-of-pain.html.

Habib, Samar. 2009. *Arabo-Islamic Texts on Female Homosexuality 850–1780 A.D.* Young-town, NY: Teneo Press.

Hannig, Anita. 2017. *Beyond Surgery: Injury, Healing, and Religion at an Ethiopian Hospital*. Chicago: University of Chicago Press.

Haraway, Donna. J. 1997. "The Virtual Speculum in the New World Order." *Feminist Review* 55: 22–72.

Harding, Rachel J. 2000. *A Refuge in Thunder: Candomblé and Alternative Spaces of Blackness*. Bloomington: Indiana University Press.

Harrison, Faye V. 2008. *Outsider Within: Reworking Anthropology in the Global Age*. Urbana: University of Illinois Press.

Hartman, Saidiya. 2007. *Lose Your Mother: A Journey along the Atlantic Slave Route*. New York: Farrar, Straus and Giroux.

Hartman, Saidiya. 2019. *Wayward Lives, Beautiful Experiments: Intimate Histories of Social Upheaval*. New York: W. W. Norton.

Haworth, John, and Graham Hart. 2007. *Well-Being: Individual, Community and Social Perspectives*. New York: Palgrave.

Hellwig, David J. 1992. *African-American Reflections on Brazil's Racial Paradise*. Philadelphia, PA: Temple University Press.

Hennessy, Rosemary. 1993. *Materialist Feminism and the Politics of Discourse*. New York: Routledge.

Higginbotham, Evelyn Brooks. 1992. "African-American Women's History and the Metalanguage of Race." *Signs: Journal of Women in Culture and Society* 17, no. 2: 251–74.

Hoberman, John. 2012. *Black and Blue: The Origins and Consequences of Medical Racism*. Berkeley: University of California Press.

hooks, bell. 1995. *Killing Rage: Ending Racism*. New York: Henry Holt and Company.

hooks, bell. 2005. *Sisters of the Yam: Black Women and Self-Recovery*. Cambridge, MA: South End Press.

Howe, Cymene A. 2013. *Intimate Activism: The Struggle for Sexual Rights in Postrevolu-tionary Nicaragua*. Durham, NC: Duke University Press.

Hurston, Zora Neale. 2011. "My Most Humiliating Jim Crow Experience." In *I Love My-self When I Am Laughing and Then Again When I Am Looking Mean and Impressive*, edited by Alice Walker, 162–63. New York: Feminist Press.

Inhorn, Marcia C. 2006. "Defining Women's Health: A Dozen Messages from More Than 150 Ethnographies." *Medical Anthropology Quarterly* 20, no. 3: 345–78.

Iwai, Yoshiko, Zahra H Khan, and Sayantani DasGupta. 2020. "Abolition Medicine." *Lancet* 396: 158–59.

Jackson, John L. Jr. 2013. *Thin Description: Ethnography and the African Hebrew Israelites of Jerusalem*. Cambridge, MA: Harvard University Press.

Jacobina, Ronaldo Ribeiro, and Ester Aida Gelman. 2008. "Juliano Moreira and the Gazeta Medica da Bahia." *História, Ciências, Saúde* 15, no. 4: 1077–97.

James, Joy. 1999. *Shadowboxing: Representations of Black Feminist Politics*. New York: St. Martin's.

Janes, Craig R., and Kitty K. Corbett. 2009. "Anthropology and Global Health." *Annual Review of Anthropology* 38: 167–83.

Johnson, E Patrick. 2018. *Black. Queer. Southern. Women. An Oral History*. Chapel Hill: University of North Carolina Press.

Johnson, Jessica Marie. 2020. *Wicked Flesh: Black Women, Intimacy, and Freedom in the Atlantic World*. Philadelphia: University of Pennsylvania Press.

Jones, Briona Simone. 2021. *Mouths of Rain: An Anthology of Black Lesbian Thought*. New York: New Press.

Jones, Esther. 2016. "Africana Women's Science Fiction and Narrative Medicine." In *Afrofuturism 2.0: The Rise of Astro-Blackness*, edited by Reynaldo Anderson and Charles E. Jones, 185–206. Lanham, MA: Lexington Books.

Kapsalis, Terri. 1997. *Public Privates: Performing Gynecology from Both Ends of the Speculum*. Durham, NC: Duke University Press.

Katz, Jonathan. 1996. *The Invention of Heterosexuality*. New York: Plume.

Keane, Webb. 2016. *Ethical Life: Its Natural and Social Histories*. Princeton, NJ: Princeton University Press.

Keeling, Kara. 2019. *Queer Times, Black Futures*. New York: New York University Press.

Keller, Evelyn Fox. 2003. *Making Sense of Life: Explaining Biological Development with Models, Metaphors, and Machines*. Cambridge, MA: Harvard University Press.

Keller, Evelyn Fox. 2016. "Thinking about Biology and Culture: Can the Natural and Human Sciences Be Integrated?" In *Biosocial Matters: Rethinking Sociology-Biology Relations in the Twenty-First Century*, edited by Maurizio Meloni, Simon Williams, and Paul Martin, 26–41. Malden, MA: John Wiley and Sons.

Kergoat, Danièle. 2009. "Divisão Sexual do Trabalbo e Relações Sociais de Sexo." In *Dicionário Critico de Feminismo*, edited by Helena Hirata, Françoise Laborie, Hélène Le Doaré, and Daniele Senotier, 67–75. République Française: Editora UNISEP.

Kline, Wendy L. 2010. *Bodies of Knowledge: Sexuality, Reproduction, and Women's Health in the Second Wave*. Chicago: University of Chicago Press.

Knauth, Danielle R. 2009. *As Faces da Homofobia no Campo da Saúde*. Brazil: Fundação Médica do Rio Grande do Sul.

Kulick, Don. 1997. "The Gender of Brazilian Transgendered Prostitutes." *American Anthropologist* 99, no. 3 (September): 574–85.

Kulick, Don. 1998. *Travesti: Sex, Gender, and Culture among Brazilian Transgendered Prostitutes*. Chicago: University of Chicago Press.

Laidlaw, James. 2010. "Agency and Responsibility: Perhaps You Can Have Too Much of a Good Thing." In *Ordinary Ethics: Anthropology, Language, and Action*, edited by Michael Lambek, 143–64. New York: Fordham University Press.

Laidlaw, James. 2014. *The Subject of Virtue: An Anthropology of Ethics and Freedom*. Cambridge: Cambridge University Press.

Lambek, Michael. 2010. *Ordinary Ethics: Anthropology, Language, and Action*. New York: Fordham University Press.

Lambek, Michael. 2015. "Living as If It Mattered." In *Four Lectures on Ethics: Anthropological Perspectives*, edited by Michael Lambek, Veena Das, Didier Fassin, and Webb Keane, 5–52. Chicago: Hau Books.

Lara, Ana-Maurine. 2020. *Queer Freedom: Black Sovereignty*. Albany: State University of New York Press.

Latour, Bruno. 2005. *Reassembling the Social: An Introduction to Actor-Network-Theory*. Oxford: Oxford University Press.

Lefebvre, Alexandre. 2018. *Human Rights and the Care of the Self*. Durham, NC: Duke University Press.

Lewin, Ellen. 1993. *Lesbian Mothers: Accounts of Gender in American Culture*. Ithaca, NY: Cornell University Press.

Lewin, Ellen, and William L. Leap. 2002. *Out in Theory: The Emergence of Lesbian and Gay Anthropology*. Urbana: University of Illinois Press.

Lorde, Audre. 1980. "The Transformation of Silence into Language and Action." In *The Cancer Journals*, 16–22. San Francisco, CA: Aunt Lute Books.

Lorde, Audre. 1984. *Sister Outsider: Essays and Speeches*. Berkeley: Crossing Press.

Machado, Gisele Cardoso de Almeida. 2011. "A Difusão do Pensamento Higienista na Cidade do Rio de Janeiro e suas Conseqüências Espaciais." In *Anais do XXVI Simpósio Nacional de História*. São Paulo: Associação Nacional de História.

Mammo, Laura. 2007. *Queering Reproduction: Achieving Pregnancy in the Age of Technoscience*. Durham, NC: Duke University Press.

Martin, Emily. 1987. *The Woman in the Body: A Cultural Analysis of Reproduction*. Boston: Beacon Press.

Martin, Emily. 1991. "The Egg and the Sperm: How Science Has Constructed a Romance Based on Stereotypical Male-Female Roles." *Signs: Journal of Women in Culture and Society* 16, no. 3: 485–501.

Matthews, Gordon, and Carolina Izquierdo. 2009. *Pursuit of Happiness: Well-Being in Anthropological Perspective*. New York: Berghahn Books.

Mattingly, Cheryl. 2013. "Moral Selves and Moral Scenes: Narrative Experiments in Everyday Life." *Ethnos* 78, no. 3: 301–27.

Mattingly, Cheryl. 2014. *Moral Laboratories: Family Peril and the Struggle for a Good Life*. Berkeley: University of California Press.

McCallum, Cecilia. 1998. "Restraining Women: Gender, Sexuality and Modernity in Salvador da Bahia." *Bulletin of Latin American Research* 17, no. 2: 1–19.

McCallum, Cecilia. 2005. "Racialized Bodies, Naturalized Classes: Moving through the City of Salvador da Bahia." *American Ethnologist* 32, no. 1: 100–17.

McCallum, Cecilia, and A. P. dos Reis. 2005. "Childbirth as Ritual in Brazil: Young Mothers' Experiences." *Ethnos* 70, no. 3: 335–60.

McGlotten, Shaka, and Dána-Ain Davis. 2012. *Black Genders and Sexualities*. New York: Palgrave Macmillan.

McGregor, Dorothy. K. 1998. *From Midwives to Medicine: The Birth of American Gynecology*. New Brunswick, NJ: Rutgers University Press.

McKinley, Catherine E., and L. Joyce DeLaney. 1995. *Afrekete: An Anthology of Black Lesbian Writing*. New York: Anchor Books.

McKittrick, Katherine. 2013. "Plantation Futures." *Small Axe* 17, no. 3: 1–15.

McKittrick, Katherine. 2020. *Dear Science and Other Stories*. Durham, NC: Duke University Press.

Meinerz, Nildes. E. 2011. *Entre Mulheres: Etnografia Sobre Relacoes Homoeroticas Femininas em Segmentos Medios Urbanos na Cidade de Porto Alegre*. Rio de Janeiro: Editoria da Universidade do Estado do Rio de Janeiro.

Mbembe, Achille. 2003. "Necropolotics." *Public Culture* 15, no. 1: 11–40.

Miller, J. Reid. 2017. *Stain Removal: Ethics and Race*. New York: Oxford University Press.

Ministério da Saúde. 2013a. "Cadernos de Atenção Básica: Saúde Sexual e Saúde Reprodutiva." https://bvsms.saude.gov.br/bvs/publicacoes/saude_sexual_saude_reprodutiva.pdf.

Ministério da Saúde. 2013b. "Política Nacional de Saúde Integral de Lésbicas, Gays, Bissexuais, Travestis e Transexuais. Brasilia-DF." https://bvsms.saude.gov.br/bvs/publicacoes/politica_nacional_saude_lesbicas_gays.pdf.

Mohanty, Chandra Talpade. 2003. *Feminism without Borders: Decolonizing Theory, Practicing Solidarity*. Durham, NC: Duke University Press.

Mol, Annemarie. 2002. *The Body Multiple: Ontology in Medical Practice*. Durham, NC: Duke University Press.

Moore, Carlos. 2012. *Racismo and Sociedade: Novas Bases Epistemológicas para Entender o Racismo*. Belo Horizonte: Nandyala Livros e Servicos, Ltda.

Moore, Mignon R. 2011. *Invisible Families: Gay Identities, Relationships, and Motherhood among Black Women*. Berkeley: University of California Press.

Moreira, Adilson. 2012. "A Homossexualidade no Brasil no Século XIX: Homosexuality in the Nineteenth Century." *Bagoas-Estudos Gay: Gênero e Sexualidade* 6, no. 7: 253–80.

Moreira, Adilson. 2019. *Racismo Recreativo*. São Paulo: Polen.

Morgan, Jennifer L. 2004. *Laboring Women: Reproduction and Gender in New World Slavery*. Philadelphia: University of Pennsylvania Press.

Morgan, Jennifer L. 2021. *Reckoning with Slavery: Gender, Kinship, and Capitalism in the Early Black Atlantic*. Durham, NC: Duke University Press.

Mott, Luiz. 2011. *Boletim do Grupo Gay da Bahia, 1981–2005*. Salvador: Editora Grupo Gay da Bahia.

Mulla, Sameena. 2014. *The Violence of Care: Rape Victims, Forensic Nurses, and Sexual Assault Intervention*. New York: New York University Press.

Mullings, Leith. 1997. *On Our Own Terms: Race, Class, and Gender in the Lives of African American Women*. New York: Routledge.

Mullings, Leith. 2002. "The Sojourner Syndrome: Race, Class, and Gender in Health and Illness." *Voices: A Publication of the Association for Feminist Anthropology* 5, no. 1, 32–26.

Mullings, Leith, 2005. "Interrogating Racism: Toward an Antiracist Anthropology." *Annual Review of Anthropology* 34: 667–93.

Mullings, Leith and Alaka Wali. 2001. *Stress and Resilience: The Social Context of Reproduction in Central Harlem*. New York: Springer Science+Business Media.

Nascimento, Abdias. 2016. *O Genocidio Do Negro Brasileiro.: Process de um Racismo Mascarado*. São Paulo: Editora Perspectiva.

Nascimento, Maria Beatriz. 1985. "O Conceito de Quilombola e a Resistência Afro-Brasileira." *Afrodiáspora* nos. 6–7:41–49.

Nascimento, Sheu. 2015. "Lésbicas Negras e a discriminação na Ginecologia." *Blogueiras Negras* January 15, 2015. https://blogueirasnegras.org/lesbicas-negras-e-a-discriminacao-na-ginecologia/.

Neto, Andre de Faria Pereira. 2001. *Ser Medico no Brasil: O Presente no Passado*. Rio de Janeiro: Editora Fiocruz.

Nguyen, Vinh-Kim. 2010. *The Republic of Therapy: Triage and Sovereignty in West Africa's Time of AIDS*. Durham, NC: Duke University Press.

O'Grady, Lorraine. 2009. "Olympia's Maid: Reclaiming Black Female Subjectivity." In *Still Brave: The Evolution of Black Women's Studies*, edited by Stanlie M. James, Frances Smith Foster, and Beverly Guy-Sheftall, 318–35. New York: Feminist Press.

Oyěwùmí, Oyèrónkẹ́. 1977. *The Invention of Women: Making an African Sense of Western Gender Discourses*. Minneapolis: University of Minnesota.

Pacheco, Ana Claudia Lemos. 2013. *Mulher Negra: Afetividade e Solidao*. Salvador: EDUFBA.

Paim, Jaimilson, Claudia Travassos, Celia Almeida, Ligia Bahia, and James Macinko. 2011. "The Brazilian Health System: History, Advances, and Challenges." *Lancet* 377: 1778–97.

Parker, Richard. 1991. *Bodies, Pleasures, and Passions: Sexual Culture in Contemporary Brazil*. Boston, MA: Beacon Press.

Peard, Julian G. 1999. *Race, Place, and Medicine: The Idea of the Tropics in Nineteenth-Century Brazilian Medicine*. Durham, NC: Duke University Press.

Perry, Keisha-Khan Y. 2013. *Black Women against the Land Grab: The Fight for Racial Justice in Brazil*. Minneapolis: University of Minnesota Press.

Petryna, Adrienna. 2002. *Life Exposed: Biological Citizens after Chernobyl*. Princeton, NJ: Princeton University Press.

Petryna, Adrienna, Andrew Lakoff, and Arthur Kleinman. 2006. *Global Pharmaceuticals: Ethics, Markets, Practices*. Durham, NC: Duke University Press.

Pickering, J. 2007. "Is Well-Being Local or Global? A Perspective from Ecopsychology." In *Well-Being: Individual, Community and Social Perspectives*, edited by John Haworth and Graham Hart, 149–62. New York: Palgrave.

Pinho, Osmundo, and Livio Sansone. 2008. *Raça: Novas Perspectivas Antropológicas*. Salvador: Editora da Universidade Federal de Bahia.

Pinho, Patricia de Santana. 2010. *Mama Africa: Reinventing Blackness in Bahia*. Durham, NC: Duke University Press.

Porta Geledés. 2009. "Revolta dos Búzios." Geledés Instituto da Muhler Negra. https://www.geledes.org.br/revolta-dos-buzios/.

Prado, Marco Aurelio Maximo, and Frederico Viana Machado. 2008. *Preconceito contra Homosseexualidades: A Hierarquia da Invisibilidade*. São Paulo: Corez Editora.

Pratt, Mary Louise. 1992. *Imperial Eyes: Travel Writing and Transculturation*. New York: Routledge.

Prefeitura Municipal de Porto Alegre Secretaria Municipal de Saúde. 2011. "Diretrizes de Assistência à Saúde de Lésbicas, Bissexuais e Mulheres que Fazem Sexo com Outras Mulheres." https://prceu.usp.br/wp-content/uploads/2021/03/protocolo_de_atendimento_para_mulheres_lesbicas.pdf.

Quashie, Kevin. 2021. *Black Aliveness, or a Poetics of Being*. Durham, NC: Duke University Press.

Rodrigues, Raimundo Nina. 2019. "The Human Races." In *The Brazil Reader: History, Culture, Politics,* edited by James N. Green, Victoria Langland, and Lilia Moritz Schwarcz, 271–73. Durham, NC: Duke University Press.

Rebhun, Linda-Anne. 1993. "Nerves and Emotional Play in Northeast Brazil." *Medical Anthropology Quarterly* 7, no. 2: 131–51.

Rebhun, Linda-Anne. 2004. "Sexuality, Color and Stigma among Northeast Brazilian Women." *Medical Anthropology Quarterly* 8, no. 2: 183–99.

Reyes-Foster, Beatriz M. 2018. *Psychiatric Encounters: Madness and Modernity in Yucatan, Mexico*. New Brunswick, NJ: Rutgers University Press.

Ribeiro, Djamila. 2018. *Quem Tem Medo do Feminismo Negro?* São Paulo: Companhia Letras.

Rich, Adrienne. 1986. "Notes toward a Politics of Location." In *Blood, Bread, and Poetry*, 210–31. New York: W. W. Norton.

Rich, Adrienne. 1993. "Compulsory Heterosexuality and Lesbian Existence." In *The Lesbian and Gay Studies Reader*, edited by Henry Abelove, Michele Aina Barale, and David M. Halpern, 227–54. New York: Routledge.

Roberts, Dorothy. 1997. *Killing the Black Body: Race, Reproduction, and the Meaning of Liberty*. New York: Vintage Books.

Rohden, Fabíola. 2001. *Uma Ciência ncia da Diferença a: Sexo e Gênero na Medicina da Mulher*. Rio de Janeiro: Editora Fiocruz.

Rosaldo, Michelle Z. 1980. *Knowledge and Passion: Ilongot Notions of Self and Social Life*. New York: Cambridge University Press.

Rouse, Carolyn Moxley. 2009. *Uncertain Suffering: Racial Health Care Disparities and Sickle Cell Disease*. Berkeley: University of California Press.

Rubin, Gayle S. 1984. "Thinking Sex." In *Deviations*, edited by Gayle S. Rubin, 137–81. Durham, NC: Duke University Press.

Russo, Jane, and Sérgio Carrara. 2013. "Sexologia e Psicanálise." Acervo Revistas Ciência Hoje, Instituto Ciência Hoje, March 2013. https://cienciahoje.org.br/artigo/sexologia-e-psicanalise/.

Sanabria, Emilia. 2011. "The Body Inside Out: Menstrual Management and Gynecological Practice in Brazil." *Social Analysis* 55, no. 1: 94–112.

Sanabria, Emilia. 2016. *Plastic Bodies: Sex Hormones and Menstrual Suppression in Brazil*. Durham, NC: Duke University Press.

Sandoval, Chela. 2000. *Methodology of the Oppressed*. Minneapolis: University of Minnesota Press.

Sansone, Livio. 2003. *Blackness without Ethnicity: Constructing Race in Brazil*. New York: Palgrave Macmillan.

Santos, Ana Cristina Conceição. 2014. "Movimento de Mulheres Negras na Cidade de Salvador: Um Olhar a Decada de 1980." In *O Movimento de Mulheres Negras: Escritos Sobre os Sentidos de Democracia e Justiça Social no Brasil*, edited by Joselina da Silva and Amauri Mendes Pereira, 161–78. Belo Horizonte: Nandyala Livros e Servicos Ltda.

Saunders, Tanya L. 2017. "Epistemologia Negra Sapatão Como Vetor de uma Práxis Humana Libertária." *Periodicus* 7, no. 1: 102–16.

Saward, Michael. 2014. "Shape-Shifting Representation." *American Political Science Review* 108, no. 4: 723–36.

Secretaria Especial de Direitos Humanos do Ministerio das Mulheres, da Igualdade Racial e dos Direitos Humanos. 2013. *Relatório de Violência Homofóbica no Brasil: Ano 2013*. https://direito.mppr.mp.br/arquivos/File/RelatorioViolenciaHomofobicaBR2013.pdf.

Secretaria de Políticas de Promoção da Igualdade Racial. 2011. *Negros e Negras Lésbicas, Gays, Bissexuais, Travestis e Transexuais (lgbt): Construindo Políticas Públicas para Avançar na Igualdade de Direitos*. https://www.mpma.mp.br/arquivos/CAOPDH/NEGROS_E_NEGRAS_L%C3%89SBICAS_GAYS_BISSEXUAIS_TRAVESTIS_E_TRANSEXUAIS.pdf.

Scarry, Elaine. 1987. *The Body in Pain: The Making and Unmaking of the World*. Oxford: Oxford University Press.

Schwarcz, Lilia Moritz. 2001. *Racismo no Brasil*. São Paulo: Publifolha.

Schwarz, Kathryn. 2002. "The Wrong Question: Thinking through Virginity." *Differences: A Journal of Feminist Cultural Studies* 13, no. 2: 1–34.

Sedgwick, Eve Kosofsky. 1990. *Epistemology of the Closet*. Berkeley: University of California Press.

Seigworth, Gregory J., and Melissa Gregg. 2010. "An Inventory of Shimmers." In *The Affect Theory Reader*, edited by Melissa Gregg and Gregory J. Seigworth, 1–28. Durham, NC: Duke University Press.

Shange, Savannah. 2019. *Progressive Dystopia: Abolition, Antiblackness, and Schooling in San Francisco*. Durham, NC: Duke University Press.

Sharpe, Christina. 2010. *Monstrous Intimacies: Making Post-slavery Subjects*. Durham, NC: Duke University Press.

Sharpe, Christina. 2016. *In the Wake: On Blackness and Being*. Durham, NC: Duke University Press.

Smith, Barbara. 1995. "Some Home Truths on the Contemporary Black Feminist Movement." In *Words of Fire: An Anthology of African-American Feminist Thought*, edited by Beverly Guy-Sheftall, 254–68. New York: New Press.

Smith, Barbara. 2000. *The Truth That Never Hurts: Writings on Race, Gender, and Freedom*. New Brunswick, NJ: Rutgers University Press.

Smith, Christen A. 2016a. *Afro-paradise: Blackness, Violence, and Performance in Brazil*. Urbana: University of Illinois Press.

Smith, Christen A. 2016b. "Toward a Black Feminist Model of Black Atlantic Liberation: Remembering Beatriz Nascimento." *Meridians: Feminism, Race, Transnationalism* 14, no. 2: 71–87.

Smith, Christen A. 2021. "Counting Frequency: Un/gendering Anti-Black Police Terror."
   Social Text 39, no. 2: 25–49.
Smith, Linda Tuhiwai. 1999. *Decolonizing Methodologies: Research and Indigenous*
   Peoples. London: Zed Books.
Smith-Oka, Vania. 2013. "Managing Labor and Delivery among Impoverished Popula-
   tions in Mexico: Cervical Examinations as Bureaucratic Practice." *American Anthro-*
   pologist 115, no. 4: 595–607.
Snorton, C. Riley. 2017. *Black on Both Sides: A Racial History of Trans Identity*. Minneap-
   olis: University of Minnesota Press.
Spillers, Hortense J. 1987. "Mama's Baby, Papa's Maybe: An American Grammar Book."
   Diacritics: A Review of Contemporary Criticsm 17, no. 2: 64–81.
Stepan, Nancy Leys. 1991. *"The Hour of Eugenics": Race, Gender, and Nation in Latin*
   America. Ithaca, NY: Cornell University Press.
Street, Alice. 2014. *Biomedicine in an Unstable Place: Infrastructures and Personhood in a*
   Papua New Guinean Hospital. Durham, NC: Duke University Press.
Strongman, Roberto. 2019. *Queering Black Atlantic Religions: Transcorporeality in Can-*
   domblé, Santería, and Vodou. Durham, NC: Duke University Press.
Sturgeon, John A., and Alex J. Zautra. 2016. "Social Pain and Physical Pain: Shared Paths
   to Resilience." *Pain Management* 6, no. 1: 63–74.
Sullivan, Mecca Jamilah. 2021. *The Poetics of Difference: Queer Feminist Forms in the*
   African Diaspora. Urbana: University of Illinois Press.
Tadiar, Neferti X. M. 2012. "Life-Times of Becoming Human." *Occasion: Interdisciplinary*
   Studies in the Humanities 3: 1–17.
Taylor, Gina A., Deana McDonagh, and Michael J Hansen. 2017. "Improving the Pelvic
   Exam Experience: A Human Centered Design Study." *Design Journal: An Interna-*
   tional Journal for All Aspects of Design 20, no. 1: 2348–62.
Telles, Edward. 2004. *Race in Another America: The Significance of Skin Color in Brazil*.
   Princeton, NJ: Princeton University Press.
Theodoro, Mario. 2008. *As Políticas Públicas e a Desigualdade Racial no Brasil 120 Anos*
   após a Abolição. Brasilia: Instituto de Pesquisa Econômica Aplicada.
Thomas, Deborah A., and Tina M. Campt. 2006. "Diasporic Hegemonies: Slavery, Mem-
   ory, and Genealogies of Diaspora." *Transforming Anthropology* 14, no. 2: 163–72.
Tinsley, Omise'eke Natasha. 2018. *Ezili's Mirrors: Imaging Black Queer Genders*. Durham,
   NC: Duke University Press.
Twine, Francis Winddance. 1998. *Racism in a Racial Democracy: The Maintenance of*
   White Supremacy in Brazil. New Brunswick, NJ: Rutgers University Press.
Valentine, David. 2004. "The Categories Themselves." GLQ: *A Journal of Lesbian and Gay*
   Studies 10, no. 2: 215–20.
Valentine, David. 2007. *Imagining Transgender: An Ethnography of a Category*. Durham,
   NC: Duke University Press.
Vargas, João H. Costa. 2016. "'Desidentificação': A Lógica da Exclusão AntiNegra do
   Brasil." In *AntiNegritude: Impossível Sujeito Negro na Formação Social Brasileira*, edited
   by Osmundo Pinho and João Vargas, 13–30. Cruz das Almas: Universidade Federal do
   Reconcavo da Bahia.

Velasquez de Souza, Larissa. 2018. "Fontes para a Historia da Ginecologia e Obstetrician no Brasil." *Historia, Ciencias, Saude* 25, no. 4: 1129–46.

Visweswaran, Kamala. 1994. *Fictions of Feminist Ethnography*. Minneapolis: University of Minnesota Press.

Vosne Martins, Ana Paula. 2004. *Visões do Feminino: A Medicina da Mulher nos Seculos XIX e XX*. Rio de Janeiro: Editora Fiocruz.

Walker, Alice. 2006. *We Are the Ones We Have Been Waiting For: Inner Light in a Time of Darkness*. New York: New Press.

Walker, Alice, ed. 2011. *I Love Myself When I Am Laughing: A Zora Neale Hurston Reader*. New York: Feminist Press.

Walker. Alice. 1983. *In Search of our Mother's Gardens: Womanist Prose*. New York: Harcourt Brace Jovanovich.

Washington, Harriet L. 2008. *Medical Apartheid: The Dark History of Medical Experimentation on Black Americans from Colonial Times to the Present*. New York: Doubleday.

Weeks, Jeffrey. 1985. *Sexuality and Its Discontents*. New York: Routledge.

Weheliye, Alexander G. 2014. *Habeas Viscus: Racializing Assemblages, Biopolitics, and Black Feminist Theories of the Human*. Durham, NC: Duke University Press.

Weinstein, Barbara. 2015. *The Color of Modernity: São Paulo and the Making of Race and Nation in Brazil*. Durham, NC: Duke University Press.

Wekker, Gloria. 2006. *The Politics of Passion: Women's Sexual Culture in the Afro-Surinamese Diaspora*. New York: Columbia University Press.

Werneck, Jurema. 2016. "Racismo Institucional e Saúde da População Negra" *Saúde Sociedade. São Paulo* 25, no. 3: 535–49.

Werneck, Jurema, Nilza Iraci, and Simone Cruz. 2012. *Mulheres Negras na Primeira Pessoa*. Porto Alegre: Redes Editora.

Werneck, Jurema. 2005. "De Ialodês y Feministas Reflexiones sobre la Acción Política de las Mujeres Negras en América Latina y El Caribe." In *Feminismos Disidentes en América Latina y el Caribe*. Edited by Ochy Curiel, Jules Falquet, and Sabine Masson, 24–40. Ciudad de México: Ediciones fem-e-libros ediciones.

Weston, Kathleen. 1991. *Families We Choose: Lesbians, Gays, Kinship*. New York: Columbia University Press.

Williams, Bianca C. 2018. *The Pursuit of Happiness: Black Women, Diasporic Dreams, and the Politics of Emotional Transnationalism*. Durham, NC: Duke University Press.

Williams, Erica L. 2013. *Sex Tourism in Bahia: Ambiguous Entanglements*. Urbana: University of Illinois Press.

Williamson, K. Eliza. 2021. "The Iatrogenesis of Obstetric Racism in Brazil: Beyond the Body, beyond the Clinic." *Anthropology and Medicine*. 28, no. (2): 172–87.

Young, Iris Marion. 1990. *Justice and the Politics of Difference*. Princeton, NJ: Princeton University Press.

Zigon, Jarrett. 2007. "Moral Breakdown and the Ethical Demand: A Theoretical Framework for an Anthropology of Moralities." *Anthropological Theory* 7, no. 2: 131–50.

Index

Page locators in italics refer to figures

abolitionist work: acts of resistance distinguished from, 114, 138; collective organizing by Black queer women, 19, 114–15; empowerment forged by an antiracist Black/queer *olhar*, 17, 66, 172n23; impact on Black lesbians' justice work, 133

adocimento psíquico (psychological sickness): the *vivência* of being Black impacted by, 63

Afro-futures: *afrofuturism* coined by Dery, 172n25; as bem-estar for Black women, 152–53; *bem-estar Negra* as the fabric of Black lesbians' Afro-futures, 150–54

Ahmed, Sara, 65

Aidoo, Lamonte, 6, 100–101

Alexander, M. Jacqui, 20, 31, 40

Allen, Jafari S., 16–17, 26, 39, 148–49, 164

Anderson, Reynaldo and Charles E. Jones, 152, 172–73n25

Angelou, Maya, 143–44

anti-Blackness: of body politics, 174n4; of Brazilian medicine, 4, 5, 8; dismantling by Afro-futures, 153; in national lesbian health policy, 13–15; of white lesbians, 13–14, 25, 123, 137. *See also* Negritude; race and racism

Bairro Dois de Julho, *34*

Barad, Karen, 121–22

Barbosa, Cléa, poem "Vivência," 21, 25–26

Barrios, Luiza, 134

bem-estar (well-being): as Afro-future by and for Black women, 152–53; collective bem-estar contextualized by Candomblé, 161–63; and the cultivation of *axé* (positive energy and forces), 153; impact of grappling with mal-estar (malaise) on, 61; sexual health viewed as *uma forma de bem-estar* (a form of well-being), 30; striving for bem-estar as fulfilling a promise to *orixás* (African deities), 18, 128, 163; theorization in Black queer studies, 18. *See also* *viver minha sexualidade* (live my sexuality)

bem-estar Negra: contradictions embraced by, 164; definition of, 143–44; as the fabric of Black lesbians' Afro-futures, 150–54; as a realm of erotic power and freedom, 145

Bhattacharya, Tithi, 175n13

Black lesbians (*lésbicas Negras* or Black queer women): as ethical subjects, 122–23; framing as *diferenciada*, 70–72; intersubjective experience of, 48; nonreproductive bodies associated with, 42; *sapatonas* (butch women) as a term for, 53, 60, 169n1; subjective strivings of, 18, 46–47, 49, 83, 115, 122, 160, 165; terms for, 169n1; *Unseen Flesh* as a story of their worth-making, 2–3, 7–13. *See also* participants

Black queer studies: bem-estar (well-being) contemplated in, 18; contribution of *Unseen Flesh* to, 4–7, 16; impact on Brazilian Black women's social movements, 133–34; transnational knowledge production of, 28–29

Black queer women. *See* Black lesbians

body scanning: countersurveillance practices to counter gyno-trauma, 53, 72–74; Hurston's body-scanning praxis, 74; as an ontological production of mindfulness, presence, and aliveness, 74–75

Brazilian medicine: abuse of power rooted in post-slavery plantation logics, 6, 95–96; ethnographic narratives as a critical tool for exposing oppressions in, 178n5; gynecologists' preconceito toward homosexuality, 89–91; heteronormativity of history-taking examinations, 62, 101–103; institutionalization of gender and sexual difference, 91–92; pervasive anti-blackness of, 4, 5; reform agenda finalized by the Ministry of Health (2013), 13; small percentage of Black gynecologists, 174n9; training in sexology, 103, 175n10; unseen flesh of Black lesbians normalized in hierarchies of domination of, 105

Browne, Simone, 73

Butler, Judith, 106, 107, 175n11

Caldwell, Kia Lilly, 11–12, 174n4

Candomblé: adherence to dress codes of Candomblé by Black lesbians, 71; collective bem-estar contextualized by, 161–163; deity Yemanjá, 33; Dora's frequenting of *terreiros*, 53; Emilia's participation in, 154; LGBTQ+ welcomed in spaces of, 127–128; orixás (African deities), 18, 128, 163; political activism and resistance of Candomblé members, 161, 164, 176n8; *preconceito* triggered by Candomblé neck beads and dress, 48, 84; religious intolerance against, 125, 138

capoeira, as an African movement to attain freedom, 150–52

Carneiro, Sueli: affirmation by the protagonisms of Black women, 144–45; "engrecendo o feminismo" (Blackening feminism) called for, 15, 124, 133; on *epis-*

temicídio, 99, 109; essay on *dor da cor* (pain of [our skin] color), 52, 69, 146; influence of, 134; on the "plenty of work" needed for a better future, 17

Chagas, Carlos, 93, 175n5

Cohen, Cathy J., 8, 134

Collins, Patricia Hill, 132, 134, 172n24

Combahee River Collective, 146

Cooper Owens, Deirdre, 42

Costa, Carlos Antonio de Paula: Brazilian Black women demonized as *onianimistas*, 95; *A Mãi da Familia* founded by, 94

Costa, Jurandir Freire, 93

Cox, Aimee Meredith: shapeshifting framed by, 116, 124, 128, 129; on social citizenship as nonnormative, 176n1

Cruz, Oswaldo, 93, 175n5

Cruz, Simone, 144–45

Das, Veena, 107

Dave, Naisargi N., 22, 115, 172

Davis, Angela, 134

Davis, Dána-Ain, 4, 5, 85, 99, 140

Davis, Dána-Ain and Karen Scott, 177n17

dehumanization (*desumanização*): of imperialist infrastructures of power, 87–88; macro- and microaggressions and microinsults directed as Black lesbians in gynecological encounters, 12, 33, 39, 44, 46, 51–52, 52, 59–60, 62–63, 82, 90, 105, 108

Dery, Mark, 172n25

Dia da Lésbica Visibilidade (National Lesbian Visibility Day), 136, 137

Edmonds, Alexander, 41

epistemic practices: auto-sabedoria (self-understanding) in social justice, 148; *epistemicide* (devaluing of knowledge) associated with the gynecological gaze, 82, 99; "epistemologia negra sapatão" termed by Saunders, 148; shape-retaining force of speaking truth to power, 131

erotic practices: Black lesbian worth-making anchored by erotic power, 2, 7, 18, 22–24, 49; erotic autonomy, 31, 33, 39–40; erotic political freedom, 35, 173n5; erotic self-making, 164; erotic subjectivity, 29–30, 39, 146, 164; and self-care, 26–29; vivência as the erotic subjectivity of the Black lesbian body, 33

Eshun, Kudwo, 172–73n25

ethics: agential orientation of Black lesbians' ethics, 132–33; dignity as an ethical quality, 121–22; embodied ethical subjectivity, 26–27, 32, 116, 122–23, 130–31, 147–49, 176–77n11; Foucault on ethics as care of the self, 132–33, 177n13, 177n21; and race, 129–30, 176–77n22; radical ethics, 115, 172; reflective evaluation for self-honing as an ethical mode, 72, 174n5. *See also* shapeshifting ethics

ethnography: of *escrevivências* (*written lived experience*), 2, 3, 144–45; Jackson's notion of flat ethnography, 172n20

eugenics movement: degeneration ideologies concerning the Black population and reproduction traced to, 95, 97; Pereira's statement that "Brazil is one big hospital," 109

Evaristo, Conceição, *escrevivências* (written lived experience) explored by, 2, 144–45

Fanon, Frantz, 117–18, 130, 176n3

Ferreira da Silva, Denise, 12–13

flesh: Black lesbians' embodiment of injury designated by, 6; body distinguished from, 6–7; Carneiro on *dor da cor* (pain of [our skin] color), 52, 69, 146; Spillers' distinction between "captive bodies and captive flesh," 51; un/gendering of, 8

Foucault, Michel: on the clinical gaze, 174n8; on clinical gazes and spaces, 82; on ethics as care of the self, 132–33, 177n13, 177n21; four aspects of the ethical, 176n4; on freedom as the ontological condition of ethics, 177n5; notion of subjectivation (asujettisement), 68; work on *scientia sexualis*, 886–887

freedom: bearing witness to worth and worth making as Black/queer freedom work, 8–9; capoeira as an African movement to attain freedom, 150–52; Emilia's drawing of a pencil as an instrument of sexual health, 155, *156*, 157; Foucault on freedom as the ontological condition of ethics, 177n5; humanizing of Negritude and anti-Negritude as a liberatory modes of being,

143–47, 153; liberatory vision of Black/queer Afro-futures, 150–54; political freedom to live *minha sexualidade* (my sexuality), 38–39; sacrifices and risks associated with gaining the freedom of *viver minha sexualidade* (live my sexuality), 25, 29, 30, 46, 116, 138, 145, 152; sexual agency and freedom gained by countersurveillance, 36, 65, 72–74, 83–84, 104; sexual health as liberatory, 30–32, 146; we are not free until all Black people are free, 134, 136

Freeing Ourselves: A Guide to Health and Self-Love for Brown Bois, 17

Garcia, Angela: on experiments of care, 106; on landscapes of affect, 64

gazes: empowerment forged by an antiracist Black/queer *olhar*, 17, 66, 172n23; ongoing colonial gaze centered on reproductive bodies as legitimizing, 41, *See also* body scanning

gazes–clinical gazes: countersurveillance by Black lesbians, 36, 38–39, 53, 65, 72–74, 83–84, 104; gyno-trauma experienced by Black lesbians due to, 18; of humane physicians, 37, 81–82; patriarchal medical gazes, 38

gender and gendering: disavowal of, 8; institutionalization of gender and sexual difference in nineteenth-century Brazilian medicine, 91

Goes, Emanuelle A., 94, 138–39

Goes, Emanuelle Freitas and Elisa Santos, 86

Goes, Emanuelle Freitas and Enilda R. do Nascimento, 5

Gonzalez, Lélia, 29, 74, 134, 137, 147

Gregg, Jessica, 37, 170n7

Guimarães, Antonio Sergio, 97

Guimarães, Marco Antonio Chagas anad Angela Baraf Podkameni, 63

gynecological trauma: *afetividade* expressed within *preconceituoso* moments of, 68; countersurveillance practices of Black lesbians', 36, 38–39, 53, 65, 72–74, 83–84, 104; of *iatrogenia* (illness caused by medical examination or treatment), 105–6; intersectional formations of, 52–53, 58, 60, 65; relationality in care as a source of, 57, 59, 65–66, 105–6, 122; unseen flesh as, 7 gynecologic racism: defined as a term, 5–6; light of the distinction between "captive bodies and captive flesh," 51–52; role of private spaces in the production of, 86; views of the Black female body as degenerative, 94–95

gynecology and gynecological spaces: Black lesbian virginity as a disruptive positionality for, 18; framing of Black lesbians as *diferenciada,* 70–72; heteronormativity of, 5, 9, 12, 19, 23, 59; and the history-taking process, 62, 101, 102–3; as microcosms of the social world of Brazil, 19, 87; projects to deterritorialize anti-Blackness in, 166; unchecked anti-Blackness of, 4

gynecology and gynecological spaces–as contact zone: Brazilian gynecology as a contact zone, 75, 81; fear of touching Candomblé female patients, 85, 163; macro- and microaggressions and microinsults directed as Black lesbians, 33, 39, 44, 51–52, 59–60, 62–64, 82, 90, 105, 108. *See also* gynecologic racism; social clinic

Habib, Samar, 173n4
Haraway, Donna. J., 109
Harrison, Faye V., 169n6
Hartman, Saidiya, 95, 150
Hellwig, David J., 170n8
Hennessy, Rosemary, 48
heteronormativity: binary gendered signs depicting underwear, 107, *107*; of conceptions about virgins and virginity, 35, 38, 174n7; of gynecology and gynecological spaces, 5, 9, 12, 19, 23, 59, 106; of history-taking examinations, 62, 101–3; as the restrictive mode of sexual subject production in gynecology, 107; of sexual health (saúde sexual), 174n7
Higginbotham, Evelyn Brooks, 100
hooks, bell, 28, 134
Howe, Cymene A., 173–74n6
Hurston, Zora Neale, 74, 144

interlocuters. *See* participants
intersectional violence: of the experience of erasure and negation, 376; gynecological trauma, 52–53, 58, 60, 65; Luciana's narrative as an intersectional window into Black queer experience of gynecologists, 11, 19, 83

Jackson, John L. Jr., 172n20
James, Joy, 13
Johnson, Jessica Marie, 17
Jones, Esther, 178n5

Keane, Webb: on dignity as an ethical quality, 121; on ethical affordance, 176n5; on the intersubjectivity of ethical life, 176n3; on race as ethical, 176–77n11
Kulick, Don, 170n7

Laidlaw, James, 68, 177n14
Lara, Ana-Maurine, 8, 169n6
Latour, Bruno, 105–6
Lefebvre, Alexandre, 177n13
lésbicas Negras. See Black lesbians
lesbofobia, 47; silencing of Black lesbians' experiences of exploitation in gynecology, 12
LGBTQ+ Diversity Month (Maio da Diversidad LGBTQ+), 124, *126*
LGBTQ+ politics and activism, Marcia's participation in, 22, 24–25
Lorde, Audre, 17, 26, 28, 67, 72, 134, 172n24; conceptualization of the erotic, 27

McGlotten, Shaka and Dana-Ain Davis, 29
McKinley, Catherine E., and L. Joyce DeLaney, 164
mal-estar (malaise): and racism and the negation of rights for the Brazilian population, 63; tug against striving for bem-estar (well-being), 61
Martin, Emily, 48–49, 108, 174n1
Mbembe, Achille, 87
medical subjectivity: broader injustice within society reinforced by gynecologists, 12, 19, 106, 109; construction of Black female queer bodies as medical subjects, 96, 102, 107, 113–14; construction of women as medical subjects, 42, 106–7; gynecological encounters as *como chega esse preconceito,* 69; gynecological encounters as sites of negotiation of and resistant to trauma triggers, 47; heteronormativity as the restrictive mode of sexual subject production in gynecology, 107

Menezes, Margareth, "Desperta (Preconceito de Cor)," 9–10
Miller, J. Reid: on ethical subjectivity, 123, 147, 176n3; on stain removal, 129–30
Moreira, Adilson, 12, 100, 148

Nascimento, Abdias, 147
Nascimento, Beatriz, 134
Nascimento, Sheu, 12
Negritude: affirmation by the protagonisms of Black women, 144–45; Brazilian Black bodies defined by, 68; gynecologic racism grounded in anti-Negritude, 68, 99; humanizing of Negritude and anti-Negritude as a liberatory modes of being, 143–47, 152, See also bem-estar Negra

O'Grady, Lorraine, 32, 173n4
olhar. See gaze
orixás (African deities), striving for bem-estar as fulfilling a promise to, 18, 128, 163

Parker, Richard, 170n7
participants: fundraiser attended by, 162; openness and passion of, 16; reactions to Freeing Ourselves, 17; Salvador visit with, 107; sexuality perceived in the broader context of their daily routines, 22, 30, 84
participants–Angela, 77–78
participants–Carmen, 149–50
participants–Cinthia, 161, 162
participants–Dora, 53–58, 59, 63, 66, 68, 72, 164
participants–Dra. Sandra: gynecologists' preconceito toward homosexuality criticized by, 89–91; training in sexology, 89; work in creating her humanizing obstetrical facility, 91, 93–94
participants–Dr. Manuel: history-taking process of, 101, 102–3; on iatrogenia (illness caused by medical examination or treatment), 105, 106; racial democratic views of, 97–98; training in sexology, 103
participants–Emilia, 154–55, 156, 157, 161, 162, 173n1
participants–Estelle, 116–121; ethical subjectivity of, 121, 122, 128; LGBTQ+ events organized by, 125

participants–Juliana, 1–5, 9
participants–Kamila, 157–160
participants–Lalia, 116–17
participants–Luciana, 11, 19, 30, 60–65, 72–73, 75, 83–85, 104; affirmation and promotion of well-being at all levels by, 143; as a guerreira (warrior) for her family, 142; masculine-gender presenting and identification of, 154; mother of, 141, 143
participants–Marcia, 22, 23, 24; capoeira event led by a friend of, 150–52; ethical subjectivity of, 122; identification as a Black lesbian virgin, 22, 23, 34, 35, 36–37; interest in Candomblé, 33; on viver minha sexualidade (live my sexuality), 22, 26; viver minha sexualidade (live my sexuality) explained by, 22
participants–Nanda, 111–12
participants–Sandra, 137
participants–Sarah, 53–54, 55–57
participants–Taina, 69–70, 146, 161, 162
Peard, Julian G., 81
Perry, Keisha-Khan Y., 33
Podkameni, Angela Baraf, 63
poetry: Barbosa's poem "Vivência," 21, 25–26; vital necessity of, 26
preconceito (prejudice): como chega esse preconceito, 66–67, 68, 69; heteronormativity of history-taking examinations, 62, 101–3; iatrogenia (illness caused by medical examination or treatment), 105–6; impact on health care access and socioeconomic inequity, 97; intersectionality of, 11, 12, 66–69, 170–71n11; Menezes's "Desperta (Preconceito de Cor)," 9–10; subtlety of institutional practices, 68; worth and worth-making in heteronormative gynecological discussions, 9, 106. See also race and racism-racial preconceito

race and racism: Bem-estar Negra as a means to clean the toxin of, 143–44; Black women as wet nurses, 95; and ethics, 129–30, 176–77n22; explaining what constitutes preconceito (prejudice) as problematic, 14–15; mal-estar caused by, 63; obstetric racism, 5, 99, 105, 177n17; racial and gender resistance work, 124;

race and racism (*continued*)
  racial *epistemicide* (devaluing of knowledge) associated with the gynecological
  gaze, 82, 99; racializing social relations in
  boa aparência, 71; "recreational racism"
  within Brazilian workplaces, media, and
  institutions, 12. *See also* abolitionist work;
  anti-blackness; eugenics movement; flesh;
  gynecologic racism; Negritude; slavery
race and racism-racial preconceito: as a
  criminal act, 97, 175n8; as a problem for
  all people, 107–8; of Brazil's *carteira de
  trabalho e previdencia* social system, 160;
  Menezes's "Desperta (Preconceito de
  Cor)," 9–10; violence of, 138
Rebhun, Linda-Anne, 170n7
resistance: community organizing by Black
  lesbians, 134, 136; lesbianism as an act of,
  17, 23, 64, 67
Reyes-Foster, Beatriz M., 105
Ribeiro, Djamila, 172n23
Rich, Adrienne, 131
Rodrigues, Raimundo Nina, 96
Rohden, Fabíola, 92, 174n8, 175n4, 175n12

Salvador: protest against Black genocide in,
  137, *139*; public resistance and protest by
  Black lesbians in Lapa, 136, *136*, 137
Salvador-Bahia: Black population of, 1; Estação Calçada, 1; racial and class divides, 1
Sandoval, Chela, 129, 176n9
Seigworth, Gregory J. and Melissa Gregg, 68
sexology: in Brazilian medicine, 103, 175n10;
  Dra. Sandra's training in, 89; Dr. Manuel's
  training in, 103; Nina Rodrigues's training
  in, 96
sexual health (saúde sexual): *cuidar minha
  sexualidade* (to take care of my sexuality),
  27, 155; as a framework for perceptual
  self-care or caring, 30–31; heteronormative
  views of, 174n7; as liberation, 30–32, 146;
  nonnormative perceptions of, 27; social
  force of *viver minha sexualidade* (live my
  sexuality), 22, 23, 27, 29; as *uma forma de
  bem-estar* (a form of well-being), 30
sexual heteronormativity. *See*
  heteronormativity
shadowboxing fieldwork, 13–16

Shange, Savannah, 114, 138, 141, 149
shapeshifting ethics: defined, 116, 128; as a
  necessary condition to survive, 140; of
  public protests, 133–34; shape-retaining
  force of, 131, 133; worth and worth-making
  of, 19, 124, 128–29, 132
Sharpe, Christina, 12–13, 20, 147, 171n12
slavery: Black women's intimacy during, 17;
  children of slaves, 95; gynecological experimentation on enslaved women, 6, 42,
  85; plantation futures represented in contemporary medical institutional practices,
  95–96; un/gendering of flesh in, 8
Smith, Barbara, 17, 134
Smith, Christen A., 8, 87, 99, 169n5
Smith, Linda Tuhiwai, 173n25
Snorton, C. Riley, 6
social clinic, 79–109 passim; as a microcosm
  of the social world from which intimate
  violence emanates, 19, 87; as a term, 19,
  82; Luciana's narrative as an intersectional
  window into Black queer experience
  of, 83
sousveillance: Browne's notion of dark
  sousveillance, 73; defined by Mann, 73
speculums, 56, *56*; Black female homosexuality as a symbolic speculum, 109;
  derailing of speculum exams by Black
  lesbians, 18, 67, 165, 336–37; sense of alienation related to, 57, 174n1
Spillers, Hortense J., 6, 51, 152–53
Street, Alice, 82
subjectivation and subjectivity: Foucault's notion of, 68; liberatory practices illuminated
  by, 68–69. *See also* medical subjectivity

Tadiar, Neferti X. M., 48
Thomas, Deborah A., and Tina M. Campt,
  164
trauma. *See* dehumanization (*desumanização*); gynecological trauma

unseen flesh: bearing witness to, 10, 138; of
  Black lesbians normalized in hierarchies
  of domination in medicine, 5, 42, 105;
  as a lens to discuss self- and collective
  agency, 109, 114; notions of unworthiness
  illuminated by, 7

virgins and virginity: as a site of resistance, 35, 38, 67; Black lesbian virginity as a disruptive positionality for gynecology, 18; heteronormative views of, 35, 38, 174n7; religious conservatism and intentional chastity associated with, 38; as a vivência (lived experience), 38, 39. *See also* participants—Marcia

vivência (lived experience): Barbosa's poem "Vivência," 21, 25–26; erotic power of, 2, 18, 26, 27, 145; escrevivências (written lived experience) explored by Evaristo, 2, 144–45; grounding of Negritude and Black culture and life in, 33, 157–59; impact of the humane medical treatment on, 37; impact of the psychological effects of racism on, 9, 63; virginity as an expression of, 18, 27, 39, See also *viver minha sexualidade* (live my sexuality)

viver minha sexualidade (live my sexuality): Black lesbians' theorizations of, 22–24, 46, 47; sacrifices and risks associated with gaining the freedom of, 22, 25, 29, 30, 46, 116, 138, 145, 152; social force of, 27; as worth-making in flesh and spirit, 145–46

Wekker, Gloria, 35, 38–39, 41, 86
Werneck, Jurema, 86, 147, 163–64

Werneck, Jurema, Nilza Iraci, and Simone Cruz, 144–45

Williamson, Bianca C., 10, 65, 66

Williamson, K. Eliza, 105

worth and worth-making: Black lesbians' visibility as crucial to, 49, 134, 136; Black lesbian worth-making anchored by erotic power, 2, 7, 18, 22–24, 49; dignity as a state or quality of, 120–21; inherited worth of Black feminist thought and labor, 133–34; and *preconceito* (prejudice), 9; of shapeshifting ethics, 19, 124, 128–29, 132; of stain removal work, 129–130; *Unseen Flesh* as a story Black lesbian worth-making, 2–3, 7–13, 145; and vivência (lived experience), 9; *viver minha sexualidade* as worth-making in flesh and spirit, 145; and worth-retaining process of Black lesbian community organizers, 134, 136

Xirê das Pretas: Black lesbian outness expressed at, 118; poster in an Aumuleto tent during, *119*

Young, Iris Marion, 170–71n11

Zigon, Jarrett, 72, 174n5